Hidden Challenges to Education Systems in Transition Economies

Sue E. Berryman

The World Bank
Europe and Central Asia Region
Human Development Sector

Copyright © 2000
THE WORLD BANK
1818 H Street, N.W.
Washington, D.C. 20433, U.S.A.

All rights reserved
Manufactured in the United States of America
First printing September 2000
1 2 3 4   03 02 01 00

The opinions expressed in this report do not necessarily represent the views of the World Bank or its member governments. The World Bank does not guarantee the accuracy of the data included in this publication and accepts no responsibility whatsoever for any consequence of their use.

The material in this publication is copyrighted. Requests for permission to reproduce portions of it should be sent to the Office of the Publisher at the address shown in the copyright notice above. The World Bank encourages dissemination of its work and will normally give permission promptly and, when the reproduction is for noncommercial purposes, without asking a fee. Permission to copy portions for classroom use is granted through the Copyright Clearance Center, Inc., Suite 910, 222 Rosewood Drive, Danvers, Massachusetts 01923, U.S.A.

ISBN 0-8213-4813-2

Library of Congress Cataloging-in-Publication Data has been applied for.

CONTENTS

Foreword	v
Preface	vii
Acknowledgments	viii
Acronyms and Abbreviations	ix
Introduction	1
1. Realign Education Systems with Market Economies and Open Societies	7
2. Combat Poverty by Increasing Educational Fairness	22
3. Finance for Sustainability, Quality, and Fairness	37
4. Spend Resources More Efficiently	58
5. Reinvent Governance, Management, and Accountability	73
6. The Role of the World Bank	91
Annex Tables	105

    A1. Total Population   *106*
    A2. School Age Population   *107*
    A3. Total Fertility Rate   *108*
    A4. Demographic Projections by Region   *109*
    A5. Preschool Enrollment Rates   *110*
    A6. Basic Education Enrollment Rates   *111*
    A7. General Upper Secondary Enrollment Rates   *112*
    A8. Vocational/Technical Upper Secondary Enrollment Rates   *113*
    A9. Overall Upper Secondary Enrollment Rates   *114*
    A10. Share of Students in Upper Secondary Education   *115*
    A11. Tertiary Enrollment Rates   *117*
    A12. Share of University Enrollments by Field of Study, Selected ECA Countries   *118*
    A13. Unemployment by Educational Level, Selected ECA Countries   *121*
    A14. Share of Registered Unemployed by Educational Level, Selected ECA Countries   *122*
    A15. Total Public Expenditures on Education   *123*
    A16. Student/Teacher Ratios in Basic Education   *124*
    A17. Wages in Education in Selected ECA Countries   *125*

References	126
Glossary	130

FOREWORD

As the transition began, countries in the Europe and Central Asia (ECA) region had reason to take pride in their education systems. They had solved problems that still bedevil several other regions of the world. Adult literacy was generally universal; participation and completion rates for children and youth of both genders were high at all levels of education; teachers came to work; students had textbooks; students from some of the countries that participated in international assessments of mathematics and science performed well; and repetition and dropout rates were low.

The Bank conducted this study of the education sector to increase the value of our contribution to our ECA counterparts. A sobering picture emerged that surprised the World Bank as much as it may surprise our colleagues in the region.

ECA education systems that were a good fit with planned economies and authoritarian political systems are a poor fit with market economies and open political systems. International evidence shows that they are not creating the best product for a market economy. Market economies—and open societies—require abilities to apply knowledge flexibly, to cope with the cognitive requirements of unfamiliar tasks, to recognize and solve problems, and to self-manage new learning. The content and structures of curricula and textbooks and prevailing teaching practices in ECA do not seem to support the acquisition of these skills.

Just when human capital is becoming increasingly important in the region, inequities in learning opportunities are increasing—to the detriment of the poor everywhere. Since the human capital acquired by parents affects that acquired by their children, lower levels of human capital in one generation can trigger less human capital and greater poverty in subsequent generations.

Enrollment rates are going in the wrong direction. A larger proportion of young cohorts is building less human capital; a smaller proportion is building more. Since 1989 the number of years of full-time education (excluding preschool) that an average six year old child in ECA can expect to achieve over his or her lifetime has declined by about two-thirds of a year. In contrast, the school expectancy for the average child in OECD countries has increased during the last decade. By 1998 the average OECD child could expect to complete almost five more years of education than the average ECA child.

Most countries have yet to control significant inefficiencies in the sector, especially in their use of teachers, nonteaching staff, and energy. Student/teacher ratios, initially low relative to other regions of the world, had dropped to an average of 14:1 across the region by 1997. Most countries are accommodating these large teaching forces by letting teacher wages fall below the average public sector wage, not by rationalizing the teaching force by reducing its size and increasing class sizes, contractual hours, and pay.

ECA policymakers are too often handling severe limits on public budgets for education in ways that compound the problems of the sector. Energy and wage bills have crowded out other inputs to education. The underfunding or nonfunding of school maintenance has created an education infrastructure crisis, especially in the former republics of the Soviet Union. Governments have cut the purchase of didactic materials such as textbooks, closed schools to conserve on the costs of heat, reduced or eliminated in-service training for teachers, and let teachers' wages fall relative to other public sector wages, thereby increasing the risk of losing the best teachers. Some governments have run up arrears in energy bills and teacher wages. They have shifted costs to familie, with unintended but nonetheless real effects on the demand for education by poor families.

In most countries of the region, goal setting and steering processes, which provide the basis for assessing the performance of the sector, are still partisan, nontransparent, weak, or missing. The managers of the sector have to cope with responsibilities incommensurate with resources and functions allocated to the wrong levels of government. Functions are missing, including policy analysis, planning, and financial management that are key to the rationalization of the sector. The efficient delivery of educational services depends on a vigorous checks-and-balances relationship between three forces: the state, the private sector, and stakeholders. However, in most ECA countries the state now dominates the delivery of educational services, unchecked by competitive processes and stakeholder voice.

The transition process has brought to the surface challenges that are much broader and deeper than anyone had anticipated at its start. As in other sectors, the job ahead for our clients and the Bank in the education sector will be technically and politically difficult. The World Bank stands ready to travel this road with our clients, mobilizing the Bank's and our partners' resources and skills to help ECA countries build excellent education systems. The Bank's commitment to economic development and poverty alleviation and our recognition of the role of human capital in realizing these objectives demand nothing less of us.

Johannes F. Linn
Vice President
Europe and Central Asia Region
1 August 2000

PREFACE

The audiences for this book are policymakers in the Europe and Central Asia region (ECA), especially ministers of finance and education, and the World Bank's top management for the region.

The purposes of this book are diagnostic and strategic. By the start of the transition, ECA education systems had solved problems that still plague other regions of the world—for example, limited access, gender inequalities, and poor quality output relative to the economic and political requirements of individual countries. Both the World Bank and our clients thought that in ECA education was not a problem sector. This report will therefore surprise many ECA governments, just as its results surprised the World Bank team that conducted the work. The team found that deep and broad problems were emerging in the sector that threatened many countries' previous achievements in education.

Thus, an important purpose of the book is as a regional alert. Another is strategic—to chart how ECA governments and the World Bank might move toward more effective delivery of educational services in the region as a whole. This book can delimit the general lines of a strategy for addressing a particular issue. It can identify approaches that seem effective in a range of countries and are thus worth considering. It can warn against actions that seem ineffective, regardless of country. But it cannot provide a blueprint that an individual country might use to move from an undesirable to a desirable state. Such a blueprint would involve too many country-specific particulars and is best developed in the context of country-specific sector work.

ECA countries can be clustered into subregions of countries that are more similar to one another in their historical, social, political, and economic contexts than they are to countries in other subregions. However, the World Bank team found that countries did not cluster neatly according to the variables used to analyze the state of education, and this complicates the design of strategy. For example, most countries showed efficiency problems, but the infrastructure crisis tended to be limited to countries of the Former Soviet Union and Albania. Underfinancing of education is scattered about the region.

The introduction points out that the issues identified for the sector cut across all levels of education but play out in different ways by level. For example, governance problems afflict all levels of education, but their nature and the strategies for dealing with them differ by level. Subsequent regional sector work will focus on particular levels of education—especially higher education, vocational/technical education, and upper secondary education. Such work will complement this book by detailing the issues and strategic solutions for those levels.

ACKNOWLEDGMENTS

Any document of this nature testifies to substantial teamwork among colleagues within and outside the World Bank. The task was managed by Sue E. Berryman with the guidance and support of the ECA education sector manager, James A. Socknat. Thomas Hoopengardner wrote the chapter on financing and, with Fredrick Golladay and Maureen Lewis, contributed broadly to the work. The thinking was richly informed—and a number of the boxes ably drafted—by ECA colleagues Maurice Boissiere, Ernesto Cuadra, Peter Darvas, Halil Dundar, Yael Duthilleul, David Fretwell, Fredrick Golladay, Marit Granheim, Michael Mertaugh, Gillian Perkins, Ana Maria Sandi, Helen Shahriari, James Stevens, and Nancy Vandycke. Anna Kokotov-Litman and Joe Emanuele Colombano provided excellent research assistance.

This education strategy takes a deeply institutional perspective. Among institutional economists within and outside the Bank who significantly influenced its thinking were Neil Boyle, Navin Girishankar, Malcolm Holmes, Philip Keefer, Brian Levy, Nicholas Manning, Elinor Ostrom, Samuel Paul, Sanjay Pradhan, and Kenneth Sigrist.

A special intellectual debt is owed to Thomas R. Bailey, director of the Institute on Education and the Economy at Columbia University. As globalization gathered force in the early 1980s in the United States, he pioneered in measuring the implications of these massive economic shifts for changes in skill requirements in the workplace. It was only a short leap to seeing the challenge that this economic restructuring posed for American schools—and, increasingly, for schools in developing nations.

A statistics and data analysis group provided the foundation for the strategy. Colleagues outside the Bank included Scott Murray of Statistics Canada, Albert Tuijnman of Stockholm University, J. Douglas Willms of the University of New Brunswick, Irwin Kirsch of the Educational Testing Service, Andreas Schleicher of the Organisation for Economic Co-operation and Development (OECD), and Albert Motivans, at that time with the United Nations Children's Fund (UNICEF). Within the Bank the group included Eduard Bos, Timothy Heleniak, and Dena Ringold.

Just when authors think that they are finished, they are in fact only halfway there. An editorial and publishing team consisting of Jenepher Moseley, the main editor for the document, Vivian Jackson, Anna Kokotov-Litman, Nancy Levine, Jennifer Sterling, and Deborah Trent wrestled arcane language to the ground, clarified tables and figures, imposed needed consistency in formatting, arranged for and reviewed the Russian translation, typeset the document, and got it into print. They brought careful and intelligent eyes to the work.

The Education Network provided financial support and encouragement as the ECA team confronted the task of writing the first education strategy for the region. We are particularly grateful to Jeffrey Waite.

This document was reviewed by several groups. Within the Bank, the ECA education team and attendees at a seminar gave time and thought to the document. Fredrick Golladay, Emmanuel Jimenez, Christine Jones, and Harry Patrinos provided careful and constructive peer reviews that helped us improve it. Reviewers outside the Bank included Nancy Birdsall of the Carnegie Endowment for International Peace; OECD staff, especially Ian Whitman; management and staff of the European Training Foundation; management and staff of the Institute of Education Policy and of the Higher Education Support Program, both of the Open Society Institute; and many of the directors of the National Foundation of the Open Society Institute.

ACRONYMS AND ABBREVIATIONS

APL	Adaptable program lending
CEM	Country economic memorandum
CIS	Commonwealth of Independent States
ECA	Europe and Central Asia
ETF	European Training Foundation
EU	European Union
FSU	Former Soviet Union
GDP	Gross domestic product
GNP	Gross national product
GRP	Gross regional product
IALS	International Adult Literacy Survey
IEA	International Association for the Evaluation of Educational Achievement
ILSS	International Life Skills Survey
IMF	International Monetary Fund
INES	Indicators of Education Systems
LIL	Learning and innovation loan
NGO	Nongovernmental organisation
NIACE	National Institute for Adult and Continuing Education
NRR	Net reproduction rate
OECD	Organisation for Economic Co-operation and Development
PER	Public expenditure review
PIRLS	Progress in Reading Literacy Study
PISA	Program for International Student Assessment
PPP	Purchasing power parity
QAG	Quality Assurance Group
TIMSS	Third International Mathematics and Science Study
UNDP	United Nations Development Programme
UNICEF	United Nations Children's Fund
VAT	Value-added tax

INTRODUCTION

Accomplishments in education were one of the triumphs of communism. At the time of the transition in 1989, adult literacy was generally universal; participation and completion rates for children and youths of both genders were high at all levels of education; teachers came to work; students had textbooks; students from some countries in Europe and Central Asia (ECA) that participated in international assessments of mathematics and science performed well; and repetition and dropout rates were low.

But the Rules of the Game Have Changed

Given such a legacy, the education sectors of the transition economies seem to have few problems relative to education systems in other regions of the world—for example, they do not have problems of low participation or gender inequities. However, the rules of the game that resulted in good educational outcomes under the requirements of communism have changed.

The rules for market economies and open political systems differ from those for command economies and authoritarian political systems. Although countries of the region differ in how far they have traveled down the road to their new political and economic destinations, all countries will ultimately have to solve similar problems in their education systems. The countries of the Organisation for Economic Co-operation and Development (OECD) are still trying to solve some of these problems, the differences between ECA and OECD countries often being more in degree than in kind.

- To deal with the uncertainties and continuous changes characteristic of market economies, students need strategic skills, such as knowing-how-to-learn skills, problem-solving skills, and evaluative skills. *Most ECA education systems focus on memorized factual and procedural knowledge, adequate for the predictability of a planned economy but not for the volatility of a market economy.*

- The years of education completed by students have to increase, as do the rates of completion of upper secondary education and participation in postsecondary education. *In several ECA countries years of education completed are declining.*

- The shift from mass to flexible production requires broader knowledge and skills than early specialization provides. *Although some ECA countries are eliminating early specialization immediately after basic education, some are not, and some are introducing it earlier.*

- The variation in students' educational attainments—whether measured by years of schooling completed or by the nature of the skills and knowledge mastered—has to be narrowed. *In general, variations in attainments are increasing, not decreasing, in ECA countries.*

- The productivity of education systems—their outcomes relative to the costs of attaining those outcomes—has to improve. *Almost all ECA countries lack a productivity focus and the information, managerial skills, and incentives needed to improve productivity.*

- Publicly financed educational services have to be accountable to taxpayers and beneficiaries for the costs and quality of these services. *Most ECA countries cannot measure service delivery in these terms, and almost none make what information they do have widely available to the public.*

- The management of education systems has to be structured to protect national, subnational, and school-level interests. *Most ECA countries have changed the management of their education systems, but generally not in ways that protect these interests.*

- Education systems have to respond to the changes in external circumstances that redefine what the larger society needs from its education system. *The region is bimodal here. Some ECA countries understand this point; others do not see that social and economic context defines educational purposes and achievements.*

These changes in the rules of the game have opened up fault lines beneath the region's education systems

Beneath the surface of ECA's education systems, then, are fault lines that, unless repaired, will ultimately undermine these systems. The region's education systems have five shared problems, each of which is discussed in a separate chapter. The final chapter lays out the implications of these issues for the Bank's business strategy.

1. *Alignment.* As touched on above, educational quality is contextual; it is not a constant under all conditions. ECA education systems that were a good fit with planned economies and authoritarian political systems do not fit open market economies and open political systems well.

2. *Fairness.* Education is an important mechanism for reducing and preventing poverty. Differences in children's learning opportunities are emerging in ECA at that very point in the region's history when human capital—summed up as skills and knowledge—increasingly determines individual and family incomes and the probabilities of intergenerational poverty.[1]

3. *Financing.* ECA countries have to realign the financing of their education systems with fiscal realities without jeopardizing the fairness and quality of educational services. Their failure to rationalize the financing of education systems is eroding the achievements of the pretransition period and undermining the sector's ability to respond to the challenges of a market economy.

4. *Efficiency.* Most ECA education systems use inputs inefficiently. These inefficiencies are the legacy of centrally planned economies, where allocation decisions were made in physical terms without the intermediation of prices or budgets.

5. *Governance, management, and accountability.* Most ECA education systems do not perform well against standards of transparent and effective governance, efficient management, and vigorous accountability to a range of stakeholders. The sector is still dominated by government, inadequately counterbalanced by competition (choice) and participation (voice).

These fault lines apply to all levels of education: preschool, primary, lower secondary, academic secondary, secondary and postsecondary vocational/technical, university, and adult education and training.[2] However, they play out in different ways at each level. For example, all levels have inefficiencies. At the preschool level they take the form of excessive numbers of nonteaching staff, such as caretakers, doctors, nurses, cooks, assistant cooks, and cleaners. For secondary vocational/technical education they lie in the facilities and equipment required to support excessively

---

1. Human capital results from investments in individuals that increase their future welfare by increasing the efficiency of their future consumption and productivity. These investments include, but are not limited to, education and training.
2. ECA countries vary somewhat in the organisation of their education systems and in the ages and grades associated with each level of education. The region's education systems have also gone through substantial restructuring over the decade, particularly at the level of vocational education. However, in general, preschool (as distinct from nursery care for children ages 0–3) includes children from age 3 to ages 5, 6, or 7. When preschool includes 7 year olds, the curriculum for 7 year old preschoolers tends to approximate that of the first grade in primary schools in other countries. Primary education can be grades 1–4/5, the normal age range being 6/7–10. The lower secondary level can be grades 5/6–8/9, the normal age range varying from 10–14 to 11–15. "Basic" education refers to primary and lower secondary education combined. After eight or nine years of schooling, students choose from among three alternatives: (1) an academic stream that leads to matriculation from secondary education and that lasts two to four years; (2) a technical/vocational stream that also leads to matriculation from secondary education and that lasts three to four years; or (3) a vocational program that does not lead to matriculation and that lasts one to two years.
Postsecondary education is quite variable in its organisation. However, there is usually opportunity for postsecondary technical instead of university training. Adult education and training target those of labor force age.

Table 1 World Bank Financing in ECA by Educational Level, 1984–99

Level of education	World Bank financing (Millions of U.S. dollars)	(Percentage of total)
Preschool	14.5	1
Basic	724.9	44
Upper secondary (vocational/technical and academic)	230.4	14
Tertiary	504.0	31
Adult training	166.9	10
Total	**1,640.7**	**100**

Note: This table is based on closed projects and those under supervision at time of writing.
Source: Authors' compilation.

narrow and specialized programs. Where important, this book discusses differences by level.

Truth in advertising—or what this paper does not try to do

This report makes no a priori assumptions about the Bank's investment priorities by level. As table 1 shows, since 1984 Bank investments in the region have ranged across the levels. It is a sine qua non that basic education has to be protected in all countries because deterioration at this level affects the incidence of poverty so strongly. Beyond this imperative, investment priorities emerge from the needs of individual countries and the feasibility of meeting them.

This book focuses on problems that are generally common to the 27 ECA countries. Countries in the region differ from one another, and by the end of the first posttransition decade these differences had increased. For example, a significant gap is opening up between the Central European and Baltic countries and other ECA countries as the former surge economically and succeed in establishing political stability and the rule of law. Despite their differences, these countries can be clustered into subregions of countries that are more similar to one another in their historical, social, political, and economic contexts than they are to countries in other subregions.[3] Figures 1 through 3 and table 2 present some of the basic demographic and economic realities of the region. Most countries have small populations (figure 1) of 10 million or less, with one country, the Russian Federation, accounting for 31 percent of the total population of the region and six of the 28 countries (including Russia) for 73 percent of the region's total.

The percentage of the population that lives in rural areas varies from 68 percent (Tajikistan) to 24 percent (Russia), with the average percentage living in rural areas being 41 percent (figure 2).

The number of ethnic groups within a country varies significantly when small minority populations are counted. Figure 3 shows the percentage of the dominant ethnicity, which varies from 98 percent (Poland) to 40 percent (Bosnia-Herzegovina).

In the last decade all countries experienced declines in total fertility rates (figure 4.1 in

---

3   The subregions are Central Europe (Czech Republic, Hungary, Poland, and Slovak Republic), Southeast Europe (Albania, Bulgaria, and Romania), the Baltic states (Estonia, Latvia, and Lithuania), the western Commonwealth of Independent States (Belarus, Moldova, Russia, and Ukraine), the Caucasus (Armenia, Azerbaijan, and Georgia), former Yugoslavia (Bosnia-Herzegovina, Croatia, Former Yugoslav Republic of Macedonia, Slovenia, and Federal Republic of Yugoslavia), and the Central Asian republics (Kazakhstan, Kyrgyz Republic, Tajikistan, Turkmenistan, and Uzbekistan). Turkey is a subregion by itself. Excluding the Federal Republic of Yugoslavia, these countries constitute the ECA lending region.

Figure 1 Six Countries Accounted for 73 Percent of the ECA Population in 1997

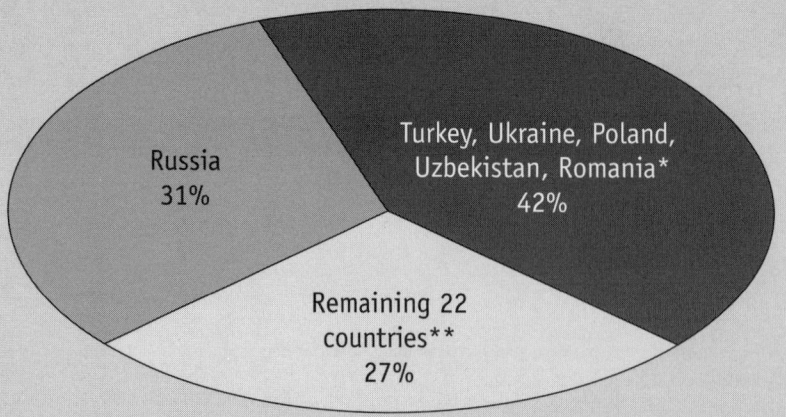

Note: *Romania - 5%, Uzbekistan - 5%, Poland - 8%, Ukraine - 11%, Turkey -13%. **Remaining 22 countries, each with less than 5% of the ECA population.
Source: Based on annex table A1.

Figure 2 Percentages of Rural and Urban Population Varied by Country in 1997

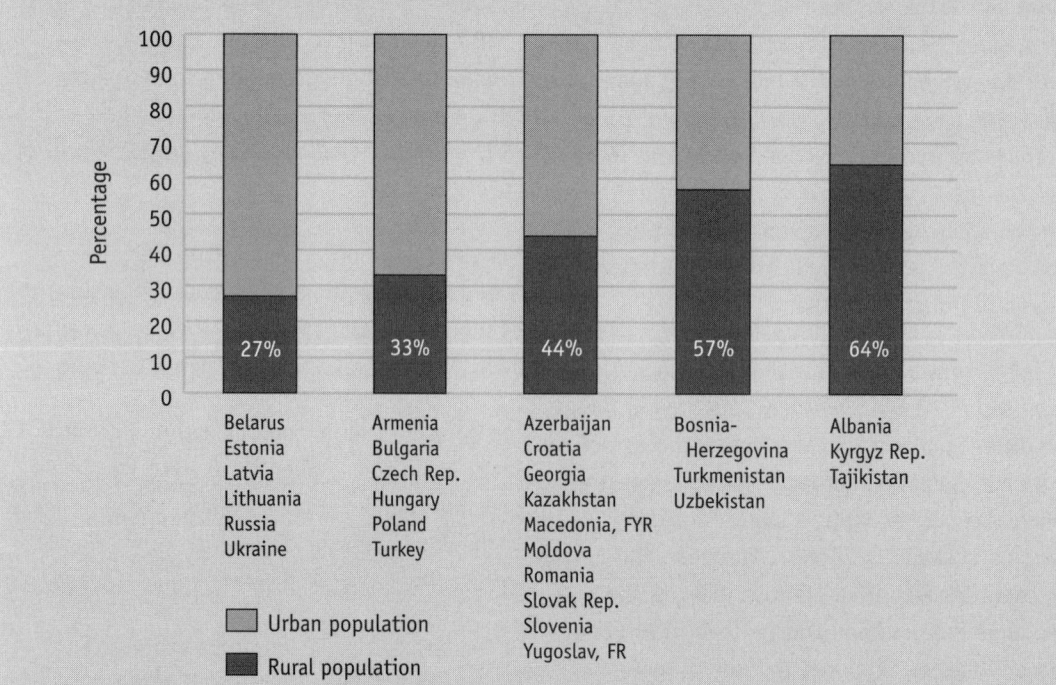

Note: Rural population in the countries listed in each group falls into a 10 percent band within an overall range of 20–70 percent. The percentage for each group is the average for individual countries in that group.
Source: Wetzel and Dunn (1998).

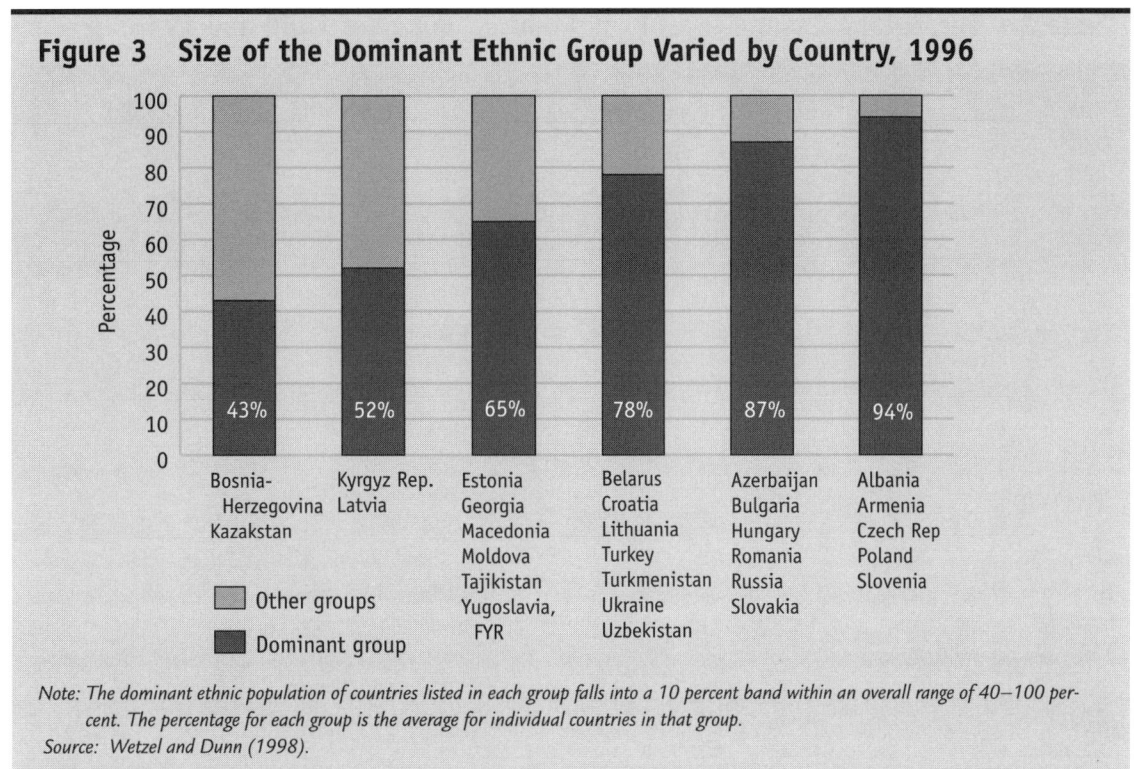

Figure 3 Size of the Dominant Ethnic Group Varied by Country, 1996

Note: The dominant ethnic population of countries listed in each group falls into a 10 percent band within an overall range of 40–100 percent. The percentage for each group is the average for individual countries in that group.
Source: Wetzel and Dunn (1998).

chapter 4; annex table A3). Between 1989 and 1997, Turkey, Albania, and the Central Asian republics show smaller declines, whereas rates in the Baltic states and the western Commonwealth of Independent States (CIS) are little more than half the rates of 1989. Most ECA countries now have rates below replacement.

The economic fortunes of the region's countries in the last decade have differed significantly (table 2). Between 1989 and 1998 Turkey's gross domestic product (GDP) grew by 73 percent; Poland's, by 37 percent; Slovenia's, by 30 percent. However, Ukraine's GDP declined by 51 percent; Tajikistan's, by 58 percent; and Georgia's, by 65 percent. Despite differences, except for Turkey the 27 countries face similar transition requirements.[4] As these affect their education systems, they have to solve similar education problems. Countries differ in the severity of these problems, in the extent to which they see them as problems, and in the form that the issues take in country-specific contexts. Where these differences are clear and important, the book discusses them.

Solutions to shared education problems have to be country-specific. This book can only map out the general lines of a strategy for addressing a particular issue. It can identify approaches that seem effective in a range of countries and are thus worth considering. It can warn against actions that seem ineffective, regardless of country. It cannot, however, provide a useful blueprint for how a country can move from an undesirable to a desirable state. These strategies necessarily involve too many country-specific particulars.

This book does not discuss the particular education problems of countries in conflict or postconflict situations. Albania, Azerbaijan, Bosnia-Herzegovina, Croatia, Georgia, and the Nagorno-Karabakh region (inside Azerbaijan but

---

4   For example, unlike other countries in the region, Turkey faces problems of participation in basic education, especially for girls at the lower secondary level.

THE WORLD BANK

Table 2. Percentage Change in GDP, by Country, between 1989 and 1998

Country	Change	Country	Change
Central Europe		*Western CIS*	
Czech Republic[a]	5.3	Belarus[a]	-12.7
Hungary[a]	6.3	Moldova[a]	-32.9
Poland	37.4	Russian Federation	-35.7
Slovak Republic[a]	11.7	Ukraine[a]	-51.1
Southeast Europe		*Caucasus*	
Albania[a]	3.0	Armenia[a]	-54.2
Bulgaria[a]	-22.0	Azerbaijan	-51.8
Romania	-10.4	Georgia[a]	-65.4
Former Yugoslavia		*Central Asian republics*	
Bosnia-Herzegovina	—	Kazakhstan	-34.5
Croatia[a]	24.3	Kyrgyz Republic	-23.5
Macedonia, FYR[a]	-1.7	Tajikistan[a]	-58.1
Slovenia[a]	30.0	Turkmenistan[a]	-28.5
Yugoslavia, FR	—	Uzbekistan[a]	4.8
Baltic states		Turkey[a]	73.0
Estonia[a]	-14.3		
Latvia[a]	-36.8		
Lithuania	-14.2		

— Not available
a. Rate is based on available data.
Sources: Authors' calculations based on GDP-PPP (purchasing power parity, based on current international dollars); World Bank, World Development Indicators *(various years)*.

claimed by Armenia) are now in a postconflict status. Russia's Chechnya region is still convulsed.

The World Bank's Goals for Education in ECA

The five fault lines identified above define the Bank's development objectives for the education sector in ECA countries:

- Realign education systems with market economies and open societies.
- Combat poverty by increasing educational fairness.
- Finance for sustainability, quality, and fairness.
- Spend resources more efficiently.
- Reinvent the sector's governance, management, and accountability.

CHAPTER ONE

REALIGN EDUCATION SYSTEMS WITH MARKET ECONOMIES AND OPEN SOCIETIES

Summary

ECA education systems must respond to the new economic and civic imperatives of emerging markets and open societies because these changes will dramatically affect the knowledge, skills, and values that citizens need.

The economic imperative. *ECA countries are moving at different rates from centrally planned economies to market economies. This shift will increasingly require workers with better information-processing, problem-solving, and knowing-how-to-learn skills. Available international test data show that ECA countries are significantly behind OECD countries in many such skills.*

The civic imperative. *Two attributes of a civic society are particularly important for economic growth. The first is a strong body of civic institutions that provide the transparency and accountability needed to attract investors. The other is a shared commitment, across social divisions, to the rules of social participation, thereby increasing trust and social cohesion. Trust reduces transaction costs; social cohesion promotes economic development by reducing the risk of political instability. If the broader society supports these civic objectives, schools can encourage both of them.*

Fundamental changes in ECA education systems will be required to achieve these objectives. Educators, supported by government, have to change the methods, content, and timing of teaching. Among other things they must realign the content of instruction with new objectives, ensure that all students attain higher levels of foundation skills, and establish opportunities for adults to adjust their human capital to new skill demands. Changes of this magnitude require a sophisticated political and technical strategy.

Over the long run, education systems only remain credible to the societies in which they are embedded, and to the citizens who pay the bills, if they meet one condition: they have to adapt to the fundamental economic, political, and social changes that affect the skill, knowledge, and value profiles that citizens need. This chapter shows how economic and political changes profoundly affect ECA education systems and discusses ways in which these systems can adapt to them. The changes required are at the core of teaching and learning.

Why This Development Goal?

Economic and civic imperatives in ECA countries are forcing changes in all major social institutions, including education. After only one decade of transition, ECA countries are moving at very different speeds toward market economies and open societies. Pressures for forward motion in these areas will persist, challenging the region's education systems to change in both obvious and subtle ways.

The Economic Imperative

ECA countries are negotiating three economic changes that affect education:

- From centrally planned economies to market economies[5]
- From protected trade based on politics to global trade based on economic comparative advantage
- From mass production to flexible or customized production of goods and services.

Figure 1.1 shows that these changes are taking place at different rates in different countries.

---

5   In fact, countries worldwide have mixed economies, in that both the state and the private sector control means of production and allocate resources. However, from the perspective of education, private sector activity has the closest link to human capital requirements.

THE WORLD BANK

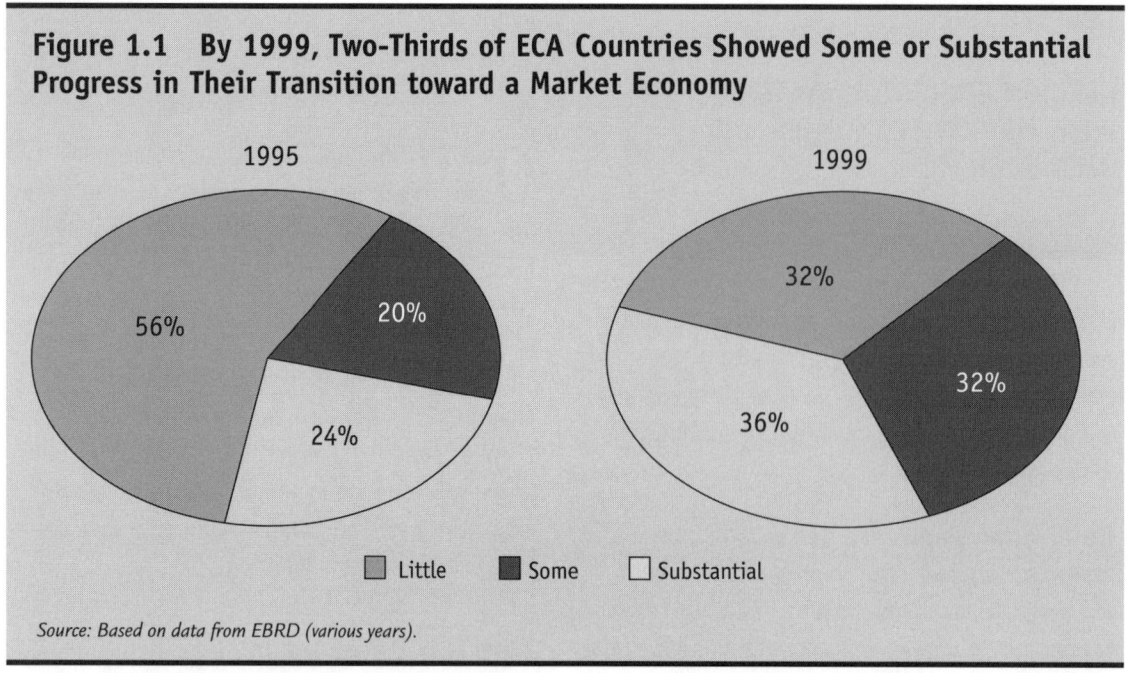

Figure 1.1 By 1999, Two-Thirds of ECA Countries Showed Some or Substantial Progress in Their Transition toward a Market Economy

Source: Based on data from EBRD (various years).

Average scores for ECA countries on nine indicators of privatization, markets and trade, financial institutions, and legal reform for 1995 and 1999 show an increasing percentage of ECA countries moving toward a market economy. Between 1995 and 1999 the percentage of laggards dropped from 56 to 32, and the percentage making some progress increased from 20 to 32. The percentage of those achieving substantial progress increased from 24 to 36.

From centrally planned to market economies. The implications of a market economy for education are radically different from those of a planned economy, but they are fairly easy to see. Price-based economies generate relationships between wages and human capital; in planned economies there is little relationship between the two. When market forces, not planning, define the skills and knowledge that workers need, the profiles of human capital required to compete in labor markets must change to let individuals adapt to rapid changes in skill demand. Market forces are also spotlighting the inefficiencies and fiscal sustainability problems of ECA education systems.

The other two economic shifts challenge ECA education systems less obviously, but both require a workforce trained to function in new ways.

From protected trade based on politics to global trade based on economic comparative advantage. Integration into the global economy imposes a discipline on domestic producers by increasing competition and clarifying comparative advantage. Integration is a stimulus for doing what producers have to do anyway in order to raise productivity, which is the key to higher wages and higher standards of living. Globalization, in conjunction with the flexible production of goods and services and expanded and cheaper communication and transport systems, gives customers more choice. Thus, moving into the global economy raises the standards for goods and services that suppliers have to meet. These higher standards prevail even within suppliers' domestic markets, since standards "leak" back and forth across national boundaries in the form of traded goods and services.

From mass production to the flexible or customized production of goods and services. Moving from mass production to the flexible production of goods and services changes the opportunities and, ultimately, the basis for economic growth. Computerized technologies have revolutionized production by allowing both long and short production runs that can respond to niche or customized markets at the cost savings of mass production. Mechanically based technologies are inflexible in that "instructions"—for example, on how to cut metal for the production of a particular model of car—are embedded in the physical tools, forcing automobile manufacturers to shut down their production lines to retool for any changes. Computerized technologies, by contrast, are functionally flexible; instructions are now embedded in computer programs that can be easily changed. Modern carmakers can now produce utility vehicles, passenger cars, and light trucks on the same assembly line on the same shop floor on the same day. Banks can vastly expand the range of their financial services by creating computerized databases and computational programs that let them customize services to their customers' needs.

Globalization and flexible production have thus combined to foster a changed profile of customer demand in manufactured goods, agricultural products, and services. International and, increasingly, domestic customers have come to expect a large, varied, and continuously improving basket of goods and services, fast delivery of orders, high and consistent quality, and low prices.

Taken together, these economic shifts put a premium on information-processing and problem-solving skills

Meeting these demands requires changes in technologies and the organisation of work. Mass production of goods and services depended on routinization and a hierarchical specialization of function, where most workers, even middle managers, were order takers. They were not expected to exercise judgment, initiative, or problem-solving skills, and most decisions were referred up the chain of command. This productive regime was predicated on slow rates of change that minimized the need for adult learning.

Under flexible production, by contrast, employers broaden job descriptions to give each worker authority over more of the component tasks of production, flatten organisational hierarchies, and introduce job rotation and team-based work. These changes simultaneously save the time lost in referring decisions up and down organisational ladders and reduce middle management and supervisory jobs. The jobs of less skilled workers begin to incorporate some of the supervisory, planning, repair, maintenance, and quality control functions previously reserved for managers or specialists.

Thus, workers even in previously lower skill jobs need higher levels of verbal and quantitative skills. Since change is the defining characteristic of globalizing market economies, workers need broader job knowledge, better problem-solving skills, knowing-how-to-learn skills, and greater initiative.

The increasing demand for highly skilled labor shows up in increasing unemployment rates for those with low educational qualifications, falling real wages for those with low skills, and increasing growth in white collar, high-skilled occupations as a percentage of total job growth.

Test data show that ECA countries are behind OECD countries in their citizens' information-processing skills

The education and training systems of ECA countries fit their pretransition economies well, and many ECA educators believe that they still have good systems. However, evidence from the OECD International Adult Literacy Survey (IALS) suggests that the region's education systems are a poor fit with modern economies (OECD 2000). The IALS defines literacy as the information-processing skills that adults need to perform literacy tasks encountered at work, at home, or in the community. The survey measures the individual's capacities to expand and interpret the meaning of verbal and quantitative texts, using three scales: prose, document, and quantitative.[6] It does not measure the individual's retention of specific information or ability to use that information in academically structured problems. Scores on these scales correlate strongly with probabilities of unemployment, wages, and per capita GDP. The amount of variance in literacy scores within a country correlates with the extent of income inequality in that country.

Four ECA countries participated in the two rounds of the IALS: the Czech Republic, Hungary, Poland, and Slovenia. Assessment results indicate that the education systems of three of these four countries (Hungary, Poland, and Slovenia) are producing the wrong product for a market economy. As figure 1.2 shows, in contrast with the results for the Czech Republic, significant shares of those 16–65 years of age in the other three ECA countries performed poorly. A comparison of the IALS data for these four countries with those for the OECD countries in the survey tells an important story.

• In three of the four ECA countries very high percentages of workers aged 16–65 tested at low literacy levels (levels 1 and 2) on all three scales.[7] (See figure 1.2.) Scores at or above level 3 predict ability to function in modern workplaces. About 75 percent of workers in each of the three low performing ECA countries tested below level 3 on the prose scale; between 67 and 75 percent, below level 3 on the document scale. Hungary performed better on the quantitative scale, although still below the OECD distribution. However, 65–70 percent of the Polish and Slovenian 16–65 year olds tested at levels 1 or 2 on the quantitative scale.

• Analyses of IALS data for all participating countries found that achieving the literacy levels required in modern workplaces (level 3 and above) was associated with having completed upper secondary education. Of the four ECA countries, the Czech Republic had the highest upper secondary completion rate for those 25–64 years of age and a significantly higher completion rate than the average for participating OECD countries. Nevertheless, two of the low performing ECA countries (Poland and Slovenia) also had completion rates above the average for the OECD countries, while Hungary's rate was only modestly lower. This suggests that the differences between the tested skills of adults in Hungary, Poland, and Slovenia and those of adults in participating OECD countries cannot be attributed to the *quantity* of education that ECA populations complete.

• The performances of those still in, or recently graduated from, school reflect most pertinently on the quality of a country's education system. Substantially higher percentages of 20–25 year

---

6 Prose literacy is defined as the knowledge and skills needed to understand and use information from texts, including editorials, news stories, poems, and fiction. Document literacy is defined as the knowledge and skills required to locate and use information contained in various formats, including job applications, payroll forms, transport schedules, maps, tables, and graphics. Quantitative literacy is defined as the knowledge and skills required to apply arithmetical operations, either alone or sequentially, to numbers embedded in printed materials.

7 *Level 1* indicates individuals with very poor skills. For example, the person may be unable to determine the correct amount of medicine to give a child from information printed on the package. *Level 2* respondents can deal only with material that is simple and clearly laid out and in which the tasks involved are not too complex. It denotes a weak level of skill but more hidden than level 1. Individuals may have developed coping skills to manage everyday literacy demands, but their low proficiency makes it difficult for them to face novel demands, such as learning new job skills. *Level 3* is considered a suitable minimum for coping with the demands of everyday life and work in a complex, advanced society. It denotes roughly the skill level required for successful secondary school completion and college entry. It requires the ability to integrate several sources of information and solve more complex problems. *Levels 4 and 5* describe respondents who demonstrate command of higher order information-processing skills.

Figure 1.2 Percentage of 16–65 Year Olds who Test at Low Literacy Levels, 1994–98

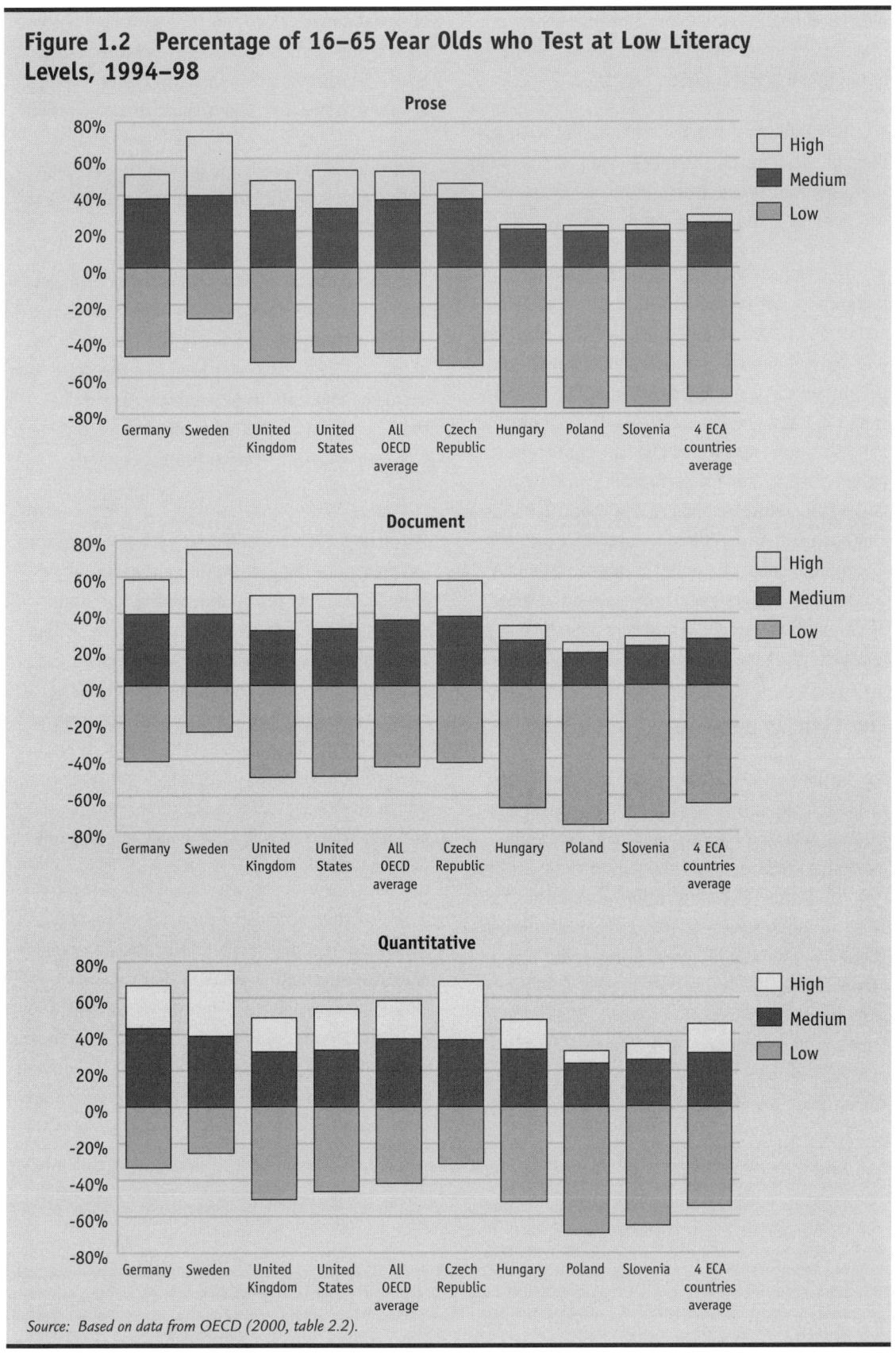

Source: Based on data from OECD (2000, table 2.2).

THE WORLD BANK

olds in Hungary, Poland, and Slovenia tested at low literacy levels than those in the same age group in participating OECD countries.[8]

- This indicates that the current education systems of the transition countries are not producing the skills that new entrants into the workplace will need as those workplaces modernize.

- Multivariate analyses show that different factors account for the literacy performances of countries that participated in the IALS. However, one factor—parental socioeconomic status—distinguishes the three low performing ECA countries from the Czech Republic and the OECD countries.[9] Parental socioeconomic status has significantly more effect on literacy performance in Hungary, Poland, and Slovenia than in the Czech Republic and has more effect than in most OECD countries. Apparently, education policy in these three ECA countries is not designed to minimize the effect of parental background—and may operate to reinforce it via mechanisms such as early tracking.

The Civic Imperative

For decades ECA countries were ruled by authoritarian regimes that controlled their populations through fear and the deliberate creation and manipulation of distrust. The region faces common civic challenges in its transition from authoritarianism to open societies. The concept of an open society is variously interpreted. However, two attributes of the civic society are particularly germane to economic development. One is having strong civic institutions that attract domestic and international investors. The other is a shared commitment across social divisions to the rules of social participation. Such commitments reduce transaction costs and increase social cohesion. Lower transaction costs increase the efficiency of economic activities, and greater social cohesion reduces the chances of the civil strife that is so disruptive to economic growth. Under some conditions, schools can encourage both of these civic objectives.

The civic basis for a state that attracts investors. Studies show that private investment correlates with investors' perceptions of the predictability, accountability, and transparency of the state. One survey of investors in 69 countries found that the ECA region performed particularly poorly on these dimensions, relative to other regions (World Bank 1997d).

The civic basis for a state attractive to investors requires more than mechanisms that let citizens enforce demands for accountability and transparency. It also requires that citizens be willing to use these mechanisms—in other words, that citizens believe that they have rights relative to the state and obligations as citizens to exercise those rights. These civic habits are poorly developed in ECA. Decades of authoritarian regimes left in their wake citizens who are often passive and fatalistic and who shift blame and responsibility to others.

A shared commitment to the rules of social participation across social and political divisions.[10] Shared rules create a basis for trust among citizens, and evidence is growing that trust and civic mindedness strongly predict better economic performance (Knack and Keefer 1997).[11] Economic development is based on human cooperation and

---

8 The average literacy skill level of Polish youth translated into a lag of 2.5–3 years of education compared with the 16–25 year olds in the full sample. Polish 16–25 year olds had completed an average of 11.2 years of education, compared with 12.1 years for the full international sample of this age group, but only 0.9 years of this difference can be attributed to the difference in years of schooling actually completed (Willms 1999).
9 Socioeconomic status is measured by parental education (OECD 2000).
10 This interpretation of "open society" is related to the concept of social capital, which is broadly defined to mean social relationships as resources that actors can use to achieve their economic interests—for example, to reduce economic risk or to acquire information pertinent to economic transactions. The economic benefits of these relationships are unintended or only partially intended; that is, they are not the main purpose of the relationship—but they are nonetheless real and persistent.
11 These terms are defined relative to items on the World Values Surveys of the University of Michigan. Trust is measured by the question "Generally speaking, would you say that most people can be trusted, or that you can't be too careful in dealing

> **Box 1.1**
>
> ## USING THE SCHOOLS TO EDUCATE STUDENTS FOR AN OPEN SOCIETY
>
> Effective participation in open societies requires capacities and perspectives that are fairly easily taught and practiced in schools.
>
> - Engendering skepticism about absolutes seems related to the acquisition of the fundamentals of epistemology: what does it mean to know something, and to what extent does a text or statement satisfy the requirements of knowing? Presenting different points of view on an issue—and using textbooks that reflect these differences—can be used to build skills in reconciling conflicting perspectives.
> - A capacity for empathy can be cultivated principally through good literature that enables a person to enter vicariously into the life of another person.
> - A strong foundation in history and the social sciences can provide an understanding of the benefits of sound social institutions and cooperation.
> - Mainstreaming education—limiting the grouping of students by ability or achievement—is a way to avoid exclusion. This implies avoiding rigid divisions between vocational and academic curricula and adopting teaching methods and curricula that allow students of different aptitudes to "succeed" in shared spaces.
>
> Classroom observations in the region indicate that many ECA countries have yet to adopt perspectives such as these. Schools tend to stress the transmission of absolute truth, blunt the imagination, and segregate students by ability, social background, and ethnicity.

exchange—on transactions. Trust increases the efficiency of these transactions. Economic activities that require agents to rely on the future actions of others are accomplished at lower cost in environments of higher trust, in part because of a lesser need for costly enforcement.

Shared rules also help citizens to see one another not as "cultural strangers" but as citizens of the same or similar communities and countries. The term *social cohesion* refers to the willingness of groups to cooperate across boundaries that normally divide them (e.g., clan, ethnic, or religious membership). Social cohesion increases economic development by reducing the risk of political instability and civic strife, both of which increase the instability of codes of social participation and the uncertainty of transactions. Studies such as Ashutosh Varshney's (forthcoming) on Hindus and Muslims in India find that the structure of civic life affects ethnic and communal violence. When groups otherwise divided by ethnic and other differences have vigorous intercommunal associations and frequent everyday engagements, there is less social space for communal violence and more constraint on the polarizing strategies of political elites.

A number of ECA countries have multiple ethnic and religious divisions that can threaten social cohesion (UNICEF 1998, table 3.3, p. 56). For example, Georgia, with a population of only 5.5 million, has multiple distinct ethnic groups and four distinct religions. Countries such as Bosnia-Herzegovina, Estonia, the Federal Republic of Yugoslavia (FR Yugoslavia), the Former Yugoslav Republic of Macedonia (FYR Macedonia), Kazakhstan, the Kyrgyz Republic, Latvia, Moldova, and Ukraine have large minority groups.

---

with people?" Civic mindedness is measured by responses to questions about whether each of the following behaviors "can always be justified, never be justified, or something in between": (a) claiming government benefits which you are not entitled to; (b) avoiding a fare on public transport; (c) cheating on taxes if you have the chance; (d) keeping money that you have found; and (e) failing to report damage you have done accidentally to a parked vehicle. (See Knack and Keefer 1997.)

Schools can be used to develop civic obligations and adherence to shared rules of the game

The school can complement other institutions in the society in socializing children to the rights and obligations of citizenship and in developing those values and perspectives that support voluntary adherence to shared codes. (See box 1.1.) Education policies relative to minorities will affect whether a country that wants to create cohesion can use its schools to do so. The European Union supports minority language instruction, and ECA countries that hope to apply for accession to the EU are moving in this direction. Minority instruction, however, imposes efficiency costs and can impose costs on individuals by restricting their mobility within the labor market. In terms of social cohesion, separate instruction can work both ways—either building social cohesion by showing respect for differences, or enforcing division.

Summary of needs

The economic and civic imperatives confronting ECA mean that individuals have to acquire the following:

- Knowledge that is broadly based, allowing a flexible response to change
- Solid foundation skills that support future learning
- Adequate metacognitive skills (knowing-how-to-learn, or executive thinking, skills) and higher order cognitive thinking skills[12]
- Substantial experience in applying knowledge and skills to unfamiliar problems
- Habits of exercising choice and voice
- Respect for differences and for shared rules of citizenship that establish the grounds for trust and cooperation.

Strategic Paths for Governments

These imperatives pressure governments to change their education systems in fundamental ways. Educators have to change what they teach (curricular content) and how they teach it (their pedagogy).[13] They have to educate the majority of students to higher standards, and they have to see education as continuous through adulthood, rather than as a process that ends when individuals reach maturity. Finally, policymakers have to change the incentives that govern the behaviors of all the players in the system in order to energize change.

Curriculum: Align the content of instruction with new objectives

Communist ideological content has been removed from most ECA textbooks. ECA education systems teach the enabling skills, such as reading, writing, oral communications, some foreign languages, mathematics, and the principles of science and technology. However, as taught, these skills' effectiveness in the modern economy is reduced in the following ways:

- The syllabus for any given grade usually includes such a large number of subjects that learning is necessarily superficial, with no time for teachers and students to reflect on and question content or for team-based and individual projects.
- The syllabus, textbooks, and learning materials structure content more as facts to be memorized than as a set of building blocks and flexible tools. Facts are an essential part of the individual's cognitive architecture; the problem is balance. In the information age, recollection of facts has become significantly less important, with the advent of the Internet and easily accessible printed materi-

---

12 Higher order thinking occurs with regard to problems that have certain characteristics: the path of action is not fully specified in advance, nor is the path to a solution mentally visible from any single vantage point; the problem yields multiple rather than unique solutions and requires nuanced judgment and the application of multiple criteria that sometimes conflict with one another; and not all of the information needed to solve the problem is available (Resnick 1987).

13 Pedagogy is defined as how teaching is conducted. Differences in pedagogy that affect how well an education system achieves certain human capital and civic objectives are discussed later in this chapter.

Table 1.1 Differences between Traditional and New Teaching Strategies and Workplaces

Traditional arrangements		New arrangements	
Teaching strategy	Workplace	Teaching strategy	Workplace
Teachers as experts convey knowledge to passive learners	Passive order-taking in a hierarchical work organisation; heavy supervision to control workers	Under teacher guidance, students assume responsibility for learning, in the process developing knowing-how-to learn skills	Workers are expected to take responsibility for identifying and solving problems and for adapting to change by learning
Emphasis on facts and on getting the right answers	Emphasis on limited responses to limited problems and on getting a task done	Focus on alternative ways to frame issues and problems	Workers deal with non-routine problems that have to be analyzed and solved
What is to be learned is stripped of meaningful context	Focus on the specific task independent of organisational context or business strategy	Ideas, principles, and facts are introduced, used, and understood in meaningful context	Workers are expected to make decisions that require understanding the broader context of their work and their company's priorities

Source: Berryman (1997, Table 6, p.14).

als, while the ability to interpret and evaluate information has become more important.[14]

- In most ECA countries the curriculum is a specification of content, not of the knowledge and skill standards that students must master.
- The way minorities within the country and groups outside the country are handled in the curriculum remains problematic in some ECA countries.

ECA's occupationally oriented secondary and post-secondary programs (including university programs) also have to be restructured if they are to reflect market demand. In most cases this means the following:

- Replacing narrow and excessively specialized instruction with broader based training in occupational families that have more academic content. For example, while Ukraine starts from a base of 1,500 specialties, Hungary has already restructured 200 occupational specialties at the secondary level into 15 families.
- Pushing more specialized training up to the postsecondary level.

Pedagogy: Change how content is taught

In the traditionally organized teaching and learning of the ECA countries, the teacher is the expert and the students are passive receivers of knowledge. This organisation discourages the open debate required for airing and tempering subgroup differences. Students do not interact with problems and content and thus do not engage in choice, judgment, control processes, and problem formulation. They have little chance to make and learn from mistakes. This dependence

---

14 In contrast to the focus on facts in ECA curricula, an analysis of the French secondary school exit examination, the Baccalaureate, shows a very different set of performance expectations for students. In biology, for example, the Baccalaureate measures the student's ability to master complex information and thematic information, to abstract and deduce scientific principles, to use scientific principles to explain, to construct and use models, to design investigations, and to interpret investigative data.

> **Box 1.2**
>
> ## AN EXAMPLE OF ENQUIRY-BASED TEACHING
>
> Social science and history classes in ECA schools normally include instruction in the country's constitution. The teacher can teach about the constitution by having students memorize it and testing them to see if they can reproduce specific points on an examination. Or the teacher can engage students in reflecting on the document. For example, the teacher can divide the class into the different interest groups that originally came together to frame the constitution. The constitution is treated as a draft, and each team proposes changes in the document consistent with the perspectives of the interest group that the team represents. The constitution is not treated as received truth but as a document that was built out of dynamic political, social, and economic forces and that can be altered in the same spirit.
>
> The difference between the two teaching approaches in this example is profound. In the second approach students learn the actual constitution better because they engage with its content. More important, because they learn that it can be interpreted in alternative ways, they develop the enquiry skills that are invaluable in a market economy and open society (Berryman and Bailey 1992).

on the teacher and on received wisdom undercuts their development of the higher order cognitive and metacognitive thinking skills valued in globalizing market economies.

Table 1.1 displays differences between traditional and new organisations of work and teaching strategies. The workplace differences correspond to the differences between work organized to support mass production and work based on a flexible production regime. Box 1.2 gives an example of traditional versus enquiry-based teaching.

Ensure that all students acquire foundation and higher order cognitive thinking skills

Before the transition, the education systems of the region were designed to serve industrialization, to inculcate narrowly appropriate skills for all new entrants into the labor market, and to minimize the difference between the workers and the elite. In practice, these goals resulted in an education system with relatively low standards because it was organized around the least common denominator. These systems also had an elitist stream that operated as an outlet for elitist pressures. Academic Olympiads were one such outlet.

After the transition, socioeconomic stratification processes are reasserting themselves, resulting in a still more differentiated education system. One stream is for the bright, the rich, and the well connected. It stresses the head at the expense of the hand. The other stream is for everyone else.

Modern economies cannot afford to discriminate between the head and the hand. Mass production economies accommodate considerable variation in the educational and skill levels of workers; globalizing market economies are much less tolerant of workers with low skills. Variations in years of education and in skill acquisition result in serious differences in employability and wage returns. To prevent the emergence of a group of youths who are virtually unemployable, ECA education systems will have to ensure that all students leave school competent in the foundation skills and in higher order cognitive thinking skills.

This does not mean that all students have to go through academic curricula at the upper secondary level. Vocational/technical programs can have substantial academic content. For the less academically inclined, instructional programs that *integrate* academic and vocational content are highly effective in delivering a quality education. For example, a high school in New York City is organized around the repair of aircraft engines. In the context of learning something that real people do in the real world, students acquire the academic foundation skills and knowledge that position them for adult learning and adaptation. The students have to use mathematics, decode the complex manuals published by the manufacturers of different kinds of engines, and exercise diagnostic and problem-solving skills.

Educating all students to higher standards also means avoiding early specialization that can stunt the development of the foundation skills for those in applied or vocational tracks. ECA education systems specialize early—sometimes before the end, and certainly by the end, of basic education, when children are 14 years old or younger. As observed earlier, excessive educational specialization reduces the ability of individuals to adapt to the broadly defined job responsibilities and rapid change that are characteristic of modern economies. Regulations that preclude later transitions between educational tracks are as damaging as early specialization. In fact, it is this structured lack of second chances that makes early specialization so damaging.

Ensure that adults can modify their human capital as skill demands change

Governments have to ensure opportunities for midcareer education and training. Most countries across the region do not have such systems. In Croatia, for example, the belief is that once an individual completes formal education, he or she is "done". Differences among countries in scores on the IALS are partly attributable to the nature and level of learning standards, the variation among school leavers in their achievement of those standards, and the society's pressures for and support of continuous learning.

The state does not have to provide or finance retraining opportunities, but it should stimulate their provision, possibly regulate them, and probably provide consumer information about their value for students. Box 1.3 gives examples of how three countries have created adult training systems.

Alter incentives to achieve the new objectives

The incentives that govern the behaviors of players in the system—from bureaucrats to students—have to support the changes just discussed. If students know that they are condemned to a low skill educational track at the age of 14, they have little incentive to strive for excellence. If the examinations that determine whether students are promoted to the next grade or gain access to university remain organized around facts and correct answers, teachers and students will continue to concentrate on facts and correct answers.

Basic to all these reforms are setting national learning standards, measuring students' learning performances against these standards, and holding educators, students, and their families accountable for meeting the standards. Unfortunately, learning assessments are not common in the region. Prior to the transition, and even today, the high degree of central control over the curriculum, the syllabus, textbooks, and teachers was thought sufficient to ensure learning. Assessments of student performance for purposes of decisions about promotion to the next grade or level were left to the teacher and tended to be grossly subjective. There was also enormous variance between teachers in the standards to which student performance was held.

Box 1.3

ESTABLISHING TRAINING SYSTEMS:
THE CASES OF SLOVENIA, HUNGARY, AND ROMANIA

In 1991 the government of Slovenia created the Slovene Adult Education Center and adult education legislation to replace the system of "workers' universities" and the outmoded training in state enterprises, which was collapsing. To some extent, the center is modeled after the United Kingdom's National Institute for Adult and Continuing Education (NIACE) and is not intended as a primary delivery agent. The center assists in preparing a foundation for adult education, maintains an information system, organizes training for adult education staff, and handles research, development, and international linkages. The government funds 60 percent of the center's outlays; the rest comes from grants and contracts.

Hungary, to facilitate its entry into the European Union, is now drafting new legislation to broaden and strengthen lifelong learning. It began reforming secondary and adult education and training in the 1980s. The system of highly specialized secondary-level training was recognized as inappropriate for a modernizing economy, but youths still needed access to this type of training at the postsecondary level, as did adult workers, and the unemployed required skill upgrading. The result has been a network of regional human resource development centers, operating as semiautonomous institutions managed by multiple bodies. The centers provide employment counseling, basic education, vocational training, small business assistance for out-of-school youth and adults, and a broad range of customized contract training for enterprises. The centers are financed by government grants, contracts for retraining the unemployed, contracts with enterprises, and individual tuition.

In Romania, where continuing education is recognized as a key element of the country's human resource development strategy, the Higher Education Finance Council is emphasizing continuing or lifelong learning opportunities for higher education graduates. This initiative addresses the issue of, for example, an excess of well trained engineers unaccustomed to functioning in the more dynamic and uncertain environment of a global market economy. The council invites competitive proposals from higher education institutions for funding to develop continuous learning programs for university graduates. These grants are expected to encourage more flexible scheduling, course duration, and mode of delivery (on-site versus distance learning). A National Training Council is also being established, in part to raise the productivity of incumbent workers. This council has a broader mandate for adult training than the continuous education programs of the Higher Education Finance Council, in that it will support programs for workers at all levels of educational attainment.

A few countries have moved to create interpretable and fair assessments and examinations. For example, Romania has established a strong National Assessment and Examination Service that has designed and now implements a new assessment and examination system, including the national learning assessment for grade 4 and the country's school leaving examinations (*capacitate* and *baccalaureate*). The service has also framed and oversees continuous teacher training in assessment of students for diagnostic purposes and examinations.

How Do Governments Get from Here to There?

In realigning education, governments can best intervene at certain points in the process. These points are defined in table 1.2 and follow the objectives for change discussed above. There are

Table 1.2 Realigning Education to Fit New Economic and Civic Imperatives

Essential changes	Points of intervention
Align content with new goals	• Change curriculum • Align textbooks, learning materials, computer-based instructional programs, and teacher guides with new curriculum
Change how content is taught	• Restructure preservice and in-service training for teachers to alter the organisation of teaching and learning in the classroom
Ensure that all students acquire foundation and higher order cognitive thinking skills	• Use diagnostic assessments of student learning • Hold players in the system accountable for the learning achievements of all students • Integrate academic content into vocational/technical training • Expand opportunities for students to move among educational "tracks"
Restructure education as continuous across the lifetime	• Ensure that students have the foundation skills that enable continuous learning • Facilitate provision of and consumer information about retraining opportunities for adults
Alter incentives to achieve new objectives	• Establish strategic partnerships with teachers • Establish knowledge and skill standards for teachers • Use these standards to determine entry into teaching and retention/promotion of experienced teachers • Set learning standards for each grade and subject for students • Administer value-added national assessments of learning • Send "report cards" to families about the performance of their children's schools • Set up consequences for poorly performing schools and recognition for schools that perform well • Align examinations for promotion to subsequent grades and levels with curricular changes and new learning standards

Source: Authors' compilation.

certain prerequisites for achieving the changes outlined in the table.

Build political support. This change agenda requires political commitment across a decade (or longer) from all of the players who affect its success. Thus, a consensus about the objectives of change must first be built among the different political parties to protect the agenda from changes in governments and ministers. Other groups critical to the success of the change agenda are bureaucrats in the education system, local governments, leaders of ethnic groups, teachers, and parents. Typically, for example, most bureaucracies around the world value the current configuration of education, whatever that happens to be, and resist policies that would alter it. Involving these groups in designing the specifics of the change agenda not only builds commitment but also helps them understand the problems that the agenda is trying to solve.

Constructing a strategic partnership with teachers is one key to sustained change. The teaching profession can be a powerful source of innovation and change—and of overt and covert resistance to change. If a change agenda fails at the level of the classroom, it fails overall. Several factors in the region are tilting teachers in the direction of resistance.

- Political and economic changes in the 1990s rendered some teaching skills obsolete and added others almost overnight. Examples include the need to retrain Russian teachers in Central Europe and the need to teach applied as well as theoretical knowledge in subjects such as mathematics and the sciences. Although there is pressure to change teaching skills and knowledge, preservice training institutions have not responded to these new demands. Governments in many countries either are not funding or are barely funding in-service training. For example, the Albanian education budget has no in-service training line. Caught between new performance standards and few means of learning how to meet them, teachers often respond to their anxiety by resisting change.

- In most countries, teachers are civil service employees. Their employment, promotion, and salaries are regulated centrally. Salaries are an issue in many countries, especially in the Former Soviet Union (FSU); see annex table A17. In some other countries teachers are not being paid at all. For example, by 1998 Moldova had accumulated arrears in the salary and benefits budget line that amounted to 81 percent of the actual expenditure for salaries and benefits in 1998.

- Teachers' unions are either left over from the pretransition period or are newly emergent, fragmented, and too small to speak effectively on behalf of the profession. In the absence of ways of coordinating members of their own profession on issues such as recruitment, standards, or training, and, in some cases, in the face of real economic pressures, teachers tend to focus on issues such as compensation and employment protection.

To involve teachers collectively, as a professional group, in reforming the sector, governments will have to reestablish mutual trust and terms of cooperation. This reform can be accomplished by framing a strategic partnership with teachers that covers a range of issues. These might include:

- Decentralization of hiring to local or school levels
- Introduction of new contracts that define teachers' workloads, including contact hours, tutorial activities, special student needs, curriculum development, and in-service training responsibilities
- Reform of preservice teacher training, separation of subject-specific university programs from professional teaching modules, and adjustment of the latter to new standards and needs
- Financing for continuous in-service training
- Keying of promotions and salary increases to teachers' performance and their participation in innovations in curriculum and teaching/learning methods
- Establishment of forums for dialogues between government, local authorities, school leaders, parent and student organisations, and teacher associations.

To change the teaching and learning process, start with the curriculum. Everything else flows from decisions about the curricular framework. That framework reflects assumptions and agreements about content, about how content should be taught, and about how students learn. The framework should include agreements on the learning standards, by subject and grade, that all players in the system are accountable for meeting. Box 1.4 shows how Hungary has met the challenge of coordinating the curriculum with learning standards.

Align textbooks, learning assessments, and examinations for students and teachers with new content standards. Textbooks and other learning materials have to be aligned with the curriculum and learning standards for a given subject and grade. The first administration of all assessments

Box 1.4

NATIONAL CURRICULUM STANDARDS IN A DECENTRALIZED EDUCATION SYSTEM: THE CASE OF HUNGARY

Hungary's national curricular framework leaves programming decisions (numbers of courses, class schedules, and hours of instruction) entirely to local authorities. The national curriculum integrates content and learning standards by defining content in terms of the skills and knowledge that students are expected to master by certain grades. Curricular performance standards give equal weight to the interests of the individual and to those of the wider community. The core curriculum is designed to use less than two-thirds of total school time, leaving one-third available for local preference. National examinations that must be passed for students to progress through the system reduce the possibilities of extreme curricula at local levels.

and examinations that incorporate the new learning standards should be for informational and diagnostic purposes only. This first experience shows all the players in the system the gaps between students' (and teachers') current performances and the ultimate goals. It clarifies the task ahead and focuses attention on getting it done. Even at this dry run stage, players need to understand the costs of failing to improve and when these costs will be imposed.

With new standards in place, start the process of retraining experienced teachers to teach new content in new ways. Typically, policymakers view teachers as conduits for instructional policy, not as actors. Studies of teachers' experiences with change agendas tell a consistent and disheartening story.

- Teachers' understanding of the content and skill changes expected of them is often quite different from that of policymakers, largely because they receive only brief and superficial training and guidance. Thus, teachers tend to change their classroom activities, but without a conceptual understanding of the reason for the changes. The result is that activities get structured in ways unintended by the change agenda.

- Like all learners, teachers interpret and carry out new instructional policies in light of their own experience, beliefs, and knowledge. In other words, they see new ideas through old lenses. If retraining is superficial, teachers merge only partially understood requirements of the change agenda with their prior beliefs and teaching practices. The result is idiosyncratic practice that approximates neither their old practice nor that envisioned by the change agenda.

- Teachers are often left to struggle with conflicts that higher level managers and policymakers should have resolved. Teachers may face a lack of alignment among the changes expected of them and the textbooks and examinations that should support these changes. Or they find that policymakers have vastly underestimated the classroom time required to cover new content and ways of learning. In these situations they resolve the conflicts in their own, individual, ways.

The message is that one-shot workshops, which define most staff development, do not work in changing teachers' classroom behavior. What does work is staff development that allows a continuous interaction between classroom practice and opportunities to reflect on that practice against clear standards and models. One method is to combine local networks of teachers that meet regularly for purposes of in-service learning; high quality distance learning materials that encourage benchmarking and reflection; and well trained facilitators.

THE WORLD BANK

CHAPTER TWO

COMBAT POVERTY BY INCREASING EDUCATIONAL FAIRNESS

Summary

As ECA economies increasingly approximate market economies, human capital will increasingly affect the prospects of individuals. Education helps create human capital. Fairness of educational opportunity is therefore important in combating poverty.

Since the transition, inequities in learning opportunities have increased in ECA. One indicator is a decline in enrollment rates, especially at the preschool and upper secondary levels. Preschool education can affect children's readiness to learn. Failure to complete upper secondary education handicaps the individual in a market economy. Enrollment losses at the upper secondary level reflect losses from vocational and technical programs as the perceived relevance to a market economy declines.

Increasing costs to families are probably affecting enrollments among the poor as a new tendency to shift education costs to families coincides with growing income gaps between families created by the transition to market economies. So far, there is only fragmentary evidence that increased private costs for education are driving down the participation of children from poor families. However, studies in other regions of the world document a clear relationship between families' demand for education and their incomes.

The downstream and intergenerational costs of seriously unequal learning opportunities may overtake the region before policymakers recognize the need to develop a solution. Preventive and equilibrating strategies include a range of education financing policies (discussed in chapter 3); low-cost alternatives to fee-based preschools; restructuring of secondary education; relaxation of the barriers to moving between tracks, levels, and programs; objective examinations for university entrance; opportunities for adult retraining; and policies that target educational access and quality in rural areas.

This chapter focuses on differences in educational opportunities that affect learning and those adult outcomes that are related to learning, such as wages, employment probabilities, and poverty. The issue is equitable opportunities to learn, such as access to an upper secondary school or to textbooks, not equal learning. Factors that create differences in learning opportunities include unequal financing, residential location (rural versus urban), parental education, family poverty, and minority status. Although the objective is not equal learning, measures of outcomes shed light on the issue of opportunity. They show when differences in inputs do not matter educationally and when they may. Unequal outcomes can have many causes. Differences in the opportunities to learn are one cause, but only one.

Why This Development Goal?

This chapter focuses on differences in learning opportunities among individuals within countries, not on differences in educational levels between countries. Education affects poverty through wages. In distorted labor markets with skewed mechanisms for distributing incomes, the fruits of greater worker productivity may not accrue to workers. However, all else equal, education builds human capital, which increases worker productivity. Greater worker productivity increases output (economic growth) and individual incomes.

Unfair learning opportunities now matter in ECA because human capital now matters

In ECA levels of human capital increasingly matter for economic growth and individuals' life opportunities and their probabilities of being poor.[15] As ECA economies start to approximate market economies, labor markets will increasingly allocate employment opportunities and wages according to variations in human capital. An individual's level of human capital will be vital in affecting the following:

- *Expected years in employment.* In 1996 in OECD countries men aged 25–64 years who had completed tertiary education could expect 5.6 more years of employment during their working lifetimes than men who had not completed secondary education. The differences in expected years of employment by education for three ECA countries were more pronounced: Czech Republic, 10.8; Hungary, 13.1; and Poland, 8.8 (OECD, *Education at a Glance*, 1998). For the only two ECA countries with reliable estimates (Czech Republic and Hungary), unemployment probabilities steadily decline as prose literacy scores increase (OECD 2000).

- *Earnings.* In 1995 women aged 30–44 in OECD countries who had completed university earned an average of 61 percent more than upper secondary graduates; for men of these ages, the difference was 57 percent. Women with upper secondary education earned an average of 32 percent more than those who had not completed upper secondary school; their male counterparts earned an average of 19 percent more (OECD 1998b). For all three literacy scales, the percentage, at each literacy level, of the population aged 25–65 that is in the top 60 percent of earners steadily increases as the literacy level increases (OECD 2000).

- *The probabilities of being trained by employers.* In OECD countries the better educated are more apt to be trained by employers, and employers reward more training with higher wages (Mincer 1993; OECD 1998b). As literacy scores increase, an increasing percentage of the population aged 16–65 reports having participated in adult education and training in the preceding year (OECD 2000).

We already see relationships linking educational attainment, employment status, wage levels, and poverty in the region. For the period 1993–95 household poverty in Belarus, the Czech Republic, Estonia, Hungary, Poland, Romania, and the Slovak Republic was closely related to the education of the household head. Households whose heads had completed only basic education were 20 to 60 percent more likely to be poor than the average household. Vocational education yielded an average probability of being poor; academic secondary education reduced that probability by about half; and, except in Belarus and the Slovak Republic, a university education virtually guaranteed that a household would not be poor (Milanovic 1998, figure 5.1, pp. 68–69).

In Georgia both the incidence and the depth of poverty were greater for the less educated (World Bank 1999e). In Bulgaria educational attainment powerfully predicted the probabilities of being unemployed: a worker with basic education faced odds of being unemployed 4 times higher than a worker with a university degree and 1.9 times higher than a worker with secondary general education. Among the employed, educational attainment explained 8.2 percent of total variance in earnings (World Bank 1999a). In Estonia better educated workers got larger pay increases,

---

15 In preparing its *World Development Report 2000/01* on the theme of poverty and development, the World Bank published a series of reports, "Consultations with the Poor," that summarized the views of 60,000 poor men and women from 60 countries. Five ECA countries (Bosnia-Herzegovina, Bulgaria, Kyrgyz Republic, Russia, and Uzbekistan) were included in the study. Notably, across the ECA region the poor perceive schools and education as essential institutions (Consultations with the Poor 1999a). In Uzbekistan receiving a good education ranked first or second among the criteria of well-being (Consultations with the Poor 1999d, p. 10). In Bosnia education was considered a "means for the society to overcome the present crisis" (Consultations with the Poor 1999b, p. 26).

were less apt to be laid off, and, if laid off, found new jobs faster (World Bank 1996b). In FYR Macedonia almost 80 percent of the poor lived in households headed by individuals with basic education or less. Analyses showed that, of all the factors considered, education had the largest positive impact on Macedonian household welfare (World Bank 1999f).

Enrollment rates are going in the wrong direction in the region

Enrollment rates are the best available measure of learning opportunities in ECA, complementary measures such as attendance and students' learning performances being scarce.[16]

Before the transition, learning opportunities in ECA were inequitable. However, unfairness seems to have been largely restricted to the noncompulsory levels.[17] Wage compression (little variation in wages) under communism meant that unequal access to education was not, as in the rest of the world, strongly associated with variations in family income. Preschool enrollments varied across countries, being especially low in Yugoslavia, Turkey, and most Central Asian countries (see annex table A5). Children in the rural areas of the Soviet Union were less likely to be enrolled in school, including preschool, than children in urban areas (UNICEF 1998, p. 43). Children from minority groups were less apt than children of majority populations to complete more than basic education (UNICEF 1998). Before the transition, father's occupation in Hungary and Poland showed almost the same pattern as for Western countries in terms of the proportion of children who obtained upper secondary or tertiary credentials. The three Baltic states and Belarus showed similar patterns (UNICEF 1998).

Since the transition, enrollments have been declining. A larger proportion of student cohorts is building less human capital and a smaller proportion is building more.[18] (See table 2.1.) Calculations show that the number of years of full-time education (excluding preschool) that an average 6 year old child in ECA can expect to achieve over his or her lifetime has declined. For comparison, in 1988 the average full-time school expectancy for OECD countries was 15.4 years (OECD, *Education at a Glance*, various years). In 1989 the average full-time school expectancy was 11.21 years; by 1997 it had declined to 10.57 years. In contrast, the average full-time school expectancy for OECD countries in 1998 was 15.4 years (OECD, various years).

Pretertiary enrollment rates have been declining in some countries for preschool and generally for basic and upper secondary education. Figure 2.1 shows the trends for preschool for the subregions. Annex table A5 shows that from 1989 to 1997 preschool enrollments increased in a few countries, such as Estonia, Slovenia, and Turkey. However, they dropped in more countries, sometimes to 25 percent of their 1989 levels. Those in this category are Albania, the Caucasian and Central Asian countries, Lithuania, Moldova, Romania, Russia, the Slovak Republic, and Ukraine.

Preschool is not compulsory, so parental demand drives enrollments at these levels more than at

---

16   There is little systematic evidence on actual school attendance. However, the Azerbaijan Survey of Living Conditions estimated an extended absence rate of 10 percent for those aged 6–16 years, as opposed to the official estimate of 0.6 percent. The rate for nonpoor families was lower than the rates for very poor and poor families (World Bank 1997a). The Armenia poverty assessment found that for rural households with children in school, only 52 percent of poor households and 68 percent of nonpoor households said that their children attended school very regularly. The poor condition of schools and lack of heat, water, and electricity were the most commonly given reasons for irregular attendance (World Bank 1996a).

17   Before the transition, ECA countries adopted policies of recruiting members of the manual working classes into institutions of higher education through a system of quotas and other preferential treatment. Analyses of the educational attainment of different classes in 10 industrialized nations, including Poland and Hungary, show that children of the nonskilled working classes are disadvantaged educationally in all 10 countries but to a lesser extent in the two socialist nations (Ishida, Muller, and Ridge 1995).

18   Gross enrollment rates for the ECA region must be treated cautiously. The age-specific population numbers are somewhat suspect, the last credible censuses having been conducted in 1989. (Most countries will conduct new ones within the next two years.) In the intervening decade civil registration of births and deaths has declined sharply, and mobility across borders has increased. The enrollment numbers are questionable for those countries, or regions within countries, engaged in conflict.

Table 2.1 Gross Enrollment Rates in ECA by Level of Education, 1989–97
(percentage of relevant age group)

Level of education	1989	1997
Preschool	51.4	41.0
Basic	94.4	90.6
Upper secondary	71.4	61.2
Academic	26.2	27.4
Vocational/technical	45.2	33.8
Tertiary	13.1	17.8
Expected years of education completed	**11.2**	**10.6**

Source: Based on annex tables A5–A11.

the compulsory level. Lower employment rates and government financing policy have both reduced family demand. With more adults at home, families need preschool less. In cases of severe fiscal constraints, governments have focused their resources on compulsory education, shifting more costs of preschool to families. The demand of poor families, whose children most need preschool services to prepare them for basic education, is particularly sensitive to increased costs. Preschool supply has also declined as state owned enterprises have divested preschools to municipalities that cannot afford to run them (figure 2.1).

"Basic" education is called basic for a reason: it is the base on which further learning builds. Thus, it is of concern that, as figure 2.2 and annex table A6 show, enrollments in basic educa-

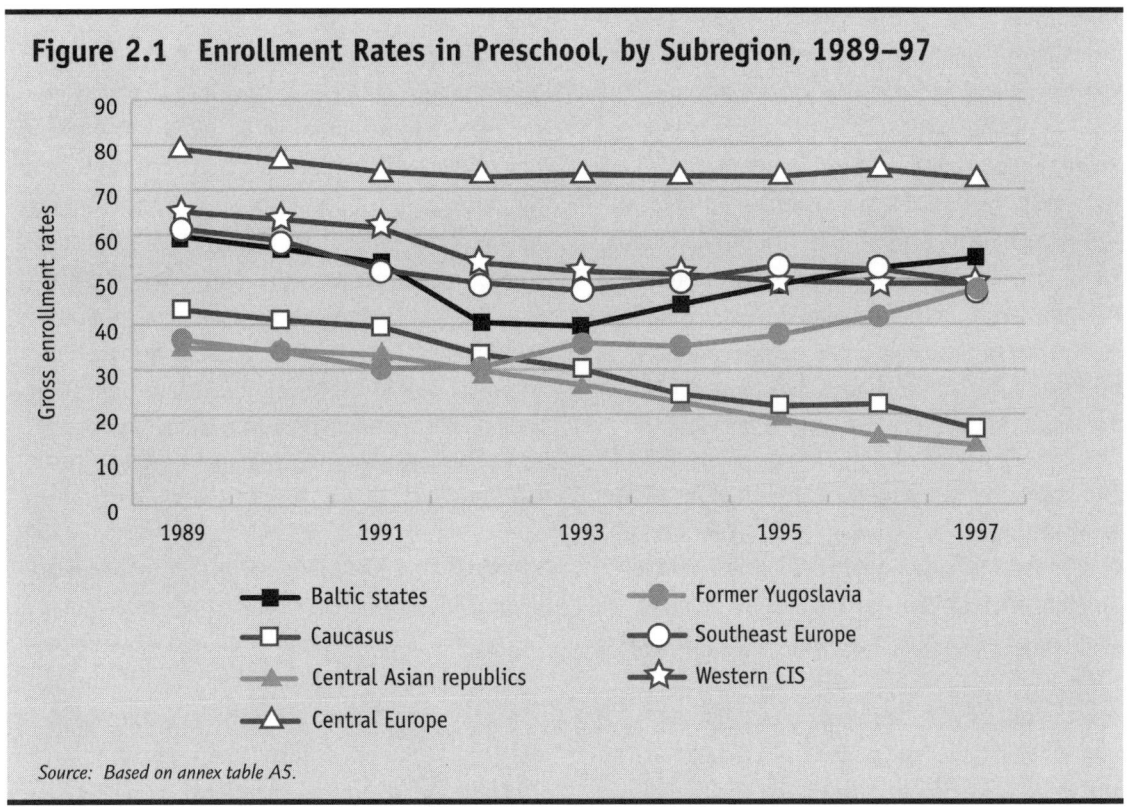

Figure 2.1 Enrollment Rates in Preschool, by Subregion, 1989–97

Source: Based on annex table A5.

THE WORLD BANK

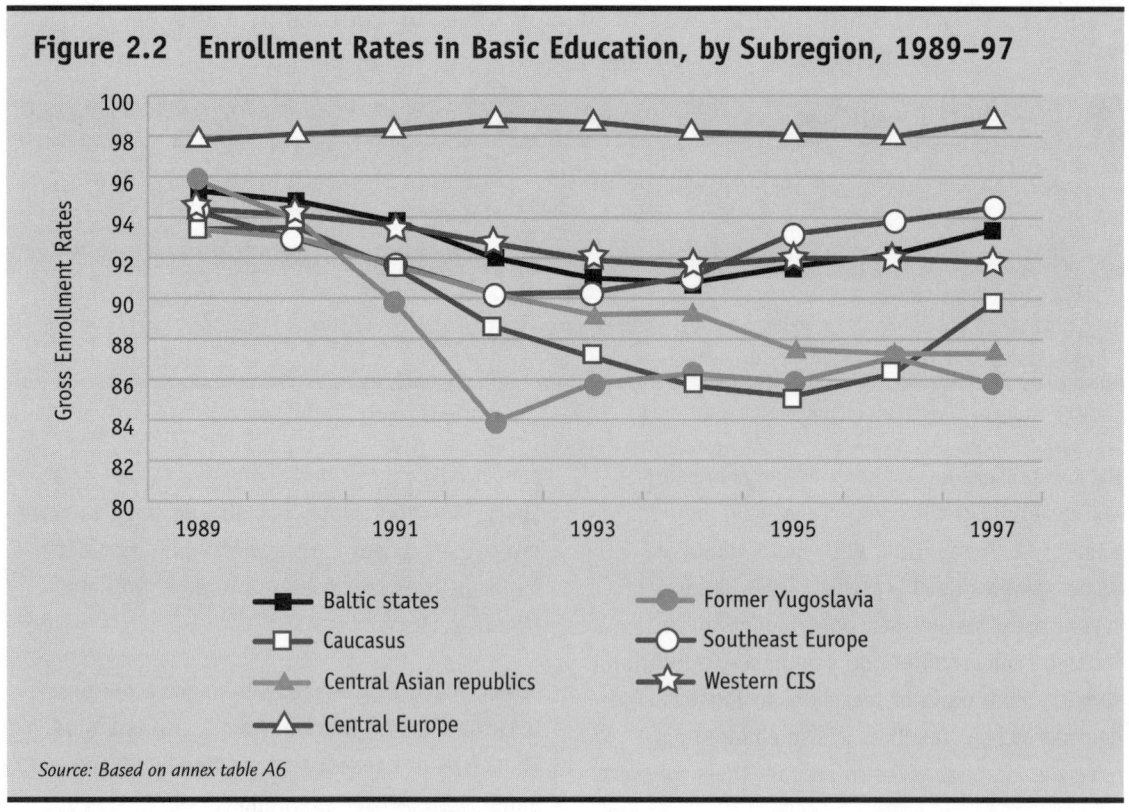

Figure 2.2 Enrollment Rates in Basic Education, by Subregion, 1989–97

Source: Based on annex table A6

tion drifted downward between 1989 and 1997 in a number of countries. In several cases, including Azerbaijan and Slovenia, the rates are stable or have even improved. In others the slippage is minor—for example in 1997, Estonia's rate was 97 percent of its 1989 rate; Latvia's, 95 percent. But Armenia, the Central Asian countries, Croatia, FR Yugoslavia, and Georgia show significant declines, some of them alarming. Armenia and Turkmenistan both had an 83 percent enrollment rate by 1997; the basic enrollment rate for FR Yugoslavia was 76 percent of its 1989 rate.

The lower and generally declining total enrollment rates at the upper secondary level signal emerging and important educational inequalities. In 1989 enrollment rates in upper secondary education (general or academic, technical, and vocational) were below the rates for basic education—substantially so for most countries.[19] By 1997 upper secondary enrollment rates, summed across the three tracks, had declined except in Croatia, Estonia, Hungary, Poland, the Slovak Republic, Slovenia and FR Yugoslavia. (See figure 2.3 and annex tables A7–A9.) In a number of countries the rates fell precipitously, by 15 to 30 percentage points. For example, Albania's rate fell from 79 to 40 percent; Armenia's, from 68 to 42 percent; Azerbaijan's, from 61 to 43 percent; Kazakhstan's, from 76 to 56 percent; the Kyrgyz Republic's, from 61 to 47 percent; and Romania's, from 91 to 67 percent. These declines account for much of the reduction in the years of full-time education, excluding preschool, that an average 6 year old ECA child can expect to complete over his or her lifetime.

Countries that had steep declines in upper secondary enrollments showed declines in all three tracks. Those countries that did not experience steep declines tended to increase their general education enrollments, their overall enrollment declines at the upper secondary level being attributable to reduced vocational/technical

---

19 This book discusses vocational programs as an entity, although, in practice, different countries handle their programs in different ways, sometimes running them as two separate tracks. Technical programs tend to be somewhat more sophisticated than vocational programs.

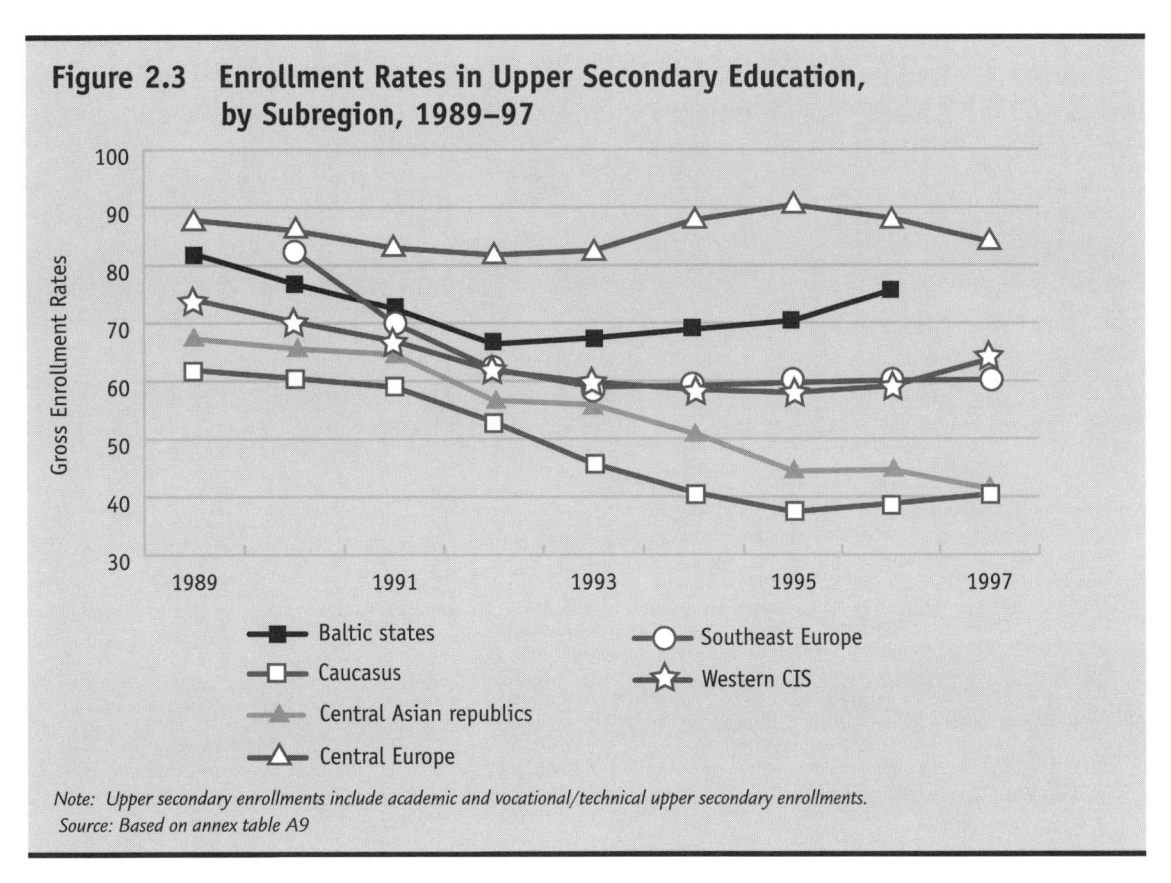

Figure 2.3 Enrollment Rates in Upper Secondary Education, by Subregion, 1989–97

[Line chart showing Gross Enrollment Rates from 1989 to 1997 for: Baltic states, Caucasus, Central Asian republics, Central Europe, Southeast Europe, Western CIS]

Note: Upper secondary enrollments include academic and vocational/technical upper secondary enrollments.
Source: Based on annex table A9.

enrollments. For the region as a whole, figure 2.4 shows that by 1997 the vocational/technical share of total upper secondary enrollments had declined to a share that only slightly exceeded the academic (general) share.

The turmoil at the upper secondary level could have been predicted. In all countries the majority of upper secondary enrollments were in the technical and vocational tracks, where, as annex tables A8 and A9 show, secondary enrollment declines are concentrated. Enrollment losses in these tracks reflect both demand and supply factors. These tracks were closely aligned with the planned economies of the region and are therefore poorly aligned with transforming economies. Students have understandably found them less attractive. They have entered the general education track at the upper secondary level or, since secondary education is not compulsory, simply left school after completing basic education.

Supply has also diminished. State owned enterprises, which ran many of these programs, either went out of business or closed their training programs. The Albanian government shut many secondary vocational schools because it lacked the resources to restore schools that had been vandalized during the civic unrest of 1991 and saw them as offering programs of low value.

The region seems to be adjusting to the increasing irrelevance of vocational/technical programs to emerging labor markets. However, the IALS (OECD 2000) clearly shows that failure to complete upper secondary education, whether academically or occupationally oriented, will increasingly place the individual at a disadvantage in ECA labor markets. The question is whether ECA countries will reverse the observed enrollment declines in upper secondary education by increasing the market value and attractiveness of upper secondary programs.

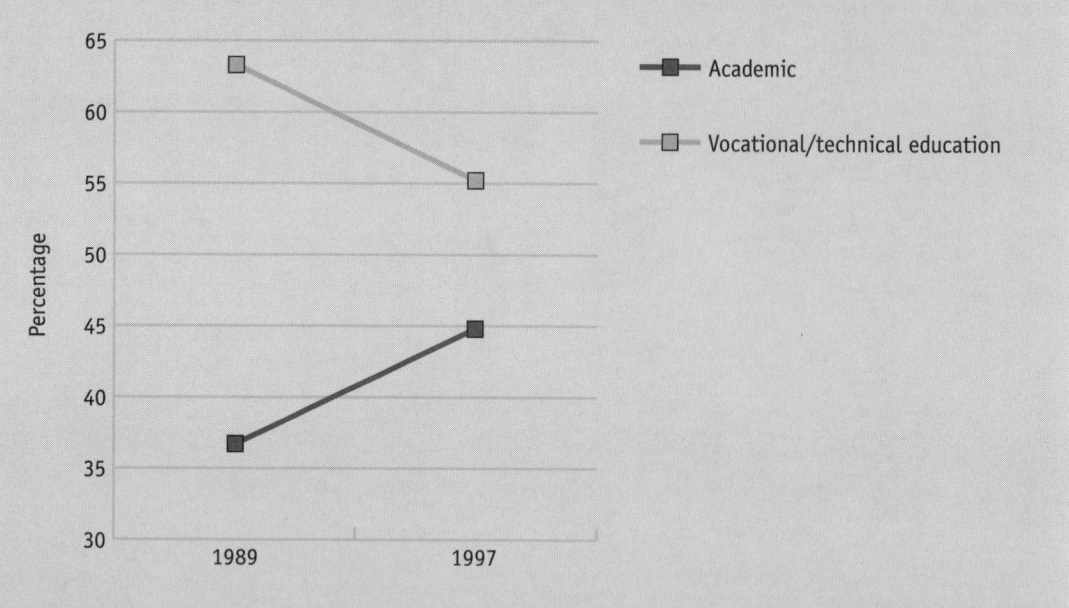

Figure 2.4 Trends in Academic and Vocational/Technical Shares of Upper Secondary Enrollments in ECA, 1989–97 *(percentage of total)*

Note: The averages for the region do not include Bosnia-Herzegovina, FYR Macedonia, Slovenia, or Uzbekistan, due to the lack of data for complete time series. For the countries where the data for 1989 and 1997 were not available, the data series for 1990/91 and 1995/96 were used.
Source: Annex table A10.

With a few exceptions, tertiary enrollment rates have either increased or remained stable across the region since the transition (see annex table A11). These statistics may indicate that individuals in ECA are responding to emerging evidence of better wage returns to more education.

Enrollment rates are related to the level of family income

Poverty assessments show that youths from poorer and less well educated families are more apt to leave school before or on completing basic education. Their lower levels of human capital can be expected to perpetuate their families' marginal economic status intergenerationally. Intergenerational poverty cycles arise through the strong relationships between parental education, household poverty, and children's educational achievements. Children of poorly educated parents complete fewer years of education and, holding constant the years of education completed, build weaker literacy skills. Because of the relationships between levels of human capital and probabilities of being poor, parents' educational legacies to their children translate into poverty legacies that, unless the cycle is interrupted, can persist through several generations.

Examples from four ECA countries show the relationship between family poverty and children's investments in education and the extent to which governments act to compensate for it.

- *Romania.* Family income and urban versus rural residence both predict enrollment rates. For the poorest decile, enrollment rates in basic education, upper secondary education, and tertiary education were 80, 47, and 5 percent, respectively. The corresponding figures for the wealthiest decile were 93, 85, and 27 percent. Government spending for education strongly favors the poor at the basic level; it is distribution neutral at the upper secondary level and only weakly favors the nonpoor at the tertiary level (World Bank 1997c).

- *FYR Macedonia.* All income quintiles had approximately the same net enrollment rates in basic education—around 80 percent. At the secondary level children from families in the poorest income quintile had net enrollment rates of 29 percent; those of the wealthiest quintile, 63 percent. At the university level the rates were 2 and 20 percent, respectively. Private spending is regressive in that poorer households spend more on education relative to their incomes than wealthier households. Public spending favors the poor at the preschool level, is distribution neutral at the basic level, and strongly favors the nonpoor at the upper secondary and tertiary levels (World Bank 1999f).

- *Bulgaria.* In 1995 enrollment in basic education did not vary much by expenditure quintile; even in secondary education, the variations were not great. However, by 1997 the net enrollment rates for basic education, while stable for the top four quintiles, had dropped by about 20 percentage points for the lowest quintile. Net enrollment rates at the upper secondary level for the lowest quintile also declined by over 10 percentage points, to a 40 percent enrollment rate. Although overall public spending is distribution neutral, it is propoor at the preschool and basic education levels and favors the nonpoor at secondary and especially at tertiary levels (World Bank 1999a).

- *Albania.* Although public spending favors the poor at the basic level of education, it strongly favors the nonpoor at the upper secondary and tertiary levels (World Bank 2000a).

The poverty assessments just discussed show a strong negative relationship between family poverty and demand for noncompulsory education. Although lack of textbooks and of instruction in the mother tongue probably reduces the enrollments of children from minority groups, in general the most powerful factor limiting enrollments is probably family poverty. International studies show that quantity of education demanded is sensitive both to family income and to the incremental costs of education that families must bear (Gertler and Glewwe 1989; King 1995). Thus it is surmised that increasing private costs for education in the region increase the negative relationship between family poverty and enrollments.

Family costs for education. The data on families' costs of education are fragmentary and elusive because costs are levied both officially and informally. For example, families make "voluntary" payments for teachers who have not been paid, or they contribute fuel to heat schools. In some cases they pay for "private lessons" from their child's teacher to ensure that the child gets a good grade. Although some governments officially charge for textbooks, others purport to provide them free. However, textbooks often turn out to be scarce, forcing parents to buy them on the private market or have their children do without. Students are now more likely to have to pay for transport to school that was previously free. Tables 2.2 and 2.3 give some information on private costs for education.

Table 2.2 shows that in the Kyrgyz Republic the poor spend a higher percentage of their per capita household expenditures on education than the nonpoor. Kyrgyz informants in both rural and urban areas reported that training manuals are costly and in short supply and that parents constantly have to contribute money to meet the needs of the school, such as heating, buses, teacher salaries, books, and supplies. They noted that the ability to pay for educational services is now an important difference between the rich and the poor. With limited household resources, "boys are being chosen, instead of girls, to attend school" (Consultations with the Poor 1999c, p. 7).

Table 2.2 Private Expenditures on Education, by Poverty Group, Kyrgyz Republic, 1997 *(Kyrgyz som)*

Expenditure category	Extremely poor	Poor	Nonpoor
Tuition	21	53	375
Books, uniforms, fees, tutors	193	228	356
School repairs, classroom supplies, teachers, field trips	36	43	64
Meals, transport, other	43	82	350
Total annual education expenditures	*293*	*406*	*1,145*
Total as percentage of per capita consumption	**16.9**	**14.1**	**13.1**

Source: Vandycke (2000).

Table 2.3 shows that in FYR Macedonia the poor pay a third more, as a percentage of per capita consumption, than the nonpoor for basic education and twice as much as the nonpoor for upper secondary and tertiary education.

Parents often have to pay bribes to get their children into university, either in a lump sum or in the form of high hourly rates, paid to those who write entrance examinations, to "tutor" their child for the examinations (Balzer 1998; Consultations with the Poor 1999c, p. 19).[20] In Moldova bribes vary in amount, depending on whether a degree in a particular field of study is expected to yield a high income. Thus, a place in a humanities department costs $2,000–$5,000, but one in a department of economics, law, or medicine costs between $5,000 and $7,000 (World Bank 1999g).[21] Box 2.1 describes these same processes for Russia and Georgia.

It seems safe to conclude that education is costing families more today than before the transition, although costs vary by country and, in fiscally decentralized systems, by subnational governmental unit. Not surprisingly, those countries under the greatest fiscal pressures seem to be shifting costs to families more than those that are less fiscally constrained. Unfortunately, it is just these countries that tend to have higher levels of family poverty.

Table 2.3 Private Expenditures on Education for the Poor and Nonpoor, by Level of Education, FYR Macedonia, 1996 *(Macedonian denars)*

	Primary education		Secondary education		Tertiary education	
Expenditure category	Poor	Nonpoor	Poor	Nonpoor	Poor	Nonpoor
Admission fee	0	0	0	96	0	4,916
Coaching	0	1,435	0	1,082	0	672
Transport	22	248	1,870	3,176	3,446	4,347
Books/supplies	1,871	2,923	1,760	3,186	2,676	3,714
Other expenditures	60	668	53	428	249	133
Total expenditures on education	*1,953*	*5,274*	*3,683*	*7,968*	*6,371*	*13,782*
Total as percentage of per capita consumption	**6.62**	**4.22**	**12.49**	**6.38**	**21.60**	**11.04**

Source: Vandycke (2000).

---

20 The poverty assessment for Azerbaijan reports that students at university there also pay their teachers for good grades, a top mark in an examination costing between US$100 and US$125 (World Bank 1997b).
21 All dollar amounts are current U.S. dollars.

> **Box 2.1**
>
> **GAINING ACCESS TO ELITE SECONDARY SCHOOLS AND TO UNIVERSITY: RUSSIA AND GEORGIA**
>
> In Russia elite secondary schools (lyceums and gymnasiums) have been emerging in the urban centers. Entry into university from these elite schools is much more certain than from regular secondary schools. Although the new schools are publicly funded, family wealth affects access. Parents often gain access for their children to elite secondary schools by donating expensive items of equipment. They pay university teachers for teaching college preparatory courses tailored precisely to the entrance requirements of their universities—examinations that are often set by these same teachers (World Bank 1999h).
>
> In Georgia education expenditures are the most unequally distributed item in the structure of family consumption. On average, a poor family sending a child to school spends annually about 2 percent of its cash budget on education. For the nonpoor the share is about 5 percent of total cash expenditures. About 10 percent of all private spending on education is for private lessons, but only nonpoor families purchase these lessons. Given the low quality of secondary education in Georgia, poor youths, lacking textbooks and access to private lessons, are effectively barred from higher education. The charge of 10 lari per month for secondary education, an amount that is half the average consumption per capita of poor families, further discourages enrollment. In fact, the data show that only 20 percent of individuals aged 16–17 (secondary school ages) from poor families are enrolled in school, compared with 78 percent from nonpoor families. Of all students enrolled in higher education, only 6 percent come from poor families (World Bank 1999d).

Family poverty. ECA has substantial poverty overall, and income inequality is growing as a predictable and inevitable consequence of the shift to market economies, where demand, not central wage setting, determines prices for labor. In 1993–95 poverty rates varied by country from 2 percent in Central Europe to 66 percent in the Central Asian republics. For ECA as a whole, the poverty headcount was estimated at 45 percent and the total number of poor was 168 million (Milanovic 1998, figure 5.1, pp. 68–69).

Greater income inequality translates into more unequal abilities to pay the costs of education. In 1987–88 ECA countries had low levels of income inequality. On a common measure of income inequality (the Gini coefficient, which ranges from 0 to 1, with 1 being the maximum), all fell between 0.19 and 0.28.[22] The average was 0.24, which was roughly equivalent to the average for those OECD countries where income inequalities are low. By 1996–98, however, ECA countries varied much more in their Gini coefficients, ranging from 0.25 in the Czech Republic to 0.61 in Armenia. At that time, the average Gini coefficient for ECA was 0.38, above the average for OECD countries in 1994–95 of 0.33. Countries such as Armenia, the Kyrgyz Republic, Russia, and Tajikistan now have Gini coefficients comparable to those observed for the most highly unequal Latin American economies. In 1998 in Russia, incomes of the top income decile were 9 times those of the bottom decile; for the Kyrgyz Republic and Tajikistan, the comparable ratio was 10; for Armenia, 35 (World Bank 2000b).

---

22 The Gini coefficient measures the degree of inequality of the distribution of earnings. It is equal to zero in the case of total earnings equality and to 1 in the case of total inequality.

Lower enrollment rates for rural populations and for marginal minority groups seem related to poverty

Rural enrollment rates. Enrollment rates are generally lower in rural than in urban areas, but the reasons for the differences are not clear. Since rural populations are usually poorer than urban ones, the gap may be largely attributable to differences in family income and parental education that affect family demand for education. However, data from a few countries in the region indicate that the quality of educational services differs between rural and urban areas. Since perceived educational quality affects family demand for education, countries may be creating lower demand by not attending to problems of quality in rural areas.

For example, in 1998, 45 percent of Romania's population lived in rural areas. A 1997 labor force participation survey showed that 27.6 percent of the working population in rural areas, compared with only 2.6 percent of the working population in urban areas, had only primary education or no formal education at all. Of students enrolled in primary education in rural areas, 3.5 were repeaters; in urban areas the figure was 2.1 percent. Rural schools are in worse physical condition than urban schools, and most rural schools lack basic teaching materials. A national assessment of the educational achievements of grade 4 students in June 1998 showed that the strongest influence on students' performance was the location of the school (rural versus urban). Variance analyses found that other factors, such as regular versus multigrade teaching, or qualified versus nonqualified teachers, had less influence on the results.

In Albania, where more than 50 percent of the population still lives in rural areas, analyses show that the most pervasive inequities in the system have to do with differences between urban and rural locations (De Waal 1999; Dudwick and Shahriari 2000; Palomba and Vodopivec 2000). The textbook distribution system is less effective in rural than in urban areas, and villages often depend on ad hoc strategies to get textbooks from urban centers to the village. Rural schools have fewer teaching materials and less equipment than urban schools. Rural schools are in worse physical condition than urban schools, students sometimes sitting under umbrellas on rainy days because of leaks in roofs. In the worst cases the schools are open to the weather, having lost walls and parts of their roofs. In urban areas 85 percent of preschools, 75 percent of basic-level schools, and 95 percent of upper secondary schools have bathrooms. The comparable percentages for rural schools are 17, 41, and 76 percent.

Rural areas have a much smaller percentage of teachers with higher education qualifications than urban areas, especially at the level of basic education (44 versus 70 percent). School inspectors confirm that many teachers in rural and remote village schools lack both subject matter knowledge and pedagogic skills. Villages with no access to a road attract qualified teachers only with great difficulty—teachers may have to walk 1.5–2 miles in hard terrain to reach the school. Urban settings offer more tutoring opportunities because the families tend to be wealthier. These opportunities make teachers reluctant to take teaching posts in rural areas, or, if they commute from urban to rural areas to teach, they leave their schools sometimes even before the end of the school day in order to return to the city to tutor.

Minority enrollment rates. Data on the enrollment rates of minority children are scattered. They are most systematically available for the Roma population. In ECA the Roma are concentrated in just a few countries—Bulgaria, Hungary, FYR Macedonia, the Slovak Republic, and FR Yugoslavia; they constitute between 8 and 10 percent of the populations of each of the first four listed (Ringold 2000).

Roma enrollment rates differ at the country level, between urban and rural areas, and across different types of Roma communities (for example, according to level of assimilation). However, the share of Roma who do not attend school is larger than among the majority population, as is the proportion of Roma who do not continue in school beyond the compulsory basic education cycle. In Bulgaria, for example, figures from the 1997 household survey showed that enrollment rates for children in the bottom expenditure quintile of the population are significantly lower than for those in the top quintile. Roma children were heavily overrepresented in the bottom quintile.

Even in countries with significant shares of other ethnic minorities, the Roma are more likely than other groups to be at the bottom of the income distribution. However, low Roma enrollment rates reflect multiple causes that represent the cumulative effects of centuries of discrimination. Poverty is only one cause.

Strategic Paths for Governments

ECA policymakers generally do not see—and have not yet had the chance to see—the downstream and intergenerational costs of seriously unequal learning opportunities. Thus, the problem may overtake the region before anybody recognizes the need to take action. Markets do not solve fairness problems. These problems are the natural responsibility of the public sector and have to be integrated into public education debate and policy.

Measure, monitor, and analyze

Are unequal opportunities for learning a problem? Where? Why? What do analyses of the data imply about appropriate policies? Few countries in the region can answer these questions because they lack the relevant data. Measures of key outcomes of education, such as learning outcomes, pinpoint whether unequal learning opportunities might be at issue. Little variance in key outcomes means that any inequalities in learning opportunities do not materially matter. Where there is substantial variance, however, it is necessary to find the predictors of this variability. This means being able to relate outcomes to the following:

- Inputs that might plausibly affect outcomes, such as variations in per capita expenditure, availability of textbooks, or qualifications of teachers
- Private costs of education
- Family factors that schools do not control but that affect children's participation and performance in school, such as family poverty, mother's education, and minority status.

Analyzing these data allows sector policymakers to assess the relationships between variations in inputs, family characteristics such as poverty, costs of education to families, and participation rates in education and training. These analyses provide the basis for policy. International studies show no necessary relationship between per child expenditures and learning outcomes. However, the fiscal crises in some ECA countries have so reduced per student expenditures as to compromise the provision of those inputs to the educational process that, studies have shown, increase learning results. Textbooks are one example.

Design and implement preventive and equilibrating strategies

Country-specific analyses of the extent, effects, and causes of unequal learning opportunities should be the basis for a country's design of an educational fairness policy.

Education finance is a major lever for ensuring fairness. Financing strategies for protecting fairness are discussed separately in chapter 3. In addition to using financing to mitigate inequitable educational opportunities, the following seven interventions should be considered.

- Restructure upper secondary education.
- Relax the barriers to moving between secondary tracks, between secondary and tertiary education, and between tertiary programs.
- Create cheap alternatives to fee-based preschools.
- Consider multisectoral strategies for improving educational access and quality in particular locations, such as rural areas, or for subpopulations, such as minority groups.
- Desegregate training opportunities by gender to eliminate or reduce wage differences between men and women attributable to gender-based occupational segregation.
- Facilitate opportunities for adult retraining so individuals can adjust to changes in labor demand.
- Create objective examinations for university entrance to reduce the relationship between families' abilities to pay bribes to university faculty and university entry.

Restructure upper secondary education. Reversing the enrollment declines at the upper secondary level requires, among other measures, creating more attractive secondary vocational/technical programs. These programs have to be restructured to adapt to changes in labor market demand. Since more and more employers can be expected to want workers with solid foundation and problem-solving skills, vocational/technical programs have to integrate the "head and hand" to continue building students' foundation skills while developing their occupationally relevant skills.

Relax the barriers to moving between tracks, levels, and programs. As discussed in chapter 1, ECA education systems tend toward early and narrow specialization. This policy deserves to be revisited. It is inconsistent with what one OECD country after another has come to understand as the education preferable for a modern economy: broad based preparation with specialization reserved for higher levels of education. It also sorts students on bases related to family poverty and parental education, thus potentially reinforcing rather than mitigating inequitable learning opportunities.

Sorting is inevitable as students move to the later stages of education. The key is to make it easier for them to transfer between tracks, to gain access to tertiary education, and to move between tertiary programs. Policymakers can take a range of steps to increase transitions across educational boundaries, in addition to the fiscal ones, such as scholarships and student loan programs (see chapter 3), that are particularly important for those from poor families.

"Easier" does not have to mean, and should not mean, lowering standards. Nonfiscal steps include:

- Ensuring that students who arrive at transition points already have the foundation skills and problem-solving skills that let them accommodate the demands of alternative tracks
- Allowing cross-registration—in other words, allowing students in one track to take courses in another
- Encouraging "second chance" programs that let individuals master the knowledge and skills needed to enter a new field of study. These programs often take the form of night courses and distance education courses available in open universities or two-year colleges.

The success of these efforts can be monitored by measuring transition rates between levels and among tracks.

Create cheap alternatives to fee-based preschools. Early childhood programs that focus on child development, not baby sitting, are an important compensatory strategy for getting poor children ready for school. Primary schools can reduce the performance gap between poor and nonpoor children, but they are working against the lost learning opportunities of the preschool years. The United Nations Children's Fund publication *Education for All?* has an excellent discussion of the facilitative role that governments can play and have played in mobilizing local communities to create quality, inexpensive early childhood development programs (UNICEF 1998, pp. 67–71). These programs have the side benefit of enabling poor mothers who cannot afford the tuition of regular preschools to work.

Whether scarce public funds should be used to increase preschool services for the poor is a different question. In terms of preparing for school, which ages most benefit from these services—the infant and very young child, or the slightly older child? Do children who attended developmental preschool programs perform better in primary education than those that did not? Are any measured differences between "treatment" and "control" groups sufficient to warrant the public expenditure?

Consider multisectoral strategies for improving educational access and quality in particular locations, such as rural areas, or for subpopulations, such as the Roma. In some cases unequal learning opportunities can be fixed with money—for example, by subsidizing poor parents so that they can buy required textbooks for their children. In other cases the causes of unequal opportunities are multivariate, cutting across sectors and affecting nonpoor as well as poor families. In Albania reducing the serious differences in educational access and quality between urban and rural areas probably requires a multisectoral rural policy—for instance, the lack of roads means that villages cannot attract and retain qualified teachers, but decisions on roads are not under the jurisdiction of the Ministry of Education and Sciences. In Romania the Ministry of National Education has launched a special program dedicated to rural education. Action plans are being based on analyses of the nature of the problem, whether access, retention, or transition.

The causes of any given problem are not always clear. For example, low transition rates from primary to lower secondary education in rural areas (65 percent) may indicate not a demand problem but a supply problem—the lack of a local lower secondary school or the lack of transport to a nearby school. Since rural areas are heterogeneous, average data showing rural-urban disparities may hide diverse conditions. Any program targeting rural areas will therefore have to be community-specific.

The strategy for minority groups, such as the Roma, whose options and choices reflect the cumulative effects of sustained discrimination has to be multisectoral and tailored to the conditions of individual communities (Ringold, 2000).

Desegregate training opportunities by gender. Although wage differentials by gender are now smaller than in the OECD countries, they can be expected to grow as wage scales decompress. Gender differences in wages operate through different wages for the same work and different wages for different work segregated into "men's" as distinct from "women's" jobs. Clearly, gender-based occupational preferences will limit women's (men's) demand for training in traditionally male (female) occupations. However, ensuring that women and men have access to training in occupations nontraditional for their gender will help reduce wage differences between men and women that are associated with gender-based differences in access to different occupations.

> **Box 2.2**
>
> **MODERNIZING THE EXAMINATION SYSTEM IN SLOVENIA**
>
> In 1991 Slovenia assessed a student's suitability for higher education in ways typical for the region. Each university faculty wrote its own tests and administered them at its own convenience. Tests were largely oral and unstandardized. A candidate did not know whether the test was comparable in difficulty to other tests within the same university, to tests for a different university, or to tests administered by the same faculty the year before. Test content was not advertised, so secondary schools with the closest informal ties with university faculties were at a distinct advantage. Personal administration of tests in widely separated locations encouraged corruption. In sum, the tests were discriminatory against the poor; they were devoid of psychometric standards; and because they favored a privileged elite, the admission process threatened the national sense of fairness.
>
> Slovenia now has a new standardized examination, the *matura*, designed by subject-specific professional committees called national matura commissions. It reflects the different professional points of view of scholars, psychometricians, and parent and teacher groups. The National Testing Center administers the test and is responsible for grading and test security. Prior to the first administration of the *matura*, Slovenian officials visited testing centers in the Netherlands, the United Kingdom, and North America to study how modern testing agencies function.

Facilitate opportunities for adult retraining to let individuals meet changing demands for labor. Many individuals in the current ECA labor forces still have years of potentially productive work ahead of them before they can expect to retire. An individual who left school in 1989 at the end of basic education, for example, is now only about 25 years of age. Skill demand is already changing, and these changes can be expected to accelerate. Minimizing structural unemployment fueled by mismatches between skill supply and demand requires retraining opportunities. Government can facilitate the supply of and individuals' access to market-responsive retraining programs. Although the issue is beyond the scope of this book, there is substantial international experience to guide governments' retraining policies.[23]

Create objective university entrance examinations. The purpose is to reduce the relationship between families' abilities to pay bribes to secondary or university faculties and university entry.[24]

Payment of bribes to faculties predated the transition, but this practice, in the form either of tutorials to prepare students for examinations that the tutor himself/herself might be writing or of outright "gifts", has worsened.

It is a pernicious practice. It excludes intellectually gifted youth from poor families from the university level. It undercuts what should be the basis for admission: merit. When merit is compromised, three things happen. First, the meaning of a university degree will ultimately be devalued because employers will not be able to trust what it is supposed to signal. Second, the country, which relies on its universities to create the highly skilled individuals needed for its economic development, will get a less competent resource than expected. And third, the practice undermines citizens' beliefs in the fairness of government.

Many countries have created objective and fair examinations for entry into university. Box 2.2 gives an example for Slovenia.

---

23 For useful examples, see Fay (1996); Meager and Evans (1998); Fretwell and Wilson (1999).
24 This proposed policy change does not redress differences among families in their financial capacities to buy their children access to lyceums, gymnasiums, and tutoring at the secondary level to prepare them to take the entrance examinations.

CHAPTER THREE

FINANCE FOR SUSTAINABILITY, QUALITY, AND FAIRNESS

Summary

Education systems in many ECA countries have been experiencing serious fiscal constraints that will almost certainly persist for the foreseeable future. Governments have tended to delay genuine adjustment with temporizing measures that increase the eventual costs of adjustment, undermine educational outcomes and fairness, and only mask fiscal shortfalls. Moreover, countries fail to position themselves fiscally to expand upper secondary and tertiary enrollments in response to the skill demands of market economies. This failure can have long-term implications for their economic growth.

Virtually all ECA countries generate revenue for education at the central level, and many of them then distribute it to localities using various sharing arrangements. Central revenue generation is transparent and efficient and can also be consistent with local control of education spending. Any supplementation with local revenues should be carefully done to avoid undermining educational opportunities for poor families or the quality of education in schools that are unable to mobilize local support. Centrally generated funds should be distributed to units of local government that are large enough to manage a school system rather than a single school, and yet small enough to be politically responsive to the local populace. The best way to ensure fairness in the distribution of resources among these jurisdictions is probably "money follows student", using a capitation-based formula.

Spending units need to improve the use of available resources by rebalancing the product line, meaning especially basic versus tertiary and general versus vocational education. They need to optimize the educational input mix, especially personnel versus didactic materials, energy, and maintenance. Each decision entails complex issues and risks that require careful consideration and management.

The major financing goals for the region's education systems should be fiscal sustainability and use of public finance to ensure educational quality and fairness. This links the theme of this chapter closely to several others in this document. Decisions about the sources, distribution mechanisms, and uses of financing affect educational quality (chapter 1), fairness (chapter 2), and governance and accountability (chapter 5). Although an efficient system may not be fiscally sustainable, reducing the inefficiencies in the region's education systems (chapter 4) will clearly help achieve fiscal sustainability.

Why This Development Goal?

This objective emerges out of two related realities. One is that the education sectors of many ECA countries are afflicted with serious fiscal constraints. The other is that these countries are reacting to fiscal constraints in ways that threaten educational quality and fairness. Education ministers in the transition countries tend to consider "insufficient funds" their most serious problem and are treating fiscal constraints as temporary crises that can be handled by "muddling through".

But austere budget constraints are not temporary. Ministries of education will face serious fiscal constraints relative to spending pressures for the foreseeable future. They cannot continue to muddle through. By failing to reconcile their education sectors with fiscal realities, they are jeopardizing educational outcomes and fairness in the medium and long term.

Many countries have reduced the resources available to education just as the prices of educational inputs have increased

The present imbalance has three immediate sources: macroeconomic declines in many countries have caused the resources available for education to drop; the true costs of energy and other inputs have surfaced; and pervasive inefficiencies in the sector have not been confronted. The latter problem is discussed in detail in chapter 4.

Macroeconomic decline has reduced the public funds available for education. Following the disintegration of the Soviet Union, macroeconomic conditions deteriorated dramatically in all ECA countries. Most countries in Eastern Europe have subsequently recovered, but as table 2 in the Introduction showed, many countries of the FSU continue to face macroeconomic decline or stagnation. Countries experiencing secular declines in GDP have tended to react by reducing public spending on education even more rapidly, causing not only an absolute decline but also a decline in the ratio of public education spending to GDP. Countries whose GDP has grown have tended to increase public spending on education even faster, increasing the ratio of education spending to GDP. These points are shown in figure 3.1.

True prices and costs have surfaced. The removal of subsidies and price distortions is compounding the effects of the decline in the resources available for education.

- *Energy.* When energy prices in the region began to reflect world energy scarcities in the early 1990s, the energy bill for ECA education sectors increased by as much as 2,000 percent in the areas with the most severe climates.

- *Infrastructure.* Maintenance of infrastructure has been deferred, resulting in its cumulative deterioration. Today this represents a hidden cost that has to become explicit.

- *Didactic materials.* In the past textbooks and written didactic materials were published by government printing houses and subsidized in ways difficult to assign to education budgets. Now, prices reflect costs to a greater extent. The effect is similar to the effect of "honest" energy prices, though smaller in magnitude. This effect may be greater now than later. A number of countries are trying to replace their entire stock of textbooks for pedagogic and political reasons, and the accelerated purchasing schedule bunches textbook costs in the short term.

- *Teachers.* Teacher salaries are a nascent source of pressure on education finances. Teacher salaries are generally below the average wage in countries of the region (see annex table A17). However, price-sensitive markets for labor are emerging. As the service sectors begin to compete for well educated workers, they are likely to bid up teacher wage rates, thus reversing the downward relative wage trend that has prevailed for several years and increasing the pressure on education budgets.

In addition to these actual and potential increases in the costs of inputs, policymakers now or in the future will be under pressure to increase upper secondary and tertiary enrollments in response to the skill demands of market economies. Even though the demographic trough that all but Albania, Turkey, and the Central Asian countries are experiencing will reduce the size of cohorts going through the system, upper secondary and tertiary educational services are generally more expensive to provide. Depending on country particulars, the net result may be increased total costs.

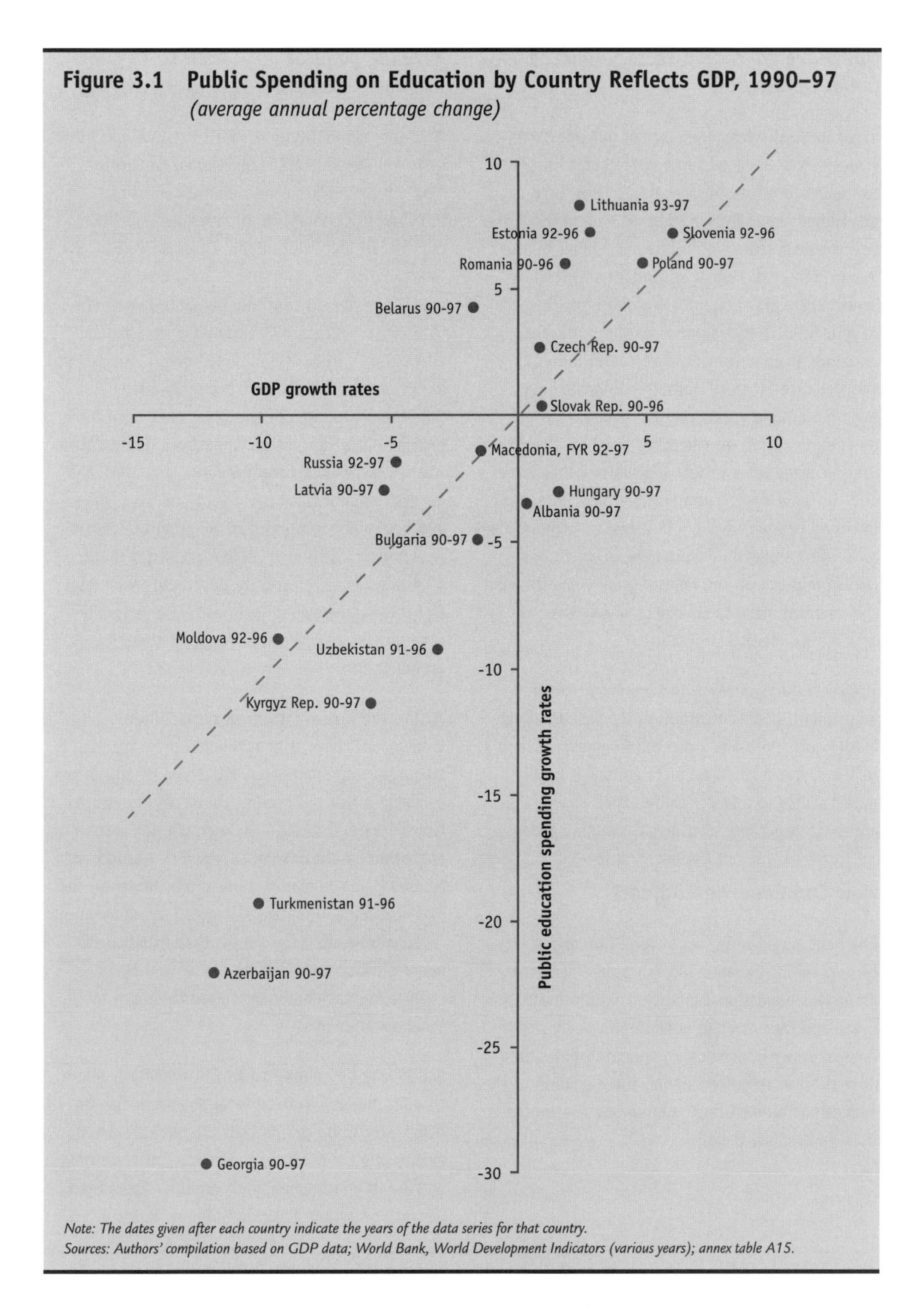

Figure 3.1 Public Spending on Education by Country Reflects GDP, 1990–97
(average annual percentage change)

Note: The dates given after each country indicate the years of the data series for that country.
Sources: Authors' compilation based on GDP data; World Bank, World Development Indicators (various years); annex table A15.

How have education sectors reacted to budget pressures?

ECA countries have generally not yet adjusted effectively to reduced funding (in some cases) or to increased prices (in all cases). They have not positioned themselves fiscally to handle what may be increased costs attributable to higher enrollment rates at the upper secondary and tertiary levels. Instead, as chapter 4 elaborates, they have tended to take temporary measures. Such measures include continuing to defer building maintenance (thereby decapitalizing the sector even more rapidly), cutting the purchase of didactic materials, not heating schools, allowing teacher wage rates to fall relative to other wages, and, in some cases, running up arrears in energy bills and teacher wages.[25] In a few cases countries have decentralized revenue generation to get fiscal problems off the central books, not because this measure necessarily makes good sense for governance, equity, or quality.

These measures increase the eventual cost of adjustment, hurt educational outcomes, and only mask fiscal shortfalls. Since the financing of inputs to the sector is often de facto shifted from the public sector to private families that vary in their ability to pay, these measures undermine fairness.

How Can Countries Adjust?

The next sections discuss several promising possibilities for sustainable and fair adjustment that maintains educational quality. This discussion is organized into revenue generation, mechanisms for resource distribution to spending units, and allocation of resources among the elements of the education "product line" and among the inputs used to produce them.

Revenue generation: Continue to generate most education revenues centrally

It is sometimes thought that most ECA education systems use decentralized revenue generation. This misperception arises from a confusion between the generation of revenues and their control. In fact, all but three countries (Bosnia-Herzegovina, Georgia, and Russia) now rely predominantly on centrally generated revenues to finance education.[26] Revenue generation for education is truly decentralized only if subnational levels of government define the tax bases and determine the rates of the taxes that raise funds for the education sector. Almost all ECA countries finance basic education primarily from national, general revenues, meaning that tax rates, bases, and administration are controlled by the central government. Although all ECA countries rely to a certain extent on locally generated revenues to finance education, such resources generally account for small fractions of total spending on education.

Within the broad pattern of central revenue generation, there is considerable diversity in spending responsibilities. Ministries of education sometimes use national funds to pay for educational inputs directly—for example, for teacher and other salaries, as in Latvia, FYR Macedonia, Moldova, and Romania. More often, however, the "vertical fiscal imbalance" created by national responsibility for revenue generation but local responsibility for spending is resolved by channeling nationally generated resources to local governments.

Funds may be channeled to the education sector through block grants to local governments—in other words, via grants that are not earmarked exclusively for education. Examples of countries with such arrangements are Albania, Azerbaijan, Georgia, Hungary, Poland, Moldova, Romania,

---

25 For example, by 1998 Moldova had accumulated fiscal arrears in the education sector that were more than 50 percent of total actual expenditures for the sector in that year.

26 Russia's oblasts (regions) are as large as most ECA countries. In Russia decentralization from national to subnational levels of government should be thought of in terms of decentralization from oblast to suboblast levels of government.

Russia, Tajikistan, and Ukraine. Sometimes, as in Armenia and Bulgaria, countries use grants earmarked exclusively for education. The Kyrgyz Republic finances some education expenditures via taxes that are shared between the national and local governments. In Latvia education is financed in part by taxes that are "owned" by localities but collected by the national government and returned to the localities where they notionally originated. In Bosnia-Herzegovina, education is financed almost exclusively in this way, via assignment to cantons of taxes administered by the Bosnian federal government. In many countries redistribution among localities is implicit—the size of grants or other transfers does not depend exclusively on where the revenue originated.

Although most ECA countries now raise revenues for the sector centrally, many countries are considering devolving responsibility for revenue generation to local governments. There are a number of reasons for continuing the present pattern.

First, central governments can raise larger amounts of money than local governments can—local governments do not yet have much to tax. National taxes such as value-added taxes (VATs), personal and business income taxes, and trade taxes have the potential to generate large amounts of revenue. The obvious candidate for a subnational education tax is a property tax. However, in many ECA countries government ownership of property that would otherwise be taxable continues to be important. In others property rights remain unclear, property markets are thin, and property values are unstable or difficult to ascertain. Duplicating national taxes or dividing a fraction of a national tax among subnational governments confuses accountabilities, and neither measure departs significantly from national revenue generation for education.

Second, the central government can administer taxes with lower administrative costs and higher compliance than local governments can. Local taxes entail administrative costs that are a multiple of the administrative costs associated with national taxes. For example, a local sales tax would strain the administrative capacities of subnational units in most countries. Since education would need only a small VAT, the costs of administrating such a tax locally are uneconomic.

Third, national taxes are neutral with respect to geographic location. Local taxation invites destructive tax competition among jurisdictions—for example via rate cuts or tax holidays.

Fourth, it is easier politically to distribute national revenues to localities in ways that help equalize educational opportunities among jurisdictions than to implement a zero-sum equalization fund or some other equalizing mechanism. Such devices necessitate confiscating resources in one jurisdiction in order to apply them to another. A common feature of ECA countries is the wide differences in tax bases (personal and business income, turnover, property) among localities; there is a "horizontal fiscal imbalance". The ratio of high to low per capita income is typically five to one or greater. If subnational governments pay for the education only of children in their jurisdictions, geographic differences in income translate into unequal educational opportunities.[27] Poor regions have poor education systems that produce poor educational outcomes that result in low incomes that reinforce regional poverty.

Data on Russia illustrate the point. The relationship between variations in gross regional product (GRP) and education spending per school age child in 79 *oblasts* (regions) and autonomous republics for which both figures are available is shown in figure 3.2. There are substantial differences in these variables and a clear correlation between them. The richest regions are able to afford the highest education spending, and vice versa.

---

27 Just as incomes vary widely among jurisdictions, so do costs. However, it seems likely that although some costs may be lower in low-income regions, others undoubtedly are not. It is likely that education costs vary between regions much less than do incomes.

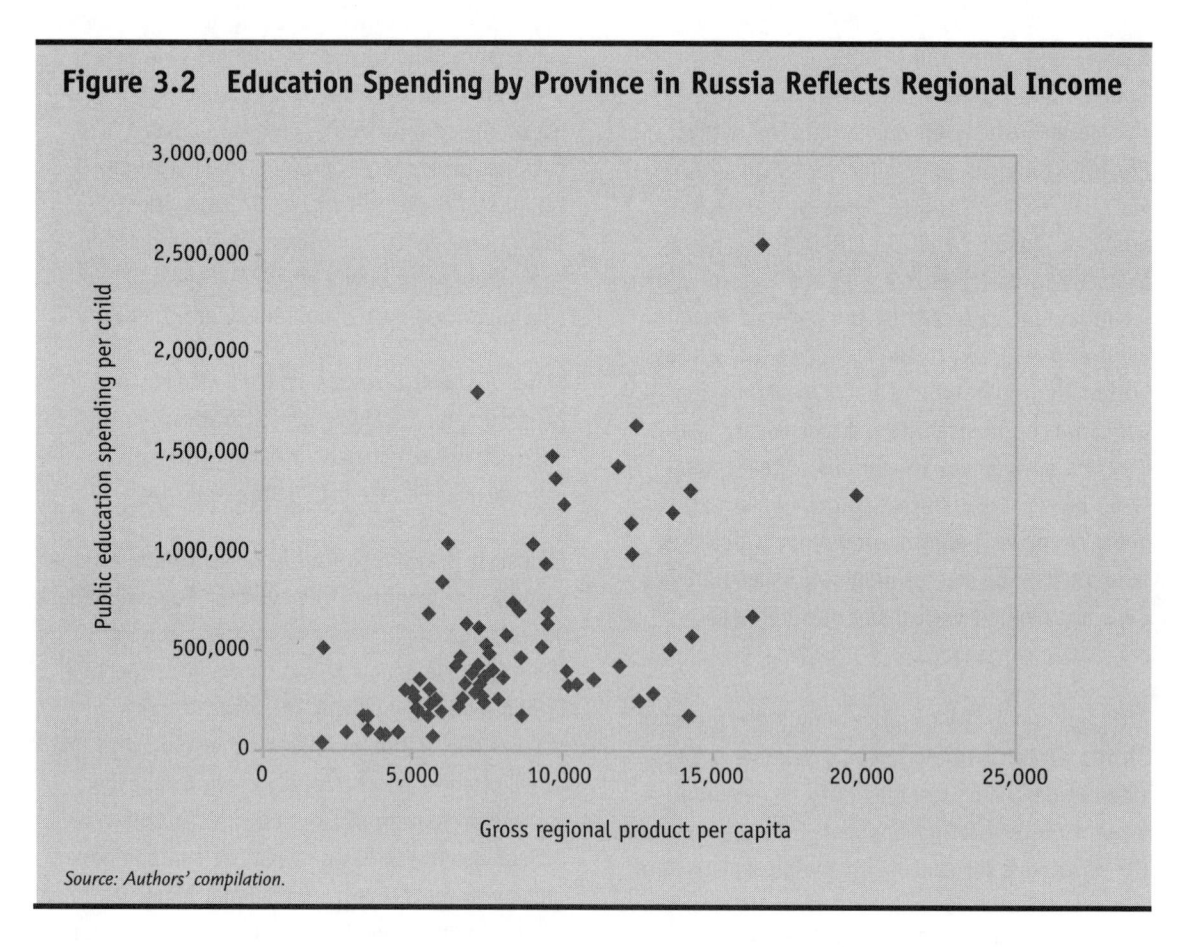

Figure 3.2 Education Spending by Province in Russia Reflects Regional Income

Source: Authors' compilation.

In a system of centralized revenue generation for education, the whole country pays for the education of all of the country's children, with citizens contributing more or less according to their ability to pay. Particularly under a system of "money follows student" (discussed below), there is at least the possibility of an equitable distribution of educational opportunity throughout the country.

As noted earlier, decisions about how revenue for education is generated and who controls its spending are separate. Centralized revenue generation does not imply centralized control over resource use, as revealed by an examination of practices in countries where revenue generation and governance are not always tied. Prior to the transition, the education sector in ECA generally had centralized revenue generation and governance. Money for education came from general state revenues, and central ministries—especially ministries of education, but also ministries such as agriculture and industry for vocational schools—controlled all aspects of the "education production function". Today some ECA countries, such as Azerbaijan and Tajikistan, are decreasing dependence on centralized revenue generation but retaining control at the center. Some Western countries, such as England, have decentralized control without decentralizing revenue generation. The United States, by contrast, decentralizes both revenue generation and governance. The point is that fiscal decentralization is not essential for decentralizing elements of education governance.

A factor that influences whether central revenue generation is consistent or inconsistent with decentralized control is earmarking. Earmarking means that centrally generated funds that are channeled to local authorities must be used for specified purposes. An earmarked education transfer (whose size might be determined by a capitation formula, as discussed below) could be used only for education, for example. Earmarking reduces the flexibility of local authorities to tailor their spending patterns to fit local circumstances, so it shifts control from localities to the center. It is difficult to confine earmarking to just one sector such as education; the arguments in support of earmarking for education can also be applied to health, water and sewer services, and locally managed social assistance, for example. Obviously, if most of the funds available to local governments are centrally generated, and if most centrally generated funds are earmarked, then local authorities have almost no discretion as to spending patterns, and central authorities have almost total control. These considerations apply to any region.

In ECA there are two additional regional considerations. First, health care is increasingly financed via health insurance systems that in effect earmark funds that are centrally generated by a wage tax. Health insurance means that education is a much larger fraction of local government spending in ECA than in many other parts of the world. The point is that earmarking education expenditures in ECA has the potential to reduce local flexibility more than it would if health care expenditures had not already been earmarked.

Second, in most ECA countries, whether centrally generated funds for education are earmarked or not, local governments spend more on education than the amount of the education transfers that they receive from the center. In such circumstances, earmarking presumably would not change spending patterns.

Accordingly, earmarking education funds is likely to be either confining or inconsequential. Therefore, earmarking education spending in ECA countries under normal circumstances is not desirable.

There may be a case, however, for temporarily earmarking education transfers in extraordinary circumstances. In a few countries—for example, Georgia and Moldova—the normal cash flow of public funds may break down from time to time, so that central funds intended for localities never reach their destination, or they may be "hijacked" for crisis management in other sectors. This might result in arrears in teacher wages, no didactic materials for schools and students, no heat for school buildings, and even the suspension of classes for lack of funds. Under such extreme circumstances, it may be useful to consider temporarily earmarking funds for education. If resources are terribly scarce and the normal cash flow of public funds is breaking down, however, one must ask whether earmarking would be any more respected than other budgetary practices and procedures.

Revenue generation: Cautiously supplement central revenues

Almost all ECA countries supplement centrally generated revenues for education with local taxes and formal user charges, and some also use informal user charges and entrepreneurial activities to raise money.

Possibilities for generating funds for education with local taxes are limited. As pointed out above, local tax bases are extremely weak in the region, and as a consequence, this source of funds is not terribly important. It is difficult to make precise comparisons among countries because they report their local revenue and spending data on different bases, just as OECD countries do. A report from the OECD in 1999 concludes, inter alia, that "…the state and local tax share of subcentral governments is a measure of only limited value when assessing the tax autonomy of lower layers of government", and "…subcentral levels of government may have limited or even no influence over taxes which—for reporting purposes—

> **Box 3.1**
>
> ## DIVERSIFIED REVENUE GENERATION IN HUNGARY
>
> In 1993 an OECD survey of Hungary found that 9 percent of total education expenditures came from nonbudgetary sources. By 1997, 80 percent of the costs of textbooks was covered by parents (up from 60 percent in 1994). From 1997 on, taxpayers may direct 1 percent of their income tax to certain listed organisations that work for the common good. This option has brought in significant extra income for some schools.
> The vocational training contribution (wage tax) paid by employers covers some 22–25 percent of the total expenses of school-based vocational training. The company contribution may be paid to the Vocational Training Fund (administered by the Ministry of Education); it may be given directly to a vocational training institution chosen by the company; or the company itself may provide training out of its contribution either for the school population or for its own employees.
>
> Most schools carry on certain economic or other activities to gain extra income. They rent their classrooms for language classes or even hold the courses themselves. In some cases vocational schools earn significant extra income by selling in-service or retraining programs for the adult labor force.

are assigned to their jurisdiction." Accordingly, measuring the precise contribution of local taxes to education revenue in ECA countries is beyond the scope of this book.

There are two dangers in overreliance on local taxes to generate revenue for the education sector. First, as mentioned earlier, differences in the fiscal capacities of local jurisdictions may translate into major regional differences in educational opportunities. Second, consolidation of schools is an extremely important issue throughout most of ECA. People are extremely resistant to allowing the school in their jurisdiction to close, and they will be even more resistant if they perceive that "their" taxes are going to support "someone else's" school in a neighboring town or village.

At the same time, some local taxes in the revenue mix may increase the sense of local responsibility and thereby strengthen local governance. Also, it would be futile, and perhaps undesirable, to restrict the amount of "own revenues" that rich localities can spend on education, just to pull them down to spending levels in the poorest areas.

All ECA countries also use various cost-recovery mechanisms to supplement tax revenues for the sector. These include user charges and entrepreneurship at the level of the school. For example, box 3.1 shows the variety of cost-recovery mechanisms that Hungary is using.

In some cases these cost recovery measures have merit. They can increase the total resources available to the sector and help cushion abrupt changes in any one funding source. They can increase quality and efficiency (for example, by expanding the role of the private sector) and a sense of ownership (by increasing the burden on the direct beneficiaries). However, all these strategies carry risks, a shared one being that total spending on education will not increase if the national education budget is cut to offset funds fully or is partially raised through supplementary sources.

Exercise caution with user charges. User charges are payments by recipients for identifiable elements of educational services. Tuition for preschool students, charges for textbooks or laboratory materials, and tuition and dormitory fees for university students are examples. A variant is public funding for education salaries, with user charges to cover nonsalary inputs. Particularly in very low-income countries or regions, schools and jurisdictions are relying increasingly on user charges to supplement public education spending.

Families of students already help support schools through their taxes. The rationale for user charges is that individual students receive a large part of the benefit from education and that therefore they (their families) should bear part of the cost directly. A family with no children does benefit from the education system, but not nearly as much as a family with children. User charges may also give parents a sense of ownership in their schools that they might not otherwise have. User charges can potentially improve the quality of education beyond what would be possible with government financing alone.

Yet there are two dangers to overreliance on user charges. First, international studies show that user charges discourage children and youths from poor families from attending school. For example, when countries have eliminated fees for primary school, enrollments have increased, often dramatically. Means-tested education vouchers for the poor are one way to deal with this problem at pretertiary levels; scholarships and student loan schemes can work at the tertiary level. Second, the schools best positioned to raise money through user charges may be in richer jurisdictions where educational opportunities are already the best. Reliance on user charges, like reliance on local taxes, may increase regional disparities.

The case for user charges for education is strongest for universities, where individual students realize the greatest share of the benefits of education. Several ECA countries have already introduced or are considering introducing tuition and fees to shift a share of costs from the taxpayer to students and their parents. Box 3.2 gives examples for Azerbaijan, Hungary, Poland, and Russia.

Politically, it is probably prudent to increase user charges for universities gradually, with the schedule of increases announced well in advance. For example, students could be asked to bear 2 percent of the cost of their education in 2001, with the share increasing 2 percent per year for all students to 20 percent in 2010. Alternatively, each successive matriculating class could be asked to bear a higher proportion of costs. For example, students born in 1982 could be asked to bear 2 percent of the costs of their education, students born in 1983 could be asked to bear 4 percent, and so on, up to 20 percent for students born in 1991. The advantages are that no students already in university would face the new regime and that the burden would not be increased after a student matriculated. The disadvantage is that different students in university at the same time would face different user charges.

An important complication is that many ECA countries have constitutional provisions that guarantee free education at all levels beyond preschool. If higher education enrollments are to increase, countries have to change or find ways to circumvent such provisions. As a former minister of finance from an ECA country observed, "These countries have constitutions that they cannot afford." The clash between a constitutional guarantee of free education and today's fiscal realities can result in bizarre behavior, as shown by the case of Poland (see box 3.2).

User charges for higher education should be complemented by student loan schemes and means-tested scholarships. However, creating an effective student loan and scholarship program requires overcoming several formidable obstacles. First, applying a means test to identify students who are eligible for state subsidies is difficult. Countries that operate subsidized student loan

> **Box 3.2**
>
> ## USER CHARGES IN HIGHER EDUCATION
>
> **Azerbaijan.** In Azerbaijan formal student fees have been introduced in public higher education institutions. Public institutions now accept a proportion of their students on a fee-paying basis. As a rule, government subsidized places are allocated to those who perform well on university entrance examinations. In 1998, of 17,000 students entering the 18 state universities, 9,400 were budget-sponsored students and 8,200 were fee-paying students. User fees collected by higher education institutions are not included in the budget and are used at the discretion of the collecting institution.
>
> **Hungary.** The 1995 higher education reform in Hungary focused on making more efficient use of public resources in higher education and shifting the burden of some costs from taxpayers to students and parents. In 1995 a tuition policy was introduced in public institutions of higher education. However, about one-fifth of the students receive partial or full waivers based on academic merit or financial need, and total tuition revenue in fact covers only a small fraction of total costs (Johnstone, Arora, and Experton 1998, p. 9).
>
> **Poland.** The constitution calls for "free" higher education "without any payment". In order to circumvent the spirit of this provision, higher education institutions choose not to apply this rule to "extramural" students. The quality of education offered to extramural students is not on a par with the programs offered to regular day students, especially with respect to the frequency of direct contact and tutoring with qualified instructors. It would also appear that fee-paying students are subsidizing day students.
>
> In the past, "extramural" students attended only weekend and evening programs. Now "extramural" students are being permitted to attend regular day classes along with day students who do not pay tuition charges. In effect, universities are trying to increase revenues by turning night into day.
>
> **Russia.** Higher education institutions in Russia are prevented by the constitution from implementing a "formal" policy of charging for tuition. However, in apparent contradiction of the constitution, a government decree in 1994 made tuition charges legal for all persons, not only "juristic persons" (i.e., enterprises and organisations). In 1995 fee-paying students accounted for about 10 percent of total admissions (Johnstone, Arora, and Experton 1998, p. 9).

schemes and scholarship programs rely on reports of income and wealth to the tax authorities to estimate ability to pay for schooling and capacity to repay loans. However, tax compliance in ECA countries tends to be low, and self-reporting tends to be inaccurate.

Second, since consumer credit is underdeveloped in most ECA countries, there is little tradition of voluntary repayment of credit and little onus attached to default. Third, enforcement of loan repayment is usually facilitated by the borrower's sense that the lender has a legitimate claim on the borrower. This sense of obligation derives from a recognition that the loan has supported the purchase of something of value and that the terms of the purchase were fair. The history of highly subsidized higher education in the region undermines this sense of obligation.

Implementing a student loan scheme also requires solving the problems inherent in lending large sums of money on a long-term basis without collateral. Students generally do not have an established credit history that might be used to assess their character. In addition, double-digit inflation in most ECA countries makes nominal interest rates on fixed rate loans very high. These rates impose large risks on borrowers if inflationary expectations are not realized. Innovative lending products that index the unpaid principal amount of the loan to a price index or that adjust interest rates frequently might be considered. Application procedures that identify a network of family members might be employed to simplify the tracing of defaulters. A variant combining features of a scholarship program and a loan scheme is an income-contingent repayment scheme (possibly associated administratively with the social security system) and a program of forbearance for persons who are unemployed, disabled, or faced with exceptional financial crises. This kind of hybrid might be used to avoid formal default and to increase the probability of eventual repayment.

Avoid or legitimize "informal" user charges. Informal user charges are payments that are neither explicit nor public. They can take several different forms. Parents may have to pay teachers for extra tutoring to compensate for low teacher salaries. Legitimate costs of education, such as the costs of heating school buildings, may be pushed onto parents or the community because tax revenues are inadequate.

"Informal" user charges are problematic. Because they are "hidden", the access of poor families to education may be reduced because the need to subsidize families that cannot afford these payments is not confronted. Hidden payments invite corruption. Finally, money raised outside government channels is not always handled in a businesslike way. In Russia, for example, head teachers do not even have bank accounts for their schools. Hungary has arrived at a solution that may be relevant for other countries in the region. Most schools in Hungary have formed their own foundations, which parents or economic organisations are welcome to support financially. Education foundations in Hungary provide a businesslike, legitimate mechanism for schools to manage nongovernment money.

Informal education payments are sufficiently important in ECA countries that they should be studied systematically, just as informal health payments are now receiving analytic attention. To the extent that the incidence of informal payments for education is unfair, limits the educational opportunities of the poor, or increases regional disparities, corrective measures may be needed. Ideally, informal payments should be legitimized by law or regulations and special provisions introduced for poor regions or poor students.

Entrepreneurship should contribute to educational outcomes. Confronted with rising costs and inadequate budgets, head teachers in some schools have resorted to renting school space to enterprises, using vocational training equipment to produce goods for sale, or charging businesses for using school computers. Universities have an even greater range of opportunities:

- The provision of short-term or specialized teaching services, such as extension or continuing courses for working adult students
- The sale of education- and research-related products, such as books, inventions, and farm products
- The sale of consultant services and applied contract research
- The privatization of various noneducation-related services such as dormitories, cafeterias, and health care
- The use of assets, such as land and facilities.

"Entrepreneurship" entails benefits and risks. It increases the resources available to the school—if the education budget is not cut to offset entrepreneurial profits. It does not harm educational quality if it is pursued without distracting school authorities from the business of education, reducing the availability of facilities to students, or detracting from the quality of their education in some other way. However, if these conditions are not met, entrepreneurship can be inferior to budgetary financing. The key point is that such entrepreneurial activities should be within the framework of the institutional mission and should support educational outcomes.

Resource distribution: "Money follows student"

If most funds for education are generated centrally, countries face two basic choices. First, what should the spending unit be—in other words, how far down should the money go? Should money be allocated to the individual student, the individual school, townships, provincial regions, or what?

In general, the money should go to a jurisdiction that is small enough to be politically accountable to the local population and yet large enough to create possibilities for shifting resources among schools. It is impossible to set precise limits; every country is different. However, a spending unit with a population of, say, 1 million may be "too big", while a jurisdiction with a population of 20,000 is almost certainly "too small". Units of perhaps 100,000 seem small enough to be politically responsive but large enough to allow flexibility. Allocating the money all the way down to individual schools (corresponding to a jurisdiction with a population of only a few thousand people) erases the flexibility to shift resources among schools and creates resistance to school consolidation. Assigning competence for different levels of schools to different levels of government, as Poland does, also reduces flexibility. If one level of government receives funding for basic education and another for upper secondary education, for example, the system's managers cannot easily smooth out demographic waves by, say, retraining teachers and shifting them between levels.

Note that the recommendation here is different than it would be in a region where there is a need to expand the number of schools. Capitation all the way down to the school level might make it easier for a group of parents and teachers to organize a new school by ensuring that funding would follow students to the new school. In ECA the problem is school consolidation, and capitation at the level of individual schools would almost certainly slow this painful but inevitable and probably necessary process.

Second, what mechanism should be used to determine how the money is distributed among spending units? Three obvious choices are to perpetuate historical patterns, use centrally determined norms, or allocate via a capitation system. Traditionally, funding in ECA countries was allocated on the basis of norms for inputs. Jurisdictions with the most school buildings and teachers generally received the most money. It is almost universally accepted now that "money follows student" (demand-side financing) is the preferred alternative. "Money follows student" simply means that funding for education is a function primarily of the numbers of students. Such systems are sometimes said to be based on capitation, or unit cost, or average cost.

The funding formula per student can be adjusted for factors that result in differences in costs, such as population density (rural schools are usually more expensive per capita because fixed costs are distributed across smaller numbers of students) or differences in the educational challenges that student bodies present. The formula must be simple and transparent, preferably with only a few (less than six) adjustment factors. Typically these factors are summarized in funding algorithms for each level of schooling.

Demand-side financing has particular application in higher education. In most ECA countries higher education funds are allocated on the basis of inputs used—for example, on the basis of the number of faculty, as in Poland, or on the basis of courses offered, as in the Czech and Slovak Republics. In a capitation or demand-side financing scheme, public funds are allocated as "block" or "lump sum" grants according to a formula based mainly on the number of students. The formula can also be designed to reward educational quality or the efficiency with which the institution uses inputs. Institutions then have the flexibility to reallocate resources as they see fit. Such approaches have the potential to improve efficiency in the use of public resources, since institutional managers have the freedom to make decisions that reduce costs and increase quality. Box 3.3 describes how Romania is introducing demand-side financing in higher education.

Capitation financing raises the following three questions: Should "money follows student" apply to private and parochial schools as well as to government schools? How much school choice should be permitted? What are the advantages and disadvantages of paper vouchers?

Should "money follows student" apply to private and parochial schools as well as to government schools? Every ECA country permits nongovernment schools to coexist with public schools. In practical terms most nongovernment schools in the region are not-for-profit and are sometimes church-related, although commercial schools for subjects such as languages, computer sciences, and accounting also exist. Although the nongovernment schools' legal basis for existence is shaky in a few countries, there is universal agreement that they should be allowed.

Questions about the public fiscal relationship to these schools then have to be answered. Most ECA countries provide no public funds for nongovernment schools, on the rationale that public schools are available to all and that they play a valuable socializing and nation-building role in addition to their purely educational function. If parents wish to use nongovernment schools, they are welcome to do so at their own expense.

In a few ECA countries nongovernment schools receive subsidies from the government, usually in proportion to the number of students they serve. In Poland, for example, nongovernment schools may receive a reimbursement of up to half the average cost of educating their students in a government school. The rationale is that nongovernment schools lighten the public fiscal burden and that this net saving for government should be rewarded and encouraged. Even with a subsidy of 50 percent of the average cost of the public schools (as in Poland), students who transfer from a government to a nongovernment school potentially reduce public spending on education. (Whether that potential can be realized depends on whether it is possible to close the excess capacity that the transfers create.)

Of all of the countries in the region, only Hungary offers a subsidy to some nongovernment schools equivalent to 100 percent of the cost of government schools. (See box 3.4.) Obviously, 100 percent subsidies to nongovernment schools do not reduce public expenditures on education. The strongest economic argument for full subsidization of nongovernment schools is that this is likely to make high quality education in nongovernment schools more available to students from poor families that cannot afford to pay full or even partial tuition. Other arguments for a 100 percent subsidy tend to be political rather than financial. Some stakeholders may believe that church schools promote family values better than government schools, for example. In some countries antiunion forces may argue for full subsidization of nongovernment schools (which tend not to be unionized) as a way of undermining the strength

Box 3.3

DEMAND-SIDE FINANCING IN ROMANIAN PUBLIC HIGHER EDUCATION

Prior to 1990, financing for Romanian higher education was a supply-side system based on central manpower planning that determined enrollments. Funds were allocated on the basis of the number of teaching positions, square feet of building space, and other planning norms. In practice, considerable bureaucratic bargaining that was not transparent also affected financing. After 1990 enrollments in public universities exploded, reflecting the pent-up demand for higher education that the limits on enrollments under the communist regime had created. However, some of the traditional fields, such as heavy industrial engineering, that faced declining demand continued to be funded on the old basis, whereas funding of new fields such as economics, social sciences, and humanities did not keep pace with rapidly increasing enrollments.

To improve resource allocation in public higher education, Romania introduced a funding principle of "resources follow the students". The core recurrent funding of the basic teaching mission of the university is based on a formula that reflects the unit cost per student in various fields of study. The National Higher Education Financing Council (NHEFC), established in 1995, conducted studies of unit costs to provide the empirical basis for the funding formula. Thus, the budget allocation to individual universities depends on the demand for different fields of study as expressed by the preferences of students, the unit costs of education in that field of study, and the overall budget envelope.

Beyond the core recurrent financing, the new system includes complementary financing allocated on a competitive basis among universities for research and capital improvement proposals. Research projects go through a peer-reviewed competition organized by the National University Research Council; capital improvement projects go through a peer-reviewed process organized by the Capital Grants Committee of the NHEFC. Romanian universities have also been granted more financial as well as academic autonomy, along with accountability guidelines for how funds are to be used. Within broad accounting categories (block grant funding), universities are not as constrained as in the past by the detailed line item accounting of the centrally controlled system (Dinca 1998).

Box 3.4

DEMAND-SIDE EDUCATION FINANCE IN HUNGARY

Hungary's central budget provides local governments and operators of nongovernment schools with education grants based mainly on the number of students. In practice, local governments spend about twice as much on education as is provided by the state education grants. The rest comes from state grants for other purposes, local taxes, the share of general income taxes transferred to local governments, and other local revenues. Some 30 percent of the yearly budget of local governments is devoted to education.

Registered operators of nongovernment schools are automatically given the same normative state grants from the central budget as local governments. In addition, operators of church schools receive the amount that the local governments spent on their schools above the normative state grant in the previous year.

Besides the normative support, an obligatory 7 percent of all public education expenditure goes for the development of public education programs and technology, the development of teachers' in-service training, and other activities defined by law.

of the education unions. Others may wish to weaken local governments by eroding one of their most important programs.

Governments can realize some of the equity benefit of subsidizing nongovernment schools without sacrificing all of the public financial benefit from having a share of students in nongovernment schools. Nongovernment school vouchers for students from poor families, with the subsidy element a function of income, achieve these joint objectives. For example, there could be a 50 percent subsidy for the general student body, with students from poor families being subsidized at 75 or 100 percent, depending on income.

Whether or not nongovernment schools receive public funding, central authorities have an obligation to regulate them to protect the national interest in educational quality and social cohesion. As discussed in chapters 1 and 5, this regulation can take the form of accreditation, licensing, learning standards, learning assessments of students, and a core national curriculum.

How much school choice should be permitted?
In theory, school choice should provide students with the opportunity to "vote with their feet" by leaving weak schools and enrolling in strong ones, and more school choice is generally desirable. However, the importance of school choice should not be exaggerated. The average share of the population that lives in rural areas in ECA is 41 percent. For rural students, school choice has no practical significance because there is usually only one school within manageable range. School choice has the greatest value to students who live in urban areas with multiple schools that are geographically accessible. Even so, its value to consumers is restricted. As chapter 5 points out, where population density or availability of transport allows students to attend any of several schools, it is not the students who choose the best schools; it is the best schools that choose the students. This generates a vicious circle: the best schools attract the best students, who achieve the best test scores, which results in the best school ratings, which attract the best students. Even in urban areas, for all but superior students school choice may have little significance.

What are the advantages and disadvantages of paper vouchers? De facto, in a school system where money follows students, there is a choice of whether to use a voucher system. The advantages of moving beyond capitation financing to physical paper vouchers seem political. The disadvantages seem financial.

• Paper vouchers that may be "spent" at either public or private schools are a way of pushing public spending for private and parochial schools up to 100 percent.

• Paper vouchers in the hands of individual students remove discretion from local governments about how much to spend on education and on individual schools.

• Paper vouchers add to administrative costs and lessen the amounts available for true educational purposes.

Because of the costs of administration, ECA countries would be well advised to pursue the voucher principle (school choice combined with "money follows student") without using paper vouchers. This option does not require a complicated, computerized "virtual voucher" system. The voucher principle is preserved through a technique as simple as basing each year's budget on the previous year's enrollment. The public debate about paper vouchers should include an honest disclosure of the costs of administration, so that if the public does choose paper vouchers, it is an informed choice.

Allocation of resources: Reconfigure the product line and optimize the input mix

Given available funding, how should it be used? Four kinds of choices must be made: who should be the beneficiaries; what should be the product mix; what should be the input mix; and how can efficiency of input use be ensured? Choices should optimize the sector's fiscal sustainability, quality, and fairness.

This chapter focuses primarily, but not exclusively, on the second and third of these four choices: the levels and types of education produced, the inputs used to produce them, reconfiguring the product line, and optimizing the input mix. Chapters 2 and 4, respectively, focus on equitable educational opportunities among beneficiaries and on efficiency.

Reconfigure the product line. In many cases the costs of providing the educational services for which spending units are responsible exceed their resource envelopes. In these cases countries or localities must redefine the scope of public educational services. Many have been implicitly redefining them by closing schools or converting to fee-based provision. However, these ad hoc adjustments are usually being made in ways that damage the nation's human capital stock or subgroups of citizens, such as the poor. Resizing the public responsibility has rarely been explicitly, transparently, or strategically conducted.

Each country has to decide for itself what levels and types of education it most wants to protect and for whom. Decisions about reconfiguring public responsibilities for education inevitably involve decisions about the distribution of educational opportunities among groups. The implications of these choices for fairly distributed opportunities have to be confronted along with decisions about the scope of publicly financed services.

BASIC EDUCATION. International experience provides some guidelines for setting priorities. Most international education experts agree that universal compulsory basic education (grades 1 through 8 or 9) should have first claim on public education resources, simply because a sound education in these grades lays the base for subsequent learning. Publicly supported mandatory education is a fiscally achievable standard in all ECA countries. Increasing the efficiency of the input mix (see chapter 4) may secure adequate financing for basic education, even in fiscally stressed countries. However, in countries experiencing extreme fiscal pressures, meeting this standard may require additional actions in the form of two types of reallocation. One is reallocation to education from defense, money-losing state owned enterprises, and other state-financed activities. The other is reallocation within education—for example, from higher education to basic education.

When financing for basic education has been secured, governments can expand public services in other directions.

PRESCHOOLS. Accumulating neurological evidence shows that children are primed to learn during the first years of life (e.g., Shore 1997). It is clear that children who receive developmentally appropriate stimulation before they are six years old can be educated at lower cost and to higher levels than children who do not. The issue for education systems is whether preschools are a cost-effective way to provide that stimulation.

Restoring the former childcare system probably would not be as cost-effective in improving educational outcomes as devoting the same resources to basic education instead. In pretransition days, enterprises provided preschool services to their employees, but the main purpose was childcare that could free parents to work, rather than the cognitive development of the children. Following the collapse of communism, enterprises began facing hard budget constraints that compelled them to cut spending that did not contribute directly to profitability. Preschools were early casualties. In most cases attempts have been made to transfer the financial responsibility for preschools from enterprises to municipalities. However, municipalities have often lacked the means to finance preschools, and they have had either to close them or to introduce user charges to finance them. As a result, only children from families that can afford to pay are able to attend preschool in most ECA countries. It is important to bear in mind, though, that what has been lost to lower-income families is childcare, not a calculated learning experience.

If it could be demonstrated that a high quality preschool experience can make a lasting difference to a child's educational attainment, an evidence-based case for state support for quality preschools, with a priority similar to that for basic education, could be made. So far, though, the evidence is ambiguous. What little evidence there is suggests that quality preschools do give children an advantage in the early years of basic education but that this advantage tapers off after several years.

Until better evidence is available, it is not possible to conclude that preschools for the general population should be given higher priority than basic education. In the short term the emphasis should be on increasing access to preschool for poor families by means of demand-side financing techniques such as capitation financing, supplemented as necessary by local funding.

The impact of preschool and other early childhood developmental experiences on life-long learning is an important area for further research.

VOCATIONAL EDUCATION. Specialized secondary vocational education is costly in fiscal and human capital terms. In most ECA countries students choose between academic and vocational education streams early—typically, after eighth grade. The percentage enrolled in vocational/technical upper secondary education varied in 1997 from 16 percent in Albania to 85 percent in the Czech Republic. Although, as figure 2.4 shows, the vocational/technical share of upper secondary enrollments has declined since the transition, in most ECA countries more than half of the students are enrolled in vocational/technical, not general, upper secondary education. (See annex table A10.)

This has two consequences. First, early specialization, especially in narrowly defined vocational tracks, is inconsistent with survival in the dynamic market economies of the future (see chapter 1). These markets are characterized by uncertainty and rapid technological and product change that require workers able to learn and adapt. Workers need a command of the foundation skills—good literacy and quantitative skills that can be flexibly deployed—and the higher order cognitive and metacognitive skills. They do not need to acquire in public schools detailed vocational skills that are rapidly rendered obsolete by the rapid change characteristic of modern workplaces.

Second, specialized secondary vocational education tends to cost two to four times as much per student as general education. However, as noted in chapter 1, broad based vocational/technical training that strengthens foundation and higher order skills in the context of real things that real people do in the real world can replace expensive, specialized secondary vocational training. This strategy of integrating secondary academic and vocational training results in about the same unit costs for academic and vocational training. For countries that have not yet reformed their upper secondary vocational/technical systems, replacing specialized with broad based vocational/technical training will, in the long run, yield savings that can be used to finance increased upper secondary enrollments in countries where enrollment growth outstrips demographic decline.

HIGHER EDUCATION. ECA countries are trying to expand university enrollments rapidly, a goal consistent with the human capital demands of the market economies that are emerging in the region. However, if governments are successful in rapidly expanding enrollments, and if public spending per student remains constant, higher education will absorb an increasing share of public spending on education, endangering public spending on other levels of education that should have higher priority.

Instead of allowing public higher education spending to crowd out other levels, ECA countries can bring down the cost per student and increase the portion of the cost that is borne by the student. Bringing down the cost per student is a matter of efficiency, as discussed in chapter 4. Increasing the cost share borne by the student is discussed in the earlier section on diversifying the sources of education finance.

The challenge is to expand the quality and quantity of this part of the education "product line" without allowing higher education to crowd out other public spending on education.

Optimize the input mix. Coping with tightly constrained resources requires that education managers consider very carefully the input mix and the quality of inputs that go into the education production function. In a number of countries essential educational inputs such as textbooks, school maintenance, teachers' in-service training, and supplies and teaching aids are being squeezed between the education budget and utility costs. As price-sensitive labor markets develop, these nonteaching inputs will be squeezed out by an increasing wage bill for teaching forces that are often inefficiently used.

REALLOCATE RESOURCES FROM ENERGY TO OTHER EDUCATIONAL INPUTS. Especially in colder countries, the prime target for freeing up savings is energy. Now priced at market levels, it is consuming between 30 and 50 percent of total education expenditures, as opposed to less than 5 percent prior to the transition. Freeing up funding for other uses by conserving energy will take sustained cooperation among sectors of government—and will take time. As chapter 4 points out, energy-conserving school designs can gradually reduce energy use as new schools replace old ones. However, this process will take years. Insulating school walls, double-glazing windows, and installing meters so schools are billed only for energy used will reduce the energy bill somewhat faster.

RATIONALIZE THE TEACHING WAGE BILL. The generally low wage levels for teachers in the region do not currently make the teacher wage level a prime target for freeing up savings. However, as price-sensitive markets for labor emerge, the region's generally inefficient use of teachers will become very costly.[28] In the shorter run, if governments use teachers more efficiently, thus reducing their numbers, they can increase teacher wages. Obviously, the net effect on the budget of paying more to fewer teachers depends on the size of the wage increases and labor force reductions. However, calculations show that reasonable labor force reductions and increases in wages should result in a lower wage bill, leaving some room for increasing spending on nonteaching educational inputs.

As noted in the Introduction, school age cohorts are declining in size, but there is nothing automatic about realizing the potential savings from this demographic decline. If governments do not downsize the teaching force in accord with small-

---

28   Not all countries use teachers inefficiently. For example, in Albania in 1998 wage expenditures constituted 83 percent of the total recurrent budget, 8 percentage points more than the average for OECD countries. This left 17 percent of the recurrent budget to cover all other costs of running the system, such as utilities, textbooks, teaching materials, school maintenance, scholarships, welfare services, and in-service teacher training. The high percentage going to staff salaries in Albania may seem to reflect an inefficient use of teachers but in fact signals a highly constrained recurrent cost budget (2.8 percent of GDP). Relatively high student/teacher ratios and a very low percentage of nonteaching staff place the total staff in the system, as a percentage of the total employed population, well below the OECD average.

er school age cohorts, teachers will be even less efficiently used. If governments act to capture this "demographic dividend", they can use the savings to increase teacher wage rates and pay for nonteaching educational inputs.

As with energy conservation, rigidities in the system make it difficult to adjust the educational input mix by decreasing the number of teachers. In some schools, for example, classes may already be as large as the size of the classrooms permits, so the only way to increase class size would be to undertake major reconstruction projects. Some schools may have only one teacher for a particular subject such as biology or a foreign language, in which case it is difficult to adjust downward when the number of students declines.

Yet there are many cases in which some adjustment is, in fact, possible. If classrooms are not filled to capacity, it may be possible to combine them. For example, four classes of 15 students could be combined into three classes of 20 students. It may be possible for teachers in special subjects to divide their time between schools. For example, a language teacher might spend mornings at one school and afternoons at another. In very small schools it may be desirable to combine grades, so that one teacher in effect covers two or more grades. In some cases it may be possible to consolidate schools. These are all difficult solutions, but without such solutions, it is impossible to see how teachers can be given pay raises and the tools to do their jobs.

ALLOCATE RESOURCES TO INFRASTRUCTURE, ESPECIALLY IN THE FSU. The underfunding—often nonfunding—of school maintenance has created an education infrastructure crisis in ECA, especially in the former republics of the Soviet Union.[29] Schools are deteriorating. A major school construction drive started in these countries in the early 1960s and lasted about 20 years. Schools were constructed quickly in order to meet quantitative targets (number of classrooms, square meters of schools) without regard for quality or durability. Fifteen to 25 years later, this initially shoddy construction has combined with many years of deferred maintenance to result in an infrastructure with rotting window and door frames, deteriorating roofs, and inadequate insulation. Some of these schools are in such poor structural condition that they present a physical danger to the children and teachers who use them.

It is impossible to estimate the total value of the repairs required in the region, although estimates for Albania ($270 million) and Latvia ($850 million) suggest the magnitude of the problem. Data from these and a few other countries suggest that correcting the infrastructure problems resulting from deferred maintenance would absorb at least double or triple the annual education budget.

Continuing to neglect school maintenance amounts to borrowing from the future at exorbitant interest rates because it will cost much more to rehabilitate schools in the future than it would to repair them in the present. Paying down the rehabilitation bill can be financed with a special bond issue or by borrowing from an international lender such as the World Bank in the context of a broader reform program. Although governments may be reluctant to borrow for this purpose, the reality is that a liability already exists. Every day that a roof leaks results in additional interest charges in the form of rotting timbers and other water damage. Unarrested deterioration is as much a deduction from the national wealth as interest payments—in fact, a greater deduction in cases where the implicit interest rate on the deferred maintenance is higher than the real cost of explicit borrowing.

Almost all countries need a strategy for financing deferred maintenance and routinizing capital

---

29 Education infrastructure in the Czech Republic, Hungary, and the Slovak Republic does not follow the Soviet pattern. School buildings, although old, are usually solidly built. In fact, they are almost too solidly built in that it is almost impossible to reconfigure themæfor example, to change classroom size.

THE WORLD BANK 55

investments. Such a strategy might contain this sequence of actions:

1. Define needs by measuring the physical condition of education buildings and the ways in which they are used.
2. Give first priority to closing or rehabilitating schools that pose safety hazards for children and second priority to buildings that, because of deferred maintenance, are rapidly deteriorating.
3. Develop the basis for making capital investments and maintenance a routine part of education finance.

First, define the infrastructure problem. Measuring it is the first step toward managing it. ECA countries with centralized education systems should consider an architectural inventory of education buildings, preferably in the context of creating a school mapping database. A school mapping database with architectural data on the physical status of each school and the ways in which the building is being used lets policymakers judge the wisdom of using funds to repair a school. Census data in the database may indicate that it is wiser to close a school than to repair it, or, in anticipation of closure in a few years, to invest only in safety repairs, not in fundamental rehabilitation. Latvia and Romania have undertaken architectural surveys of schools, and Albania, in the context of developing a school mapping database, is starting to add engineering information on schools to its database.[30]

The architectural inventory approach can be criticized because it centralizes control and because it requires examination of all school buildings when only a small fraction can actually be repaired. An alternative is to provide procedures and standards for localities to use in defining their own problems and to invite proposals that would be funded on a competitive basis. Localities with serious problems could commission an analysis of one or all of their schools, but localities with schools in minimally acceptable condition would not need to undertake this expense.

Second, whatever approach is used to define needs, the problem of setting rehabilitation priorities remains. Ordinarily, first priority should go to safety and second priority to stopping rapid deterioration. (See box 3.5.) The fiscal responsibility for repairs may rest with levels of government that lack the financial resources to pay for them. In this case central governments should consider establishing a national school repair fund to which local school authorities can apply for emergency assistance. In the absence of a tax increase, such a fund will have to be financed through reductions in spending on other inputs or through borrowing.

Third, plan ahead. It is important to reach a steady state where expenditures for education buildings, maintenance, and equipment are routinely integrated into decisions about education finance. The decision framework for capital financing should:

- Make explicit the tradeoffs among all educational inputs—for example, if a new building is to be constructed, what other inputs must be reduced?
- Clarify the recurrent cost implications of capital investments in a budget framework that links the two.
- Make explicit the tradeoffs across time—for example, what cannot be afforded later if a new building is constructed now? Expenditure choices should neither starve the present nor beggar the future.

At local levels, capital expenditures are "lumpy" over time. A smooth flow of resources for capital expenditures can be created by setting up a centrally funded capital allowance based mainly on the numbers of students. This smooth flow can be transformed into lumpy expenditures through

---

30   The Romanian survey covers structural soundness, student capacity, and total size, but it is not a true architectural survey because it does not cover current use.

> **Box 3.5**
>
> **SCHOOL SAFETY CONCERNS IN ALBANIA**
>
> The physical state of schools in Albania is among the worst in the region. Poor initial construction, lack of proper maintenance even before the transition, and two episodes of popular unrest in the 1990s, when schools and other public buildings were looted and vandalized, have left a physical stock that violates minimum safety and health standards and the minimum conditions for teaching and learning. Many schools lack heat, have no glass in the windows, and are open to the elements. When schools have been rehabilitated, it has sometimes been found that only the roof was holding up the walls or that the walls were so badly rotted that the whole school had to be pulled down, to be replaced by a new one.

borrowing. If private capital markets are not well developed, as is the case in most of the region, a revolving fund that extends loans for education infrastructure is a mechanism for converting a smooth revenue stream into the lumps required for capital outlays. The revenue stream is pledged against future repayment of loans from the revolving fund. If private capital markets are well developed, it is possible to hypothecate the revenue stream as collateral for a commercial bank loan.

Many design questions would have to be answered for a "steady-state" system to work in practical terms. First, would an adjustment be required to reflect different initial endowments of education infrastructure among schools and localities? One way to do this would be to base an interest-free grace period and maturity structure on the initial capital stock as revealed by an architectural inventory of education buildings. Second, should the interest rate on loans from the revolving fund be below market interest rates in order to offset an inherent bias toward overspending on salaries and underspending on other essential education inputs? Third, should a capital budget be earmarked exclusively for school buildings, maintenance, and equipment? This strategy offsets the political pressure that teachers might otherwise bring to bear on local authorities to use the capital component for teacher salaries, but it conflicts with any effort to decentralize allocation decisions.

An alternative system that provides most of the same incentives is one in which private owners such as banks, insurance companies, and pension funds lease or rent buildings to the government (and the private sector) for educational purposes. In this case lease payments or rents become just another recurrent cost.

CHAPTER FOUR

SPEND RESOURCES MORE EFFICIENTLY

Summary

In general, ECA education systems consume more resources than are required to reach their goals. Depending on the country, the education sector may consume at least double the resources employed per basic and secondary student in the West.

Much of today's inefficiency is a legacy of pretransition economies, when planners, not market forces, determined wages, subsidies, and prices. These inherited inefficiencies interact with new realities. The sector has to pay much higher prices for some inputs, especially energy, and it has less public financing available for the sector. Demographic trends will exacerbate today's inefficiencies because ECA education systems are sized for larger student cohorts than will be going through them in the near and medium term. The sector has responded with measures that can seriously affect learning outcomes. Teachers' wages have been deferred or allowed to fall, textbooks and school maintenance are underfinanced, and costs are shifted informally to parents.

ECA governments must develop interpretable measures of outcomes, such as student learning, to monitor the efficiency of their education systems. Meanwhile, governments can improve efficiencies by targeting action in four resource areas: facilities can be consolidated and rationalized; a large, low-wage teaching force can be replaced with fewer, better qualified, higher paid teachers; energy conserving measures can be introduced; and goods and nonteaching services can be contracted out on a competitive basis. Governments should also re-examine four policies for their efficiency implications: curriculum, minority language instruction, early specialization, and education of special needs children.

Since it usually costs money to save money, governments must analyze the tradeoffs between the initial costs of securing savings and the expected savings. They will have to develop sophisticated political strategies that will ensure affected stakeholders accept specific efficiency reforms.

Even countries in the region with expanding economies have to manage scarce public resources efficiently. Efficiency in the education sector is defined as getting better student outcomes (such as more learning) for the same resources, the same outcomes with fewer resources, or better outcomes with a different input mix that costs less or the same.

Why This Development Goal?

In general, ECA education systems use more resources than they need to achieve their objectives. Countries of the FSU, such as Latvia, Moldova, Russia, and Ukraine, have particularly egregious efficiency problems.

These inefficiencies stem from the incentives of the pretransition period, when planners, not market forces, determined wages, subsidies, and prices. There were no mechanisms for determining the total costs of anything and therefore no incentives to contain costs. Budgeting norms for different levels of education, in many instances adopted in the 1930s, were never tested for cost-effectiveness.

Space norms resulted in wasted space—for example, large lobbies and highly specialized laboratories and workshops that were, and remain, underutilized.

Staffing norms encouraged inefficiencies. For example, resources were allocated by classroom. Each "class" got a teacher and teaching aids. These budgeting rules encouraged schools to minimize class size in order to maximize the number of teachers and teaching aids. The regional tradition of using, after grade 4, subject-specific teachers who had not been cross-trained in cognate, or "adjacent", fields interacted with smaller schools to create diseconomies of scale. Most teachers were certified to teach a single, narrowly defined subject. For example, a physics teacher would not have been cross-trained to teach chemistry. As a result, except in the largest schools, teachers might not teach more than two or three hours per day.

Methods of capital budgeting did not allow, let alone force, tradeoffs between investment and operational costs. The results were designs that minimized construction costs by increasing operating costs, especially for heating, lighting, and routine maintenance. Chapter 3 pointed out that the majority of school buildings now in operation throughout the region were constructed between 1960 and 1980 to energy-inefficient building standards, using prefabricated concrete panels, single-pane windows, and poorly sealed windows and doors.

Where Does This History Leave ECA Today?

Depending on the country, ECA education systems may consume at least double the resources employed per basic and secondary student in the West. Schools that were not built to conserve energy consume, on average, between two and three times as much energy as modern school buildings in OECD countries. For example, the average Danish school consumes about 100 kilowatt-hours per square meter per year, in contrast to Latvia's typical 285 kilowatt-hours per square meter per year. Space per student is one-third to two times higher than in the West. For example, in Georgia average total space per pupil is 9 square meters, as opposed to an average of 6 square meters for a number of OECD countries.

The numbers of teachers are two to three times as great, as a result of small class sizes, light teaching loads, and the practice of having teachers trained to instruct in only a single subject after the primary grades. For example, in Georgia for grades 1 to 11 the average student/teacher ratio is about 10:1 for the country as a whole and only 3:1 for small secondary schools (Perkins 1998). In Russia federal regulations limit class sizes to no more than 25 students, but it is not uncommon for rural classes to have only 3 to 5 students. Teachers in Russia are contracted for 18 instructional hours per week. Their annual load of 666 instructional hours is light compared with that of teachers in OECD countries; for example, in the Netherlands the load is 1,000 hours per year, and in France it is 923 hours (World Bank 1999h; OECD, *Education at a Glance*, various years). Data from Ukraine show the effects of single-subject teaching in grades 5–11. In 1993 the student/teacher ratio in the primary grades (1–4) was 20:1, but grades 5–11, which used specialized teaching, had an average ratio of 11:1.

Although data on nonteaching staff are not generally available, those data that do exist hint at further inefficiencies in the FSU countries.[31] For example, in 1993 Ukraine had a ratio of 1.37 nonteaching staff to every teacher at the preschool level and a ratio of 0.71 for grades 1–11. In 1999 Moldova had a ratio for all levels of education of 1.35 nonteaching staff to one teacher, in contrast to the 1992 average ratio for OECD countries of 0.58 nonteaching staff for every teacher at all levels (OECD, *Education at a Glance*, various years). A quarter of Moldova's nonteaching staff was at the preschool level, in a ratio of 3.6 children to one nonteaching staff. For grades 1–12 the ratio dropped to 0.83 nonteaching staff to one teacher.[32]

---

31 In contrast to the FSU countries, the Czech Republic and Hungary in 1992 had lower ratios of nonteaching staff to teaching staff than the average for the OECD countries (OECD, *Education at a Glance*, various years). Although much depends on how nonteaching staff are used, lower ratios are generally preferable because they imply that the sector is reserving higher proportions of its positions for the core function of teaching.

32 Personal communication, Claude Tibi, 2000.

Box 4.1

INEFFICIENCIES IN HIGHER EDUCATION: HUNGARY

The root causes of the inefficiencies in Hungarian higher education were complex. The system of higher education had been seriously fragmented after the communist takeover in 1947. By the beginning of the 1990s, 90 higher education institutions had been established. Only three enrolled more than 2,500 students; half enrolled fewer than 500. The creation of a large number of very small institutions resulted in diseconomies of scale in institutional administration and the provision of student services. It also forced expensive duplication of courses in the basic disciplines, particularly mathematics, foreign languages, and the basic sciences. Higher education had also shifted its emphasis from instruction in the humanities, law, and theology to the laboratory and applied sciences. This shift increased demand for laboratories, workshop space, and small group instruction, all of which drove costs up sharply

The high cost of higher education in the mid-1990s was also attributable to practices of elitist education that had been adopted much earlier. Teaching relied heavily on tutorials and seminars rather than lectures. The high cost of college and university instruction stemmed primarily from the employment of exceptionally large numbers of teachers. In 1994 the systemwide average ratio of students to instructional staff in Hungary was 6.9, in contrast to between 12.9 and 29.3 in the OECD countries. The excessive use of staff was traceable to light teaching loads, small classes, and high requirements for in-class instruction. The average professor taught only 6.9 hours a week, while an OECD counterpart taught between 8 and 12 hours. Hungarian students spent an average of about 27 hours a week in class; their counterparts in the West spent only 12 to 16 hours. The intensity of direct instruction in Hungary was balanced by relatively light expectations for independent study and library work. The typical Hungarian student spent less than a quarter of the time working independently as did his or her Western counterpart. The result was that the average cost per year of higher education was $5,189 per student—about 1.4 times per capita GDP. By contrast, in Western Europe a year of higher education cost 0.3 to 0.6 times per capita GDP.

Inefficiencies permeate all levels of the system

All levels of education are inefficient, but in different ways. Student/teacher ratios in secondary vocational programs are reasonable, particularly given the safety issues inherent in vocational training and the fact that the staffing numbers include technical support staff who set up and maintain equipment. For example, in Hungary in the early 1990s the ratio was 17:1 for secondary vocational programs.

However, unless reformed, secondary vocational programs have inefficiencies. They were often set up to handle both training and production. Production requires the expensive equipment used in long production runs and facilities larger than needed for training alone. Programs may rigidly differentiate theory instructors, who must have university teacher training and sometimes teach very few hours, from practical instructors, who are technicians and work much longer hours. Common practice in the West is to use one instructor who can integrate theory and practice, thus improving the elasticity of staffing assignments.

Unreformed programs tend to have several hundred specialties with associated equipment and staffing demands. Common practice in the OECD countries and in countries such as Hungary and Romania that have been reforming their secondary vocational systems is to make instruction more

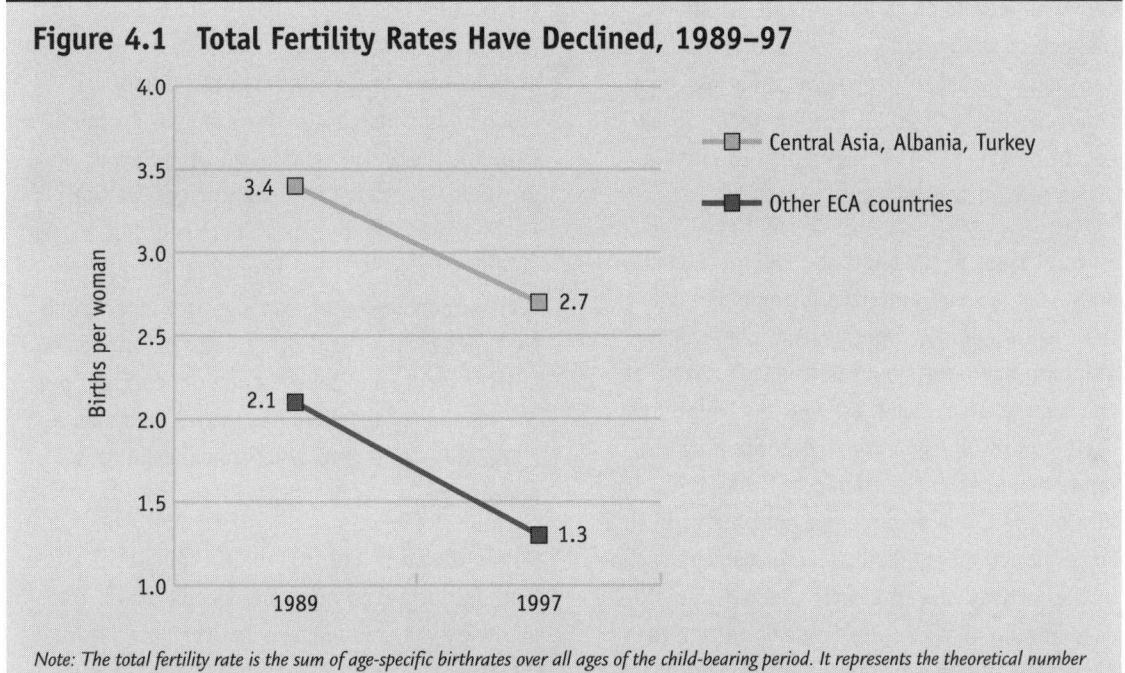

Figure 4.1 Total Fertility Rates Have Declined, 1989–97

[Chart showing births per woman from 1989 to 1997:
- Central Asia, Albania, Turkey: 3.4 (1989) declining to 2.7 (1997)
- Other ECA countries: 2.1 (1989) declining to 1.3 (1997)]

Note: The total fertility rate is the sum of age-specific birthrates over all ages of the child-bearing period. It represents the theoretical number of births to a woman during the child-bearing years, using the given year's birthrate as a constant.
Source: Authors' compilation based on averages in annex table A3.

general by reducing programs to a much smaller number of broad curricular areas and by shifting more specialized training to postsecondary programs. These broad based programs require much less capital investment.

Postsecondary vocational training that has not been modernized has different inefficiencies. In the pretransition period enterprises and secondary schools provided this training. As state enterprises close or become privatized, the former system is disintegrating. Secondary schools have governance, administrative, and delivery arrangements that reflect public school norms for teacher salaries, time and method of delivery of instruction, and type of pedagogy. These practices are often inappropriate for adult students in that they fail to take account of the individual's prior training and work experience. The public school regulatory environment limits the flexibility and responsiveness of these schools. The schools are not organized to customize training for employers on short notice, and, even if they were, they cannot levy full cost recovery because they may have no legal way to amortize equipment costs. When they are contracted to train the unemployed, payments are sometimes based on the numbers contracted, not on the final numbers trained. This arrangement means that these programs do not have incentives to increase the completion rates of their students by offering occupational counseling, using modular curricula that take account of prior experience or using open entry and exit programming. (See box 4.1 for examples of inefficiencies in higher education in Hungary.)

Demographic trends will increase today's inefficiencies

As figure 4.1 shows, total fertility rates for all ECA countries declined between 1989 and 1997, although fertility rates for Albania, the Central Asian republics, and Turkey still exceed the replacement rate of 2.1 children. In most other ECA countries, fertility rates have dropped to well below replacement. As annex table A4 shows, the size of the region's preschool age group (ages 3–6) is projected to decline by about a seventh between 1995 and 2020. The age group in basic education (ages 7–14) is expected to decline by 25 percent in this period.

Thus, at least in the short to medium term, ECA education systems are sized for more children than will be going through them. These demographics may reflect only transient factors that could be reversed, such as transition-related declines in GDP. The current declines may also reflect changes in the timing of births, resulting in a delayed, not a permanent, decline in births. For example, an approximately 40 percent decline in the fertility rate of Latvian women aged 20–25 accounts for that country's overall decline in birthrates, but these women, like women in the West, may simply be deferring child-bearing until their 30s.

The sector has not adjusted to new economic realities by reducing inefficiencies

Chapter 3 pointed out that today's education sector has to pay much higher prices for some inputs, especially energy; it has less public financing; and its input levels are still generally excessive. Utilities are now being priced at market levels, and the share of the education budget being devoted to energy inputs has risen from less than 5 percent at the beginning of the 1990s to 25, 35, or 40 percent of the total education budget, depending on the severity of the climate.

One might expect the pressure of utility costs on education budgets to be accommodated by an increase in student/teacher ratios. In fact, these ratios have declined over the decade in most ECA countries. In 1989 the average ratio was 16.2:1; by 1997, it was 14.4:1. (See annex table A16.) The dynamics underlying these declines differ, but the bottom line is the same: more teachers in proportion to students. In some cases the number of students has declined but the number of teachers has increased—for example, in the Czech Republic, Poland, Romania, and the Slovak Republic. In other cases the numbers of both students and teachers have declined, but student numbers have declined disproportionately to teacher numbers—for example, in Bulgaria and FR Yugoslavia. In still other cases the numbers of both students and teachers have increased, but the number of teachers has increased disproportionately—for example, in Armenia, Belarus, and Russia.

Russia is one of the three ECA countries that uses true decentralized financing in education. One might expect this practice to stimulate efforts to increase efficiency. As box 4.2 shows, in some cases it has. However, fiscal decentralization in the region often does not allow true budgetary autonomy at local levels. Too frequently, local authorities still have to use the old central norms in constructing their budgets. Thus, they cannot even change the input mix to take advantage of local conditions and changed relative prices (Klugman 1997a, p. 37).

The sector is adjusting to new economic realities in ways that will ultimately damage educational quality and fairness

Educators' wages have been allowed to fall. The sector has generally adjusted to budget constraints in two ways. One is to allow the real wages of staff in the sector to decline (see annex table A17). In Armenia teacher salaries in 1990 were 65 percent of the average wage in the country; by 1997, they had dropped to 44 percent of the average wage. In the Kyrgyz Republic teachers were paid 75 percent of the average wage for the country in 1990, but by 1997 their wages had

> **Box 4.2**
>
> ### RUSSIA'S SAMARA OBLAST REDUCES PER STUDENT COSTS
>
> The senior education administration staff of Russia's Samara oblast concluded that the root causes of unfavorable staffing ratios and high per student costs were (1) the formulas by which the oblast was allocating budget to schools; (2) the fungibility of oblast subventions to *raions* (districts), which left raions free to divert to other sectors allocations intended for education; and (3) the small size of many schools, especially those in very rural and remote parts of the region. The traditional system of education finance was "supporting the process but not the results" of education, the level of financing going to an individual school being more a reflection of history than of rational choices based on evaluations of economic tradeoffs. The region decided to experiment with a capitation system, where money follows students, the per student allocation being modified by a small number of factors known to affect per student costs, such as rural location. Although raions and school directors were given more flexibility in how they spent their subventions, these funds were earmarked for education and could not be spent in other sectors. After careful costing, the region started a long-term program of consolidating schools into clusters in order to benefit from the economies of scale of larger classes (World Bank 1999h).

dropped to 61 percent of the average. Wages for teachers in Tajikistan dropped from 88 percent of the average wage in 1990 to 49 percent in 1996. Analyses of labor markets and poverty in Bulgaria found that being in a social service job, including education, rather than in a manufacturing job doubled the risk of low wages (Rutkowski 1995). Lengthy delays in the payment of salaries, coupled with very high rates of inflation, have further eroded the value of salaries and wages.

When unemployment levels decline and teachers' wage expectations adjust to new market rates for educated labor, the sector's primary means of absorbing the fiscal consequences of inefficiencies will no longer be available. Governments also run the risk of igniting processes of "adverse selection" in which wages are too low to retain teachers of quality, thus leaving the field to poor performers. The analyses of the teaching force needed to assess whether these processes have started in the region have not been done but should be done. International studies show that once these processes start, they are very hard to reverse. Since teachers tend to stay in the occupation until retirement, low quality teachers also adversely affect the learning achievements of several generations of students.

The sector is seriously underfinancing nonwage inputs, with consequences for the maintenance of infrastructure, the provision of textbooks, and private costs to parents. The second adjustment by the sector is that it has scaled back budgets to the vanishing point for inputs other than labor. In some cases it is shifting the costs to families. Several ECA countries have almost eliminated budgets for building maintenance, textbooks, other teaching materials, in-service training, or heat. Either these inputs are not being provided, or parents are paying the costs.

Chapter 3 showed that by deferring maintenance, the region is accumulating a very large bill for rehabilitation. The estimated bills for Albania and Latvia have already been cited. In Georgia more than 75 percent of all school buildings are now in urgent need of rehabilitation or reconstruction—up from less than half in 1992. The costs of necessary rehabilitation are now estimated at about $250 million (Perkins 1998).[33]

---

33 Analyses for other countries show that routine maintenance of schools is cost-effective over time. One study estimated that routine maintenance saves 13 percent per school over a 21-year period.

THE WORLD BANK

The textbook story is similarly troubling, especially for the FSU countries.

- Latvia's budget for textbooks now covers the costs of one-third of one textbook per student.

- In Georgia parents are responsible for the full costs of textbooks. As a result, 90 percent of the required textbooks are available for children up to grade 3, 50 percent are available for children up to grade 8, and only 15 percent are available up to grade 12.

- In Azerbaijan the government pays for textbooks for grades 1 to 4, and parents pay for textbooks in the later grades. Only 30 to 35 percent of the required textbooks end up being provided.

- The Belarus government funds all textbooks, but budget constraints result in only about half of the required textbooks being provided.

- The Moldovan government has started a textbook rental scheme. However, the unwillingness of the government to place rental fees in hard currency accounts that will protect them against future devaluations of the local currency jeopardizes future textbook provision. Poverty levels preclude pricing textbooks at levels that will compensate for the devalued local currency, and the government cannot afford to cover the shortfall.

- In Russia the percentage of textbooks provided by oblast budgets varies from 6 percent (Chelyabinsk) to 65 percent (Irkutsk).

- In Tajikistan the government pays for textbooks, but this financing arrangement results in only 5 to 15 percent of the required textbooks being provided (information provided by International Book Development, Ltd., 1998).

Small or nil budgets for teaching materials and in-service training of teachers have made it difficult to introduce new curricula and teaching methodologies. These constraints have particularly affected countries that are attempting to readopt the national language of instruction and to reintroduce teaching of the history and culture of the nation into the school curriculum.

Strategic Paths for Governments

Cross-national studies show that student learning outcomes and per capita gross national product (GNP) are not closely related. This implies that governments at comparable income levels can and do make policy choices that differ in their effects on learning outcomes (Mingat and Tan 1998). In making these choices, governments should consider both sides of the equation (inputs relative to outcomes), since the efficiency of an education system is measured by resource use relative to the outcomes achieved.

Focus on the relationships between the resources consumed and the outcomes secured

In general, the ECA region still focuses on inputs, not on outcomes and not on the relationships between inputs and outcomes. The region does measure some outcomes, such as enrollment and completion rates, but the bottom line of an education system is what students know and know how to do. Most ECA countries lack interpretable measures of student learning. This means that most ECA countries have no basis for monitoring the system's efficiency, as measured by resources used relative to learning achieved.

Even in the absence of measures of student learning, international experience shows that a number of efficiencies can be achieved in ECA systems without hurting (and in some cases probably improving) learning outcomes. In their efforts to increase educational efficiency, governments should focus on four types of resources: facilities, teachers, utilities, and goods and nonteaching services. They should revisit four policies in terms of their broad effects on efficiency: curriculum, minority language instruction, early specialization, and policies on special needs children.

There are numerous opportunities for reducing costs, and two points need to be kept in mind:

- Except for energy use, the potential savings from single interventions are generally modest. Better efficiency is achieved by taking a number of interrelated actions that cumulate into substantial savings. These interventions cannot be used to "buy" countries out of macroeconomic crises, even though the education sector consumes a significant share of the public budget.
- Many efficiency measures cost money before they can save money. Some, such as adopting energy-efficient standards for new construction, will save money only over many years. Most will take time to implement.

Given these realities, improving efficiency requires good databases about inputs—for instance, school mapping databases should be used to make school closure decisions. Cost-effectiveness or cost-benefit analyses are needed for all decisions. These analyses may reveal unexpected cost-benefit (cost-effectiveness) tradeoffs. For example, the numerous small rural schools typical of many ECA countries are inefficient. However, in view of the costs of the road infrastructure and transport required to consolidate students in fewer schools with better economies of scale, it may be cheaper to maintain a large number of small schools for the present. Over the longer run economic considerations that affect individuals' residential choices will solve the problem by depopulating these small villages.

Cost-benefit (cost-effectiveness) analyses must reflect the fact that inputs into the delivery of education can be "lumpy". You cannot close 1.5 classrooms; you can only close 1 or 2 classrooms.

In other words, averages can be misleading. If the average class size is 16, the apparent efficiency solution may be to increase the average to 25 students. However, in reality the average class size in urban areas may be 35 and in rural areas 10. The objective has been more than achieved in urban areas and will fail to be achieved in rural areas unless schools are consolidated.

Focus on four resource targets

Facilities. Three strategies for managing the physical stock are proposed:

- Consolidate existing schools.
- Identify least-cost alternatives for managing changes in the size and geographic distribution of the school age cohort.
- Improve the efficiency of building standards for new schools.

The first two strategies require the existence of school mapping databases. These show the geographic distribution of schools in the country, with each school described by its construction type, the number and dimensions of classrooms and other spaces, the number of students by grade, the numbers and types of nonteaching staff, the numbers and types of teachers, and so on. They show distances between schools, the state of roads, and census trends by age for each catchment area.

The efficiency of the existing infrastructure can be increased by closing small schools and consolidating students in larger schools. For example, in Russia's Novgorod oblast about 70 percent of schools and 50 percent of teachers are located in rural areas, whereas only 25 percent of students live in rural areas (World Bank 1999h). Closures save on utilities, maintenance, teachers, and nonteaching staff, including administrators. Where possible, managers should close the least energy-efficient schools, those in the worst physical state, and the smallest and therefore least efficient schools. Decisions to operate minority language schools, distances between population settlements, the availability of public transport, the state of the roads during winter, and options for disposing of unneeded schools all affect opportunities to use this strategy.

Efficiencies can also be increased by using each building for a particular level of education—primary, middle secondary, or upper secondary. Many schools now cover grades 1 to 11, but this arrangement does not make the most efficient use of specialized facilities, such as laboratories, or of subject-specific teachers. Obviously, this strategy is most feasible in large towns and cities with multiple schools.

Maintaining the efficiency of the infrastructure across changes in the size and geographic distribution of the school age cohort requires that ways be found to resize infrastructure at minimal cost. Right now, given declining birthrates, governments need to assess the fiscal benefits of selling schools relative to the costs of "mothballing" them if they cannot be redeployed. If the number of school age children increases, policymakers can increase class sizes up to a point, introduce double shifts, rent facilities, or, if the increase in students is expected to be short-term, buy mobile classrooms that are inexpensive, can be constructed on-site in a week, and last 5 to 10 years. All these strategies are cheaper than investing in new permanent infrastructure, although at some point it becomes more efficient to build a new school.

Policymakers have to adjust not just to periodic shifts in birthrates but also to varying degrees of internal and external migration. For example, in Albania birthrates are declining, citizens are emigrating legally and illegally to other countries at unknown rates, and villagers are moving out of the mountains into periurban areas. Population shifts of this magnitude require frequent estimates of the population by location and age structure and projections of internal migration patterns if governments are to keep the education infrastructure approximately aligned with population numbers and their geographic distribution.

In terms of future construction, the strategy is to change space norms and construction standards to conform to international standards for space utilization, energy efficiency, and minimized maintenance costs. Experiments and costing under local conditions can clarify cost-benefit (cost-effectiveness) tradeoffs for a given standard. For example, the Moldovan ministry responsible for school buildings found that double-glazing the windows in a classroom increased room temperature by 8 degrees Celsius, relative to the same room with single-glazed windows.

Teachers. Inefficient student/teacher ratios do not translate into large shares of the public education budget because the job of a teacher has become redefined as part-time with poor pay. These conditions are not conducive to a professional ethos or to attracting and retaining high quality teachers.[34] Governments need to consider gradually substituting a much smaller, better paid, full-time teaching force for a larger, poorly paid, part-time teaching force. This change may not save money, but it should improve efficiency by improving student outcomes via the higher quality of those attracted into teaching.

There are a number of strategies for reducing the number of teachers:

- Use multigrade teaching in small schools.
- Postpone specialized curricula to postsecondary education.
- Increase class sizes by consolidating schools or classes.
- Increase teaching loads in exchange for better pay.

---

34   To survive on low pay, teachers have incentives to take actions that can damage the integrity of the system. They are encouraged to seek opportunities to give private lessons to augment income, even to the same students that they teach during the publicly financed part of the day. They also tend to become dependent on "gifts" from parents and thus indebted to the better-off families able to afford these gifts.

- Cross-train teachers in related subjects.
- Use high quality distance learning to augment or substitute for subject-specific teaching, especially in rural areas.[35]
- Relate government subsidies of teacher training colleges to the projected supply of and demand for teachers over a 10-year period. This action ensures that money available for preservice training buys what the nation needs. By not subsidizing the training of many more teachers than the system needs, it also reduces political pressures on the government to hire excess supply.

Restructuring the teaching force as a smaller, full-time, better paid force requires a sophisticated political strategy, information, and analyses—for example, projections of expected retirements from the teaching force, estimates of the costs of layoff and early retirement packages, and models that calculate the recurrent costs of a smaller, better paid force.

Utilities. The earlier discussion about facilities identified energy-efficient construction standards and space norms as a way to conserve energy in new construction. Several strategies can improve energy use in existing buildings:

- Better insulation of schools (walls and roofs)
- Double-glazed windows
- Properly sealed doors and windows
- Meters (for billing individual schools for their energy use)
- Revised school year (school closed during the coldest months and open during the warmer months)
- A reduced school week (from six to five days), with total annual instructional hours maintained either by increasing the number of instructional hours per day or by extending the school year into early summer

Again, decisions to retrofit a school need to be based on cost-benefit (cost-effectiveness) analyses that take into account the expected life of the school and its current physical state. They need to be closely coordinated with plans to close schools.

Construction, goods, and nonteaching services. Construction includes new construction and major repairs. *Goods* include textbooks, workbooks, teacher guides, teaching aids such as maps and laboratory equipment, vehicles, computers, and so forth. *Nonteaching services* include maintenance services for buildings and equipment, medical staff, cooks, cleaners, teacher trainers, and guards.

The one efficiency rule for all these goods and services is that the government should contract them out on a truly competitive basis whenever feasible. For example, urban preschools, instead of having nurses and cooks on staff, can contract for medical and food services. (Rural areas probably do not have the alternative sources of supply required for competitive contracting.) Privatization of the textbook industry should be encouraged. However, if the domestic publishing and printing industry is poorly developed, contracting out may merely replace a public with a private monopoly, producing few (if any) efficiency savings. In that case a staged strategy, using international competitive bidding, can be introduced to stimulate the development of a truly competitive domestic textbook industry.

To secure efficiencies, the contracting process has to be transparent and competitive, and the government has to monitor and enforce the contracts. The intent to contract for services must be widely advertised; requests for proposals must specify exactly what the contractor will be expected to provide and when and spell out the penalties for late or poor performance; the evaluation criteria for selecting the winner must be

---

35 At the postsecondary level, open universities serve a similar function.

clearly specified in advance; and the evaluation committee must not include individuals with a vested interest in the outcome of the competition.

Governments must monitor the performance of the contractor. Terminating the contract is usually not the optimal penalty for poor performance because, unless the services or products being purchased are not needed soon, the government pays a price in lost time in service or product provision. Better options may include reducing payments to the contractor in proportion to the lateness of the delivery of the service or product. For example, if a publisher gets the textbooks to the schools two months late, payments due the contractor are cut by a percentage specified in the contract. Another option for unsatisfactory performance of a service, such as maintaining school grounds, is to truncate the contract. For example, a two-year contract might be reduced to one year. In serious cases of poor performance the contractor can be declared ineligible for contract renewal or for bidding on other contracts with the government.

Revisit four policies

Certain policies affect the efficiency of the system fairly broadly, in that they increase the need for facilities, staff, and textbooks. The educational wisdom of some of these policies is not always clear.

Curriculum. Compared with other regions, the curriculum at each grade in the ECA region tends to include a large number of subjects, some addressed for only one or two hours a week. Chapter 1 points out that this policy fragments the instructional focus of the classroom and encourages a superficial acquisition of skills and knowledge.[36] Each of the many subjects also requires a subject-specialized teacher and a textbook. Governments should consider reducing the number of subjects now covered in each grade, thereby enhancing the depth of students' learning and saving on subject-specialized teachers and textbooks.

Minority language instruction. Governments support minority language instruction for sound policy reasons. One is to demonstrate respect for ethnic differences as a way of keeping the social peace; nothing is more damaging to a country's economic development, its education system, or its people than ethnic warfare. Another reason is educational. Studies show that starting the schooling of the child in his or her mother tongue can enhance the child's educational progress

However, as noted in chapter 1, there are downsides to this policy. Unless the minority language policy can be designed to move minority children from their mother tongue to fluency in the national language, minority language students can face reduced labor market access and mobility. The policy can, although it does not have to, maintain social division.

This policy also broadly affects educational efficiency. Depending on how the provision of minority language instruction is organized, it can increase the number of less efficient, small schools.[37] It requires all textbooks to be published in each of the minority languages, reducing the length of print runs and raising unit costs.[38] It complicates the deployment of teachers because the teacher's and the school's language of instruction have to be matched.

---

36 Fragmented curricula seem to lower student performance. For example, the analyses of science and mathematics curricula for over 40 countries suggested that one reason for the weak performance of American students in the Third International Mathematics and Science Study was the curricula in these subjects, which were "a mile wide and an inch deep". American eighth grade science curricula typically covered 50–60 topics, in contrast to Japanese and German science curricula for these grades, which covered less than 10.

37 Minority language instruction can be offered in more efficient ways. For example, Romania and Hungary try to integrate minority language instruction into schools where the general curriculum is taught in the majority language. Only some subjects are taught in the minority language, such as language classes in the minority language students' classes.

38 For example, the Romanian Ministry of National Education funds some textbooks in all minority languages, for a total of 11 languages, including the majority language, Romanian.

Although minority instruction is an important (and volatile) political issue, civic groups and governments should confront the labor market and efficiency implications of supporting multiple minority languages of instruction. In the debates about this issue, a consensus may emerge that social cohesion can be enhanced in ways that are less costly to individuals, the society, and the taxpayer.

Specialization of programs. As was discussed in chapters 1 and 2 minimizing specialization until the postsecondary level lets individuals strengthen the foundation skills required for adapting to unpredictable skill demands. Moving in this direction also increases efficiency, in that the facility and equipment costs associated with highly specialized vocational training at the secondary level diminish. In fact, a policy of broad based vocational training at the secondary level results in about the same unit costs for both academic and vocational training.

Special needs children. These children include orphans, children who have been removed from abusive or dysfunctional families, and physically and mentally handicapped children. In all countries they cost more to care for and educate. However, in the ECA region the care of these children is not always humane or efficient. For example, Romania uses 70,000 staff for 98,000 special needs children. An orphanage in Syzran City, Samara oblast, Russia, had 85 staff and 67 children (World Bank 1999h). Misdiagnoses, especially of minority children, also seem common in the region. Aside from the effect of a misdiagnosis on a child's life, it adds considerably to the cost of educating that child. In addition to re-evaluating the staffing norms that now prevail in special needs institutions, governments should consider mainstreaming the most able special needs children. Introducing this policy requires retraining teachers in those methods of child-centered teaching that are in fact preferable for all children. For children who require boarding, it requires retaining boarding facilities but using regular schools to provide educational services.

Summary of the important alternative strategies: What will they save, what will they cost, where might they not work?

Table 4.1 summarizes the main strategies discussed above in terms of the types of savings they can generate, what it will cost to achieve these savings, and local conditions that may limit their usefulness. As the table shows, it often costs money to save money. For this reason and as argued earlier, the tradeoffs between initial costs and expected savings must be analyzed to see if the strategy ultimately saves money. Poorer ECA countries face a limit on all costly interventions: finding the money to implement them.

Politically, efficiency reforms are hard to manage. The political economy of securing efficiencies is difficult in any context. Efficiency reforms usually involve concentrated losses and diffuse benefits. When benefits are diffuse, beneficiaries are unlikely to mobilize for change, and losers are apt to organize against the change. Those likely to bear the costs include teachers' unions, villagers whose schools are being closed, and education officials who have to acknowledge failings in the system. Others are also likely to bear costs: monopoly providers of goods and nonteaching services who now have to compete to win contracts, and education officials who run political risks to secure savings without those savings necessarily accruing to the sector.

In many countries around the world inefficiencies coincide with the need to expand children's access to education, making it possible to combine politically popular reforms and unpopular reforms. For example, if enrollments increase and the number of teachers remains the same, student/teacher

Table 4.1 Increasing System Efficiency: Main Strategies, Costs, Savings, and Limits

Intervention	Intervention costs	Savings	Limits to intervention
Consolidate schools	• School mapping databases • New roads/road repair • Transport • Expansion of schools used to consolidate students • Layoff packages for redundant teachers	• Administration costs • Utility costs • Maintenance costs • Fewer teachers	• Minority language policy • Distances too great to consolidate schools • Lack of roads and/or transport to consolidate students • Political constraints: teachers' unions; leaders of villages whose schools will close
Divides schools by grade levels requiring common facilities and teaching	Retrofitting school with special facilities (e.g., laboratories) required at the educational level served by that school	More efficient use of subject-specific teachers and facilities	Limited to large towns and cities with multiple schools or to villages clustered close together
Use larger classes, double shifts, and rental space to handle enrollment increases	Rental costs	Elimination of costs of building new schools	• Political constraints: teachers may resist larger classes; parents may resist double shifts • Rental space may not be available
Use energy-efficient construction standards and international space norms for new construction	• Adaption of international energy-efficient standards to local conditions • Enforcement of construction standards and space norms in new construction • Possible higher initial capital costs	• Utility savings • Maintenance savings	None
Use multigrade teaching in small schools	Training teachers in multigrade teaching	Fewer teachers	Useful in very small schools that cannot be consolidated; difficult to use in upper secondary grades
Postpone specialized curricula to tertiary education	• Costs of closing specialized facilities; layoff packages for specialized faculty • Costs of designing broader programs, equipping them, and training faculty	Approximately the same unit costs for vocational secondary as for academic secondary education	• Requires a feasible reform strategy competently implemented • Political constraints: resistance from redundant faculty
Increase class sizes	• See "Consolidate schools," above • Layoff packages for redundant teachers	Fewer teachers	Political constraints: resistance from redundant faculty and from teachers with larger classes
Increase teaching loads in exchange for better pay	• Relative costs of more, poorly paid teachers versus fewer, better paid teachers • Layoff packages for redundant teachers	Perhaps no savings, but, as part of move to smaller, better paid teaching force, higher quality teaching	Political constraints: • Teachers' acceptance of changed conditions of work • Resistance to layoffs

Cross-train teachers in related subjects	Costs of incremental preservice training	More efficient use of subject-specific teachers	Cross-training best completed during preservice training. Converting the practicing teaching force to a cross-trained force will therefore take years
Make use of distance learning	• Costs of equipment required to deliver distance learning • Costs of curriculum and materials	Fewer teachers; better learning	Depends on delivery technologies selected. There are fewer limits to "low-tech" and low maintenance technologies
Extend government subsidies to teacher training colleges on basis of projected teacher demand	Projections of teacher supply and demand	Training costs only for number of teachers needed	Political constraints: resistance from teacher training colleges if number of subsidized enrollees reduced
Retrofit schools to conserve energy	• Analyses of tradeoffs between retrofitting costs and expected savings across projected life of school • Construction costs	Utilities	Money for retrofitting
Change instructional calendar to conserve energy	Few	Utilities	May be limited to nonagricultural districts, depending on the effect of an extended school year on a farm family's need for children's labor
Open up to competition the provision of goods and nonteaching services	Learning to run a competent and transparent contracting process and to enforce contracts	Services purchased as needed, competition lowers their costs	Difficult to implement in countries with high levels of corruption

Source: Authors' compilation.

ratios increase without anyone having to be fired. Unfortunately, inefficiencies in ECA education systems coincide with demographics that argue for shrinking the system, at least over the medium term. The region is also running relatively high levels of unemployment.

These factors suggest that compensating losers will be key to gaining efficiencies. Uncompensated losers, even if they cannot prevent the introduction of policies designed to increase efficiencies, will attempt to circumvent or dissipate them during implementation. This evasiveness is why efficiency gains may be briefly realized, only to vanish with time—eventually, losers find ways to minimize their losses. Incentives to pursue or acquiesce in efficiency measures can include:

- Reasonable layoff or early retirement packages for redundant staff
- In the context of a good labor redeployment program, retraining of teachers who are already well educated and can be retrained for other professional services
- A phasing in of broad competition for the provision of goods and nonteaching services
- Free and reliable transport for students whose village schools have been closed
- Flexibility for policymakers at different levels of government in allocating resources between different inputs
- Return of savings to the sector for reinvestment.

CHAPTER FIVE

REINVENT GOVERNANCE, MANAGEMENT, AND ACCOUNTABILITY

Summary

Most ECA countries have just started to confront the demanding requirements of governance, management, and accountability in the efficient delivery of educational services.

Governance *refers to the steering function for the education system—setting goals and monitoring the sector's progress in achieving them.* ***Management*** *refers to the effective implementation of goals. Since processes for setting goals are undeveloped in so many ECA countries, the basic tasks of sector managers are ill defined, and in general, the sector's management falls far short of good public management standards.* ***Accountability*** *refers to the mechanisms that stakeholders can use to assess the sector's performance and pressure the state to represent their interests. In ECA, pretransition accountability systems are no longer valid*

Restructuring the sector's governance, management, and accountability has to be the highest priority for governments. Goals set for the sector should be limited in number, measurable, and accepted by stakeholders. Management of the sector can probably only be significantly improved in the context of a comprehensive public administration reform. In the meantime, however, the sector can reallocate functions among management levels, re-engineer ministries of education where needed, and measure the sector's performance. Governments can strengthen the sector's accountability through better checks and balances among rules and standard setting, competition (stakeholders' "choice"), and participation (stakeholders' "voice").

The state is intimately involved with education systems. It provides educational services, finances and regulates them, and collects and publishes information on them. The private sector, both profit-making and nonprofit, also provides services, and private financing plays a greater or lesser role in paying for education, depending on the country and the level of education. However, in most countries, and certainly in ECA, the state is the dominant player.

Since the state takes these actions on behalf of its citizens and taxpayers, questions immediately arise as to how well it represents their interests. Is the education sector doing the right things?[39] Is it doing the right things in the right way? What mechanisms do stakeholders have for monitoring the state's performance and holding it accountable for its actions?

The sector's governance, management, and accountability arrangements determine the answers to these questions. *Governance* refers to the sector's steering function—how the goals for the sector are set and monitored; *management* refers to how the implementation of goals is organized. *Accountability* refers to the mechanisms that stakeholders can use to assess the sector's performance and to bring the state to honor their interests.

These three dimensions are interrelated. The vigor of the accountability mechanisms in a country affects the transparency and inclusiveness of goal setting. The nature of the goals determines whether managers of the system have clear signals or directives—an issue of some importance, since too many or confusing goals undermine the efficiency of management and the basis for accountability. The management of the sector determines the quality of the statistical and policy analysis capacities needed to increase the realism of reform goals and to report on progress in achieving them.

---

[39] "Doing the right things" is known as allocative efficiency, which refers to the way resources are distributed among different possible uses—for example, between health and education or between primary and higher education. Conceptually, allocative efficiency is similar to the idea of external efficiency in education.

Why This Development Goal?

Distortions in the governance, management, and accountability functions make the achievement of other objectives problematic. Improving these functions seems to be a sine qua non for straightening out other problems.

Given this reality, it is unfortunate that ECA education systems tend to fail on these three key dimensions. Although research on governance, management, and accountability in the region, especially for the education sector, is thin, there is substantial experience with ECA governments to draw on. With notable exceptions, this experience reveals the depth of reform that is needed, especially in countries of the FSU.

The first of the next three sections evaluates patterns of governance—how well countries in the region are setting and monitoring goals for the sector. The second section, on management, assesses how well the sector is being managed and whether it meets the standards of good public administration. The third section explores the question of whether frameworks exist for improving the accountability of the state for efficient service delivery.

Governance

A country's political, economic, and social environment frames what people need from an education system. Major changes in context, such as ECA is experiencing, normally force countries to rethink and debate the goals for their education systems. As the implications of globalization for education began to register, the United States entered noisy debates about goals. Chile, as it emerged from the repressive Pinochet regime, did the same. Tunisia, as it watched the ravages of Islamic fundamentalism next door in Algeria, rethought its goals for education to stress an education that emphasized tolerance. But many ECA countries have not engaged in these processes effectively.

Goal setting and monitoring—the roles of governance—are missing

Except for the Baltic states and a few countries in Eastern Europe such as Hungary, Slovenia, and, increasingly, Romania, goal setting processes are unfocused—or at best, nontransparent. Measuring how well goals are being attained is even rarer.

In the early years of the transition the ECA countries tried to replace communist ideological content in curricula and textbooks. Understandably, the rethinking of goals was based more on political reasoning than on sound analysis. Thus, public debates, to the extent that they occurred in the region, generated mainly political slogans, important as an impetus to education reforms but insufficient for effective goal setting.

In the second half of the decade the most progressive countries moved toward goals that were clearer, better debated, and more frequently monitored. In some ECA countries goal setting debates have occurred for subparts of the system, especially vocational and technical education. The Czech Republic is an example (Hendrichova, Svecova, and Slavikova 1999). However, in many other countries of the region the historical tradition of setting goals as an ideal vision rather than as a practical tool for setting priorities for the sector has persisted. What have often amounted to scattered initiatives are not organized around a small number of coherent, feasible, and measurable goals that define the reform direction for the sector.

Weak, absent, or nontransparent governance seems related to management and accountability problems. As discussed later, managerial functions that support goal setting and measurement are missing in most education ministries, specifically the policy analysis/planning and financial management functions.

Another problem lies in the sources of pressure to rethink goals. Education bureaucracies are inherently conservative. Although occasionally a minister of education with substantial vision leads a re-evaluation of the direction for the system, these pressures tend to come from outside, not from within, ministries of education. Often, although rarely in ECA, the pressure arises from other government players such as parliamentary committees, ministers of finance, councils of ministers, or prime ministers and their deputies.

Outside government, parents typically do not exert pressure for change. Parents are conservative—they want schooling that looks like what they received. More likely sources of pressure are employers who need skills that they cannot find and the dense networks of civic associations that characterize democracies. However, most ECA economies have not yet developed to the point where employers face important skill shortages—although when they do, if the experience in the West is any guide, they will probably become vocal advocates of change. The associational life of ECA countries is also still very thin, and the mechanisms by which citizens can register their preferences are poorly developed.

Management

The next two sections deal with management from two points of view. One analyzes the functions and decisionmaking powers in the sector: their completeness, their distribution among levels of government, their clarity, and their consistency. The second assesses how functions are conducted relative to standards of good public administration.

Management functions and powers have not been rationalized

A number of questions can be asked about functional responsibilities and powers. Are functional responsibilities and powers allocated to plausible levels of government? Are important responsibilities missing? Is authority over decisions ambiguous? Are responsibilities and the resources needed to meet them aligned?

Allocation of functional responsibilities and powers among levels of government. This topic embraces questions about centralized and decentralized funding, operational responsibilities, and decision-making powers. Since chapter 3 discusses the allocation of funding responsibilities, that issue is not discussed here except incidentally.

Countries can distribute responsibilities and powers among levels of government in various ways and still secure reasonably efficient service delivery. The size of the country—its population numbers and territorial size—and the presence or absence of geographically concentrated ethnic groups affect these distributions. For example, decentralizing certain responsibilities may make sense in large countries such as Poland, Russia, Turkey, or Ukraine but not in small countries such as Albania, Estonia, or Slovenia.

A limited number of criteria can be used to judge the distribution of responsibilities and decision-making among levels of government in ECA countries. Does the distribution:

- Protect national interests in creating human capital, in keeping variances in human capital low (fairness), and in promoting social cohesion?
- Secure economies of scale (supply efficiency)?
- Maximize opportunities for competition or customer choice?[40]

---

40   Choice is one key to holding the state accountable for efficient service delivery: it gives customers, such as families and employers, options among service providers. Choice presumes competition among what have often been monopoly providers, and competition is theoretically assumed to improve the efficiency of services.

Table 5.1. Where Should Decisionmaking Responsibilities and Powers Be Lodged?

Locus of responsibility	Decisionmaking responsibilities and powers
Central	• Leading improvement of sector by setting fiscally responsible priorities and designing and overseeing the implementation of change programs • Generating financial resources • Insuring quality of inputs and outcomes by, for example, establishing a standards-based national curriculum in the foundation skills; assessing whether students are meeting these standards; and creating and enforcing knowledge and skill standards for teachers • Publishing credible information on performance of system • Protecting interests of poor and minority groups at all levels of education • Protecting social cohesion • In centrally financed systems, using financing formulas to create incentives for subnational levels to increase efficiency • Setting health and safety standards for the sector • Making economy-of-scale decisions to open or close national-level institutions, such as universities
Intermediate (provincial level)	• Making economy-of-scale decisions for regional level institutions (e.g., to open, close, or consolidate institutions across small local jurisdictions) • Making such decisions for other issues most efficiently resolved across spaces larger than small local jurisdictions (e.g., allocation of teachers among schools.)
Local/school level	Making factor mix, not product mix, decisions—at the school level as often as feasible

Source: Authors' compilation

- Maximize opportunities for "voice"—that is, the participation of users and beneficiaries in decisions about the system?[41]
- Align responsibilities and the resources needed to meet them?

Depending on country-specific conditions, achieving one objective may undermine the achievement of another. For example, nonexperimental evidence suggests that local decisionmaking, although it may increase voice, can also decrease equity and social cohesion (Prud'homme 1995; Lockheed 1997). Decentralization is expected to increase civic voice. However, in developing democracies local elections that are the obvious mechanism for registering voice on issues of social policy may in reality be decided on grounds of personal, tribal, or political party loyalties, not on civic grounds (Prud'homme 1995). In other words, the verdict is certainly not in on centralizing versus decentralizing decisionmaking powers as a way of increasing voice.

Table 5.1 suggests one distribution of functional responsibilities and powers among government levels that is consistent with the objectives just listed.

---

41 Voice is another key to holding the state accountable for efficient service delivery. It is defined as citizens' or customers' willingness and ability to exert pressure on service providers to perform. Voice can take various forms, from local elections to community power over the selection of school headmasters.

The assignment of decisionmaking responsibilities is very fluid in the region. However, several problems associated with the distribution of functions and decisionmaking powers among levels of government have emerged. In basic and secondary education a number of countries still centralize educational decisionmaking; examples are Croatia, FYR Macedonia, and Uzbekistan.[42] Highly centralized systems, usually overwhelmed by operational decisions, are unable to focus on strategic planning and issues of national policy. They are not easily held accountable by civil society. For example, in Croatia, where the Minister of Education appoints school principals, when ministers change, so do principals, especially heads of important secondary schools. Schools are accountable to the party in power, not to the civil society, except very indirectly via national elections.

Although recent legislation is expected to remedy the problem, the Czech Republic has lacked an intermediate (regional) management level. The central level has been overloaded with administrative tasks and has been unable to focus on strategic issues. The country has lacked that level of government best able to manage a restructuring of vocational/technical education that reflects subnational economic realities and economies of scale (Hendrichova, Svecova, and Slavikova 1999).

Missing functions. An analysis of management arrangements shows that important functions may be missing. The most obvious are:

- Leading the sector's improvement
- Setting learning standards and ensuring educational quality
- Monitoring performance, especially by publishing information on the system's performance and measuring it against performance in countries selected as comparators
- Ensuring educational fairness.

These are functions that belong at the central level, but they are often missing even in centralized systems in the region. For example, in Romania performance monitoring is nominally lodged at the central level but appears to be no more than a paper function. Although this is now being remedied, thus far there is no standardized reporting, performance grading, data analysis, or other feedback information. Inspection reports and academic performance results are confidential (Ivan and others 1999).

In countries that have decentralized responsibilities for basic and secondary education, such as Russia and Ukraine, the ministries of education have lost many of their former functions to subnational levels. At the same time, they have not assumed responsibility for functions that manifestly belong at the center.

The information responsibility of the central level is particularly important for accountability—a society cannot hold its education sector accountable without credible information on its performance. All countries in the region have education statistics. However, the statistics in Albania, Bosnia-Herzegovina, Georgia, FYR Macedonia, Moldova, and Turkey are judged to be rudimentary (World Bank 1999c). Most ECA countries measure inputs to the sector, not outcomes; they rarely measure private sector educational activity; and financing data may aggregate expenditures on educational services that differ in their costs—for example, secondary academic versus vocational/technical education. In other words, statistics in the region do not support policymaking well.

The statistics that do exist are often not made publicly available, especially by the FSU countries. Ukraine is flagrant in maintaining the secrecy of data on the sector, and Romania has recently

---

42 Other levels of education can have patterns of centralization and decentralization that differ from those at the basic and secondary levels. For example, even in countries with centralized decisionmaking for basic and secondary education, decisionmaking for preschools may be decentralized. Decisionmaking for secondary vocational education conforms to that for secondary education, but decisionmaking for postsecondary vocational training differs markedly from that for secondary vocational education. The postsecondary vocational level is governed in multiple ways and tends to use one of three general models or all three models in the same country. Universities tend to have substantial autonomy.

increased the "confidentiality" of information on student learning and the managerial performance of schools.

Contradictory, unclear, or overlapping allocations of powers to different or to the same levels of government. Is authority over decisions ambiguous? As discussed later in this chapter, the incentives prevalent in the region are rules that are hierarchically imposed and enforced. The result is often excessive numbers of rules that are poorly coordinated, contradictory, unclear, and therefore idiosyncratically interpreted. In Romania intricate, parallel, and overlapping responsibilities among the many boards under the jurisdiction of the Ministry of National Education result in "endlessly contradictory information" (Ivan and others 1999).

Case studies show overlapping responsibilities for the same function between two or more levels of government without rules for adjudicating shared authority. For example, in Russia both the oblast and central levels organize textbook production and distribution; the central, oblast, and school levels develop teaching and assessment methods, design school programs, and set performance standards (Klugman 1997a, p. 19). The Hungarian education system shares responsibilities between levels of government for a number of functions, such as teacher appointments, salaries, and in-service training. The result has been problems of ambiguous boundaries and a need for coordinated action.

The same level or unit can also be assigned responsibilities that constitute a conflict of interest. In Romania, for example, school inspectorates run hundreds of schools and assess their own management (Ivan and others 1999).

Misaligned responsibilities and resources. This problem shows up in most ECA countries, although it takes different forms.

Since some accountabilities properly lie at subnational levels, highly centralized systems violate the principle of aligning decisionmaking powers and accountabilities. By definition, they do not give these levels the powers they need to meet their responsibilities. An important example is accountability for student learning. Since learning problems ultimately have to be solved at the level of the classroom and school, the school is the natural unit to hold accountable for learning outcomes. A centralized system means that the school has no control over decisions that affect its ability to deliver on its obligations.

Money, like decisionmaking authority, does not always follow responsibility. As state owned enterprises shed preschools and vocational schools, local levels of government are assuming responsibility for preschools, but often without the resources they need to cover costs. With similar effect, countries have responded to fiscal pressures at the center by allocating inadequate block grants to local governments for basic and secondary education. Countries of the FSU, however, generally have vertical fiscal imbalances, created by national responsibility for revenue generation but local responsibility for spending (Klugman 1997a, figure 2, p. 8; Wetzel and Dunn 1998). Thus, in Kazakhstan in 1994 local education expenditure as a share of local revenues ranged from 23 to 204 percent, 6 of the 21 oblasts having education expenditures that exceeded their total local revenues (Klugman 1997a, table 4, p. 10). Transfers from the center to subnational levels and from oblast to *raion* (district) levels reduce revenue disparities at local levels (Klugman 1997b; Stewart 1997; Wetzel and Dunn 1998), but final revenues at local levels are low relative to the costs of educational services that have to be provided.

Chapter 4 pointed out that budgetary responsibility may be decentralized, but with budget rules still set by the center. These include wage rates for teachers, student/teacher ratios, and minimum levels of expenditure. These central norms undermine opportunities for local government to improve technical efficiency or to use its fiscal resources to reflect the preferences of local beneficiaries.

Management of the sector falls far short of standards for good public administration

Even where functions and decisionmaking powers are complete and are sensibly allocated among levels of government, functions may be performed well or poorly. How well do ECA countries manage the sector, as measured by criteria for good public administration?

To some extent, this question boils down to a question about the effectiveness of the country's overall public administration. Public sector administration can be judged on several dimensions (World Bank 1999b), but the focus here is on policymaking capacities and operational efficiency. Factors external to government (e.g., politics) affect government's management performance, but governments do control key subsystems. Table 5.2 shows one analytic framework for assessing how well organisational functions are performed (Joyce and Ingraham 1997).

An analysis of individual countries, using the criteria in table 5.2, conveys how far short of good international practice the public administrations of most ECA countries fall. Even the Czech Republic, Estonia, and Hungary, although they have made considerable progress, still have to travel some distance to reach international standards (Nunberg and Reid 1999). Embedded as they are in a country's prevailing standards for public administration, ECA education systems share the same failings.

At the same time, the education sector can independently improve its public management. For example, in a number of countries school principals have been selected not on merit but on the basis of loyalty to the party in power or have been elected by teachers. Thus, managers in primary and secondary schools, as well as in higher education, can benefit from professional management training.

Accountability

"Accountability" in education refers to the mechanisms that stakeholders can use to assess the sector's performance and to bring the state to honor their interests.[43] These interests have to be balanced to ensure the efficient and responsive delivery of services. This section analyzes the three conditions required to achieve this balance.

1. A framework for the delivery of educational services with three mechanisms operating in a checks-and-balances relationship to one another: rules and standards, competition (choice), and participation (voice)
2. Disaggregation of education into different goods and services susceptible to different incentive regimes
3. Involvement of multiple stakeholders, not just the state, in the design, delivery, and monitoring of services.

Condition 1: The incentive framework has three mechanisms operating in a checks-and-balances relationship to one another: rules and standards, competition (choice), and participation (voice)

The key to efficient and responsive service delivery is a checks-and-balances relationship among the interests of three groups: the public sector (government and professional educators), the private sector, and the civic society (taxpayers, users, and beneficiaries). Each of these three actors plays

---

43 There is a large literature—e.g., the new institutional economics literature—on the issue of accountability. Papers that relate the implications of this burgeoning literature to service delivery problems include Paul (1991, 1994) and Girishankar (1999). The framework used here relies heavily on work by both Girishankar and Paul, especially the former.

THE WORLD BANK

Table 5.2 Criteria for Competent Public Management

Function	Criteria for evaluating performance of public administration
Financial management	Accurate revenue and expenditure forecasts; one-time revenues not used to finance on-going expenditures; countercyclical or contingency planning devices used; budget adopted in a timely way; investment and cash management systems balance return on investment and risk avoidance; management of long-term debt; accurate and audited financial statements; accurate assessments of the cost of delivering programs and services; relevant information on the future financial impacts of government actions
Management of human resources	Clear and understandable personnel system; insulation from political interests and pressures; workforce planning and strategic analysis of needs; timely hiring on the basis of merit; control of hiring; maintenance of appropriate skill mix among employees; ability to reward and discipline employees appropriately; cooperative labor-management relations
Management of information technology	Systems useful to and used by managers; coordination of technology from the center; multiyear information technology planning process in place; well trained staff and users; system cost justified by benefits it yields; system allows information to be transmitted to citizens and other stakeholders; right information to right people at right time
Capital management	Strategic analysis of long-term capital needs; use of appropriate information and analyses to differentiate good from bad capital purchases; integration of capital budget with planning for operating budget; appropriate maintenance
Managing for results	Strategic, results-oriented plan provides basis for developing performance measures; involvement of stakeholders in selection of desired results and in evaluating progress; appropriate measures of activity outcomes; use of these measures for policymaking, management, and evaluation of an agency's progress toward its goals; clear communication of results to citizens, elected officials, and other stakeholders
Integration or alignment	Actions align financial, human resource, information, and capital subsystems around performance goals; those components include leaders whose vision is clearly communicated to subordinates, leaders able to motivate employees to achieve the organisation's goals, information technology systems well integrated with other management systems, leaders who use information to evaluate progress toward goals, and budget priorities aligned with current policy priorities

Source: Joyce and Ingraham (1997).

according to different rules. The public sector uses rules and standards to establish the framework for service delivery; the private sector uses competition and choice; and the civic society uses participation or voice.

- *Rules and standards* are used to regulate the goods and services provided. Rules and standards should be framed in consultation with various stakeholders. However, the state, in the form of bureaucrats, technocrats, and quasi-state groups, such as subject-matter associations of teachers, is usually the central player. The aforementioned groups are better positioned to represent national interests and professional knowledge.

- *Competition* (choice) can be used when multiple suppliers are available. Because it gives purchasers choices among goods and services, competition improves efficiency by forcing suppliers to reduce costs and improve quality. Although private sector players are those most likely to be subject to competition, capitation financing, vouchers, and other mechanisms can be used to create competitive markets among public providers.

- *Participation* (voice) takes the form of stakeholder participation in the definition of input and outcome standards; using information on the performance of the public or private sector to press for improved performance; and using information to choose among educational options. The central players for exercising voice include beneficiaries, users, taxpayers, and civic groups. Users will vary according to the level of education in question—for example, employers are vocal about training services.

Theoretical and analytic work shows that the state cannot be trusted to supply educational goods and services efficiently or to respond to the preferences of beneficiaries and users without the competitive checks of markets or the exercise of voice by beneficiaries and users. *However, these same studies also show that efficiency and responsiveness decline if any one of these players dominates.* Mechanisms for strengthening accountability carry their own distortions. Thus, it is the checks and balances among the three mechanisms that result in the most efficient and responsive provision of services.

Markets are not self-regulating. In the absence of rule setting and standard setting by the state, they cannot be counted on to supply educational goods and services that respect national interests or the interests of taxpayers, beneficiaries, or users. Similarly, beneficiaries and users cannot be trusted to represent communal interests in the absence of rule setting and standard setting by the state. The state and professional groups provide an important check on beneficiaries and users for at least three reasons.

- In addition to the positive benefits of education captured by the individual, such as higher wages, education has positive benefits for the collectivity. These include lower crime rates, better health practices that limit the spread of infectious diseases, more vigorous and better informed voter participation, contributions to economic growth that are not entirely captured in higher wages of individuals, and—depending on occupational structures and labor markets—more equal incomes and therefore less chance of social unrest. However, neither children nor parents can be trusted to invest sufficiently in education to realize its collective benefits. Children are too young to make these choices on their own behalf. Relative to their parents, they are also powerless to enforce choices that are to their benefit but not to that of their parents. Parents' investments in their children's education are significantly determined by their own levels of education and their socioeconomic status. Thus, poor parents with little education are apt to value the benefit to them of the child's labor in the fields more than the delayed benefit of education for the

Figure 5.1 Checks and Balances between Interest Groups and Mechanisms Enhance the Delivery of Educational Services

Players and mechanisms

PUBLIC SECTOR *(GOVERNMENT AND PROFESSIONAL GROUPS)*:
Rules and standards

PRIVATE SECTOR:
Competition (choice)

TAXPAYERS, USERS, BENEFICIARIES:
Participation (voice)

Source: Adapted from Girishankar (1999).

child. To counter these choices, the state enacts and enforces laws that require families to send their children to school up to certain ages.

- The socioeconomic status of participants drives the exercise and effectiveness of voice. In the absence of state efforts to protect the interests of the poor and minorities, wealthier and more powerful parents will dominate ("capture") decisions about the allocation of services at the expense of poorer families.

- There are information asymmetries that favor the state over beneficiaries, users, and taxpayers. The latter voice preferences based on what they can observe. For example, if teachers do not show up for work, parents can observe their absence and demand ways of ensuring teachers' commitment to their jobs, such as giving communities or parent associations the right to hire and fire teachers. However, they are poorly positioned to see or understand important dimensions of education. For example, in the absence of credible assessments of student learning, educational quality is hard to judge. Parents do not readily understand the implications of a market economy for the skills and knowledge that their children need. Professional groups are better positioned to see these links and to represent them in state regulated learning standards.

Figure 5.1 shows the checks and balances among interest groups and the mechanisms that they use to govern their interactions with the education system.

Most ECA governments do not balance the use of these three mechanisms, and the result is weak accountability of the state to the civil society for the efficient delivery of educational services. Governments tend to rely almost exclusively on hierarchical rules as incentives in the education sector, bureaucrats and teachers usually being reduced to order takers with no scope for initiative. Governments do not make much use of competition (choice) and participation (voice) to counterbalance rules and norms. Although governments bid out the provision of some services and goods, these are not always true competitions. State and private sector actors are too frequently in collusion with each other.

Condition 2: Education is disaggregated into different goods and services susceptible to different incentive regimes

ECA's record here is not good. Most ECA governments treat education as a single bundle of services instead of disaggregating the services into activities according to the optimal arrangements for delivering them.

The characteristics of goods and services vary in ways that imply the optimal mechanisms for delivering them. The same framework is not optimal for all of the inputs into service delivery. Nor, incidentally, is the same framework necessarily optimal for all stages of an activity, whether that stage be design, operation, or monitoring (Girishankar 1999). For example, in a ports project, government, in the form of its technical experts, and voice, in the form of inputs by shippers, may be the optimal arrangement for designing the port. The market, in the form of a contract to a private firm, may be the optimal arrangement for operating the port. Government may be optimal for monitoring and enforcing the contract.

The characteristics of goods and services that affect the choice of the mechanisms for providing them are expressed in the form of the following questions and answers.

- *Can multiple suppliers compete to provide the good or service?* If so, choice or markets can be exploited competitively to improve the efficiency of the goods and services delivered. For example, in the case of computers, a number of vendors can provide the same equipment. Families in small rural communities rarely have choices among schools provided by the state, but some competition can be introduced by opening to competition the management of the school. Urban families have choice among the city's multiple providers of primary or secondary education. Since students often expect to move to the location of a university, this gives them choices and creates competitive pressures on tertiary institutions.

- *How precisely can the desired characteristics of the good or service be specified and measured?* Measurable goods or services favor the use of markets as a way to improve the efficiency of service delivery. For example, it is easy to specify good custodial services and to use visual inspection to check on the quality of the service provided. ("Is the school clean?") It is much harder to specify good teaching. In the absence of agreed teaching standards, visual observation is not much help in measuring teaching quality—observers, whether parents or school inspectors, do not know what to look for or how to judge what they see.

- *Is information about the quality of the delivered service equally available to all players—users, beneficiaries, and suppliers (often government agents)?* Beneficiaries and users may be able to observe quality better than government agents, in which case voice is an important component of the framework.

In the interests of simplification, table 5.3 gives examples of educational goods and services that differ only in terms of supplier choice and the ease with which their quality can be measured. These can be goods and services that a ministry of education or a district education office provides to itself, such as accounting services or information systems, or that government provides for the public.

The items in type I are standardized goods or services. Providers of these goods and services can be changed without particular disruption to the purchaser. Items in type II are services that can be opened to competition, but the competition is organized around bidding for the market. Once the contract is signed or the concession let, choice

Table 5.3 Educational Goods and Services Differ in the Multiplicity of Providers and Ease of Measuring the Quality of the Product or Service

Quality of good or service	Can multiple suppliers provide the good or service?	
	Yes	No
Easily measured	**Type I** • School furniture • Vehicles • Standard teaching aids • Equipment • Supplies • Textbook printing	**Type II** • Custodial services • Food services • Book publishing • School construction services • Utilities, accounting, and payroll services
Not easily measured	**Type III** • University level education • Postsecondary vocational/technical training • Urban preschool services • Urban basic education • Urban upper secondary education	**Type IV** • Rural preschool services • Rural basic education • Rural secondary education • Curriculum and learning standards • Measures of learning outcomes (examinations, assessments) • Statistics on educational inputs and outcomes

Source: Adapted from Girishankar (1999).

is severely reduced because those who let the contract incur monetary and time costs if they change providers. For example, a contract to construct a new school can be awarded on the basis of competitive bids, but once the contract is signed, changing contractors in midstream entails construction delays that may be unacceptable.

Condition 3: Multiple stakeholders, not just the state, are involved in the design, delivery, and monitoring of services

Again, the record of the education sector in most ECA countries is not good. ECA governments tend to define government as the only intermediary for delivering educational services, rather than defining the services as needing multiple intermediaries and stakeholders.

The nature of the good or service has implications for the institutional arrangements that best ensure efficient service delivery. Table 5.4 shows that competition (the market) is the mechanism of choice for type I goods and services. Type II goods and services also rely on competition. However, the "sunk costs" associated with type II contracts—that is, the costs to the contractor of switching suppliers—mean that market mechanisms cannot be used as readily to enforce compliance. Public officials have to enforce the contract by monitoring how well the supplier is meeting the contract provisions.

Markets and choice. Most countries in the region use at least limited forms of public competition to buy standardized goods and services (type I). However, contracting out (type II goods and services) is still in its infancy. Contracting out does not automatically increase the efficiency of

Table 5.4 Incentive Arrangements for Different Categories of Goods and Services

Quality of desired good or service	Choice: availability of multiple providers	
	High	**Low**
Easily measured	**Type I** Markets: competition *in* the market with contracting	**Type II** Markets and government: competition *for* the market with audits of supplier performance by government
Not easily measured	**Type III** Markets, government, and participation	**Type IV** Government and participation

Source: Adapted from Girishankar (1999)

service provision (Keefer 1998). Several conditions have to be in place for contracting to benefit efficiency. For example, procurement practices have to be transparent if providers are to innovate. Governments also have to be able to make credible commitments to compensate providers for innovations that improve quality or reduce costs. Credibility hinges on a secure environment for contract and property rights—again, a condition that many ECA countries do not meet well.

Services of types III and IV depend heavily on checks and balances between rules and standards and participation by the users and beneficiaries of the services. Type III services differ from type IV services only in that users have choices among providers. In other words, competition (choice or markets) can be used together with government rules and user or beneficiary voice to ensure efficient service delivery for type III services. In theory, urban families have choice, or chances to "vote with their feet", by virtue of having more access to private schooling and chances to exercise choices among public schools. Rural citizens in ECA have almost no choice of educational services unless the school's management is subject to competition or rural dwellers migrate to urban areas.[44] As already noted, on average, 41 percent of the populations of ECA countries lives in rural areas (Wetzel and Dunn 1998).

The laws of many ECA countries support the entry of private schools into the market, although countries differ in their obstacles to entry. The vigor of the private sector market also depends on the extent of public subsidy to private schools and the relative wealth of families in the country (UNICEF 1998, p. 83). A number of countries allow parents to choose among public schools regardless of residence (UNICEF 1998, p. 82), although tracking, which can sometimes start at age 11, constrains parental choice. Parents may also need subsidies in order to exercise choice, such as capitation financing, which can take the form of vouchers, scholarships, or even subsidized transport. With some exceptions in certain countries or provinces, however, ECA as a whole does not use capitation financing; no ECA country uses vouchers; and, as noted in chapter 2, scholarships for the poor are diminishing.

The limited supply of university places relative to demand turns choice on its head after basic (and sometimes after primary) education. Universities and the lower and upper secondary schools that virtually guarantee entry into university choose students, not vice versa.

Participation and voice. Voice is very weak in the region. A variety of mechanisms can support voice—for example, parent-teacher associations;

---

44 Distance learning provides a type of exit in that it increases learning options for students in rural communities.

THE WORLD BANK

election of local government officials who have the authority and resources to respond to voice; complaint procedures; public hearings; legal challenges through the courts; elected oversight boards for each school or each municipality; the community's right to fire the head of the school; publication of the results of each school's performance in local newspapers; citizen surveys of corruption in the sector, with the results published in national and local newspapers and discussed on television; and client service surveys that assess consumer satisfaction with education.[45]

Beneficiaries in ECA countries, however, do not have a rich array of ways for expressing voice and little tradition of using those means that do exist. Several ECA countries impose legal or political constraints on mechanisms for expressing voice, such as constraints on the press. For example, Bulgarian law stipulates that each school is to have a school board, but the working of the law restricts the opportunities for voice. Only a limited number of schools have boards, and principals who fail to establish school boards are not subject to sanctions. Even where school boards exist, they have advisory powers only, in part because school policy is almost entirely determined by decisions made at other levels of government (World Bank 1998a).

Citizens also need to have formed habits of using available channels of voice, and these habits are still weak in the region. For example, a Romanian working group that analyzed the sector's governance and accountability noted:

> The Romanian educational organisation neglects the legitimate interest and demands of the beneficiaries because it functions in a vacuum of external accountability. The beneficiaries of education (students, parents, communities, and industry) do not express their expectations or dissatisfaction because they lack the structure and culture of participation. (World Bank 1998c)

Decentralization and voice are often equated. However, they are not the same. Decentralized governance is more conducive to the exercise of voice because clients have more access to those making decisions about the sector. However, clients need channels, such as local elections, to make themselves heard. These channels need to be protected from capture by local subgroups, usually the elite of a community.[46] Unlike water supply, where the quality of the supply in the community is uniform, the quality of a community's educational services can differ depending on the beneficiaries. Powerful members of the community can commandeer resources to create high quality schools for their children, leaving families with weak voice to fend for themselves.

Strategic Paths for Governments

Since most ECA education systems have governance, management, and accountability problems that undermine the sector's abilities to solve other problems, attending to them must be a priority.

Governance: Re-evaluate the goals for the sector

What do the leaders and citizens of the country need from the education system? Is it giving them what they need? Can this question be answered at present? If not, how is it going to get answered?

Well-defined goals are necessary for focusing the energies of all players in the system and for accountability. Goals must be limited in number (no more than five and preferably fewer) and stable over a reasonable period of time. When goals

---

45 Client service surveys are primarily useful for evaluating visible dimensions of the school. Do teachers show up for work? Is the school building in reasonable physical condition? Do the children have textbooks? Is the physical equipment in the playground kept in safe condition? Client surveys are not as useful for less visible dimensions such as learning achievement.
46 Especially at the community level, beneficiaries with naturally stronger voice—the better educated and wealthier—are often also providers or are connected to them in networks. They have disincentives to use voice or exit and are inclined to prevent others from using these options. See Paul (1991).

multiply, managers responsible for achieving them are forced to ignore some or to vacillate between them, with the result that progress in reaching goals is ragged. When goals shift rapidly, managers do not have enough time to achieve any one of them, and reforms that are prematurely abandoned simply mean wasted time and effort. Goals should be targeted on ends, not means, and progress in achieving them must be measurable and measured.

Goals must be understood and accepted as legitimate by all the parties that are key to their achievement. Stabilizing goals across governments and ministers of education requires a broad political consensus. And a goal-driven reform requires that the wide range of players who implement it understand its objectives. This means conducting extensive and inclusive debates about goals. It also means investing in a communications strategy that clarifies the nature and reasons for agreed goals. In the absence of a shared understanding among the major players about the direction for the sector, they will be unable to coordinate and effectively target their efforts.

Management: Measure, measure, measure

Trusted information on the performance of the sector is the key to realistic goal setting, better management, and greater accountability. Without relevant data on the sector, all the players are flying blind. What does not get measured does not get fixed.

Start with an audit. Put together a working group of users, bureaucrats, and education professionals to assess what is known about the sector at each level of education. What information on performance is publicly available?

Assess and strengthen the capacity of the education statistics unit. An international expert in modern education statistics systems should assess the capacity of the country's education statistics unit. Statistics staff should be (or should become) familiar with new data collection standards, methods, and tools. They should be protected from political pressures. They should use computers and software to process, store, share, and disseminate information efficiently. Depending on the results of the assessment, develop a strategy for helping the unit reach international standards for statistics agencies.

Evaluate how education policymakers use statistical information in their decisionmaking. A country's education statistics system is only as strong as the information and analytic demands placed on it by education policymakers. Demand drives quality. Using donor aid, a Middle Eastern country built a respectable education statistics system, but since education policymakers did not use the data in their policymaking, the system gradually fell into disrepair. As one observer noted, "They built a statue without a head."

Design and implement a system of performance indicators. Selection of performance indicators should be based on broad consultations with stakeholders and policymakers to identify the information that they want for judging performance. The OECD countries have substantial experience in identifying such indicators (OECD, *Education at a Glance,* various years). OECD policymakers and stakeholders can attest to the policy relevance of different candidate indicators.

ECA countries should exploit the substantial technical experience of participants in the OECD's Indicators of Education Systems (INES) project to help them with the technical work of validating measures, collecting and analyzing data, and publishing results. ECA countries need to benchmark the performances of their education sectors against those of other countries. The OECD framework for some core performance variables would allow comparisons with other nations, including some ECA countries. The Czech Republic, Hungary, Poland, and, for a few variables, Russia are already participating in the INES project.

Special international assessments provide other chances to benchmark the performances of education systems (see chapter 1). Several ECA governments have already participated in some of these assessments: the Czech Republic, Hungary, Poland, and Slovenia participated in the IALS, as did East Germany before reunification (see chapter 1); a larger number of ECA countries have participated in the Third International Mathematics and Science Study (TIMSS). The OECD has also conducted reviews of national policies for education in several ECA countries, including Poland, Russia, and Slovenia.

Management: Reallocate functions among levels of government and reinvent the ministry of education

Again, start with an audit. Since the distribution of functions among governmental levels is very country-specific, rationalizing this distribution first requires an audit of decisionmaking by level of government and by level of education. Working groups for the audit should include those empowered to change current arrangements and those now affected by them. Several ECA countries, such as Albania, Bulgaria, the Czech Republic, Hungary, Poland, and Romania, have either completed or are now completing such audits.

For each educational level, the audit has to start with an analysis of who makes each of the major decisions. Using this database, working groups should examine the data for evidence on the following:

- Missing functions
- Contradictory or unclear allocations of powers to different levels of government
- Overlapping responsibilities for the same function between two or more levels of government without rules of the game to govern shared authority
- Misalignment of responsibilities and the resources required to meet them
- Allocation of functions to an inappropriate level of government.

Build a consensus around reallocating, eliminating, or adding functions. The analysis of the sector's governance arrangements will reveal both egregious and minor distortions. The strategy for reallocating, adding, or eliminating decisionmaking powers has to reflect a careful, country-specific assessment of the winners and losers from a management reform. Some players benefit from distortions; some lose. Attending to the political economy of reforming sectoral management will increase the chances of its success. Look for a window of opportunity. Politically, changes may be best made in the context of broad discussions within the government and the parliament about centralization versus decentralization and public sector management reforms.

If necessary and possible, start at the top by reinventing the functions of the ministry of education. Many ministries in the region have become empty shells. They no longer do what they used to do; they do not now do what they should be doing; and, by virtue of not having redefined their roles, they are unable to lead change in the sector.

Management: Support efforts to improve the administration of the public sector

Since the public administration of the education sector is so entwined with that of the whole country, the sector is somewhat limited in its abilities to significantly improve its own practices independently. However, the sector can participate

> **Box 5.1**
>
> **DECOMPRESSING CIVIL SERVICE WAGES IN GEORGIA**
>
> In 1997–98 Georgia began classifying teachers into four categories on grounds of their measured professional competence. The four categories are linked to differences in salary; those in the highest category make twice the monthly salary of those in the lowest. These new salary scales and the extension of the salary range that they represent were part of a public administration reform to decompress the salaries of public sector employees and to reward employees on the basis of their performance (World Bank 1998b).

in broader efforts to modernize the nation's public administration. For example, Albania's Ministry of Education and Sciences is a pilot ministry in that country's civil service reform. Box 5.1 describes a civil service reform in Georgia's education sector.

Accountability: Strengthen checks and balances between rule setting and standard setting, competition, and participation to improve efficiency and accountability

This section suggests ways to improve stakeholders' opportunities for choice (competition) and voice (participation).

Increase use of competition. Contracting increases the efficiency of service delivery, but only under the following conditions (Keefer 1998):

- Procurement procedures for contracting for goods and services are not corrupt. Government officials who use corrupt procurement procedures will not press for high quality and low cost provision of services and are unlikely to share with the government any cost savings that do emerge.
- Officials do not use the procurement of goods and services to gain the support of public sector workers. Those who do are likely to oppose any reform that jeopardizes the status of these workers.
- The government knows the costs of public provision. If the government does not know what it costs to provide the good or service within the public sector, it cannot adequately assess bids from private providers to determine whether contracting would save money. This ignorance is particularly costly when private competition is limited.[47]
- Legal standards and judicial processes for resolving commercial disputes are in place.
- There are enough private firms providing a service or good to sustain competition.
- The government is able to monitor contracts, especially the quality of service provision. Competition and a focus on less complex services can substitute for significant performance auditing capacity.

As noted earlier, many of these conditions are not in place in ECA countries. For example, the budget officers of education ministries or municipalities are not trained to estimate the costs of public provision. These realities argue for piloting contracting with very simple services and for a focus on getting required conditions in place.

Encourage school choice by capitation financing. Conditions needed for successful choice systems include the following:

- Meeting individuals' different preferences should not violate national interests in building human capital and social cohesion.

---

[47] Because it has the capacity to evaluate costs, the U.S. Air Force was able to conclude that contracting out engine repair to a major aircraft manufacturer would not save $4.7 billion, as the private vendor contended, but would cost the Air Force $1.3 billion. (See U.S. General Accounting Office 1997.)

THE WORLD BANK

- Families should be motivated to shop aggressively for schools that meet their preferences.
- Families should be well informed about the quality of education offered by different schools.
- There should be many suppliers of the service competing or able to gain easy access to the market.
- The service should be purchased frequently enough that users (or networks to which they belong) can learn by experience (Allen and others 1989).

As with contracting, few of the conditions for effective choice are in place in most ECA countries. Central ministries do not necessarily have the regulatory and standard setting structures to protect national interests—for example, social cohesion. Families lack objective information on the quality of individual schools that they can use to inform their choices. Again, these realities argue for focusing first on getting important conditions in place.

Expand voice in the management of the sector. As observed earlier, rural families have few resources apart from voice for disciplining service providers. However, it has been found that citizens with lower incomes and less education are less apt to use voice, and rural citizens are apt to be poorer and less well educated than urban citizens. In these cases external agents, such as nongovernmental organisations (NGOs), can be used to mobilize the local public to demand and monitor better service delivery (Paul 1991).

A number of strategies can increase the avenues for voice. These include conducting social assessments that capture the perspectives of beneficiaries and users. Other avenues are parent-teacher councils with decisionmaking powers, employer-trainer councils with decisionmaking powers, report cards on the performance of each school, and client surveys to assess citizens' perceptions of educational services and of corruption in the sector. Countries such as Albania, Georgia, Latvia, and Ukraine, for example, have conducted citizen surveys to identify corruption in various sectors, including education, thus beginning to establish a public demand for accountability and transparency in the education sector.

CHAPTER SIX

THE ROLE OF THE WORLD BANK

Summary

A country's will to change is a key determinant of lending success. Whatever the need, the World Bank should not lend to countries resistant to change in the education sector. For such countries, the ECA education sector will limit its activities to nonlending services that can help these countries benchmark their education systems against those of other countries. Countries low on need will be tapped to act as benchmark countries.

Lending to the education sector in ECA will be based on six principles.

- *The Bank will help clients achieve the five development objectives of this paper.*
- *No level of education is out of bounds for lending as long as lending at a given level promotes rationalization of the whole system.*
- *Lending will start where clients are and build from there.*
- *The Bank will not lend for humanitarian emergencies but will lend in postconflict and postdisaster situations.*
- *The Bank will only lend for infrastructure in the context of supporting policy change.*
- *Lending will reflect the Bank's comparative advantage, relative to its partners.*

Lending to the ECA education sector has higher than average risks because of volatile fiscal, legal, and policy conditions and the Bank's limited experience with ECA education systems.

The Bank's business strategy in ECA education is about changing concepts, rules of the game, incentives, and capacities. To accomplish these ends, the Bank's education sector is working with other teams and sectors in the Bank to realize payoffs from coordinated activities, such as establishing medium-term expenditure frameworks.

The role of the World Bank in the ECA education sector is to use its services to help ECA governments mitigate the problems in the region elaborated in chapters 1 to 5.

How Will the Bank's Education Sector Set Priorities for Lending and Nonlending Services?

The Bank's business opportunities in the education sector emerge out of the interaction of each country's need for change and its propensity to change. Countries differ more in their will to change than in their need to change. They differ markedly in their recognition of the issues discussed in this strategy paper and their will to deal with them.

Analyses of Bank investments across time and sectors show that a country's will to change is one of the two key determinants of lending success, the other being institutional capacity. Thus, whatever the need, the Bank has no business in countries that are resistant to change in the education sector. The fact that often the need is greatest where the will is least is painful but does not change the reality of the preconditions for lending success. This reality implies the priorities for intervention shown in table 6.1. The general rule is to analyze comprehensively but lend selectively.

The sector's lending and nonlending services will be concentrated in countries with high propensity and need to change (type I) and in countries with high need but low propensity to change (type III). As pointed out below, any categorization of countries by cells in table 6.1 has to be understood as dynamic. Countries move among the categories over time and depending on the education issue.

Table 6.1 Priorities for Bank Intervention

Need to change	Propensity to change	
	High	Low
High	**Type I** Lending services	**Type III** Limited lending and nonlending services
Low	**Type II** Nonlending services	**Type IV** Benchmark countries: use nonlending services to help other countries in region

Source: Authors' compilation.

A country is not one type for all dimensions of the sector. Experience with assessing a country's will to change shows that will is component-specific. A country may be type III relative to one domain or one level of education but type I relative to another. The government may be completely unwilling to introduce efficiency and cost recovery measures but very interested in building capacity to assess students' learning outcomes. It may be willing to modernize its vocational/technical training system but unwilling to disturb its university system.

A country is not one type for all seasons. Type I countries can shift to type III, and vice versa. The first reality (I→III) implies the need to manage risk (see below). The second reality (III→I) implies the need for the Bank to be ready to construct an intelligent lending response quickly. This means having up to date knowledge about the country in the form of Bank-financed sector work, public expenditure reviews, poverty assessments, and studies financed by other organisations, such as UNICEF, the OECD, and the Asian Development Bank.

Lending to type I countries is noncontentious. Perhaps the greatest contribution that the Bank can make to type I countries is to challenge the public policy goals of the changes that they want to make. Although these countries are trying to improve, they understandably often seize on reforms that fit pretransition habits, such as regulating higher education. Ministries do not always think through what they expect an initiative to achieve or the conditions required for its success. For example, the concept of vouchers is popular with ministries of finance, but they usually have not determined what they expect vouchers to achieve or the conditions required for achieving those policy goals. Their objective may be to use vouchers to create the competitive conditions that will improve educational quality. However, the usual absence of interpretable information in ECA countries about the learning produced by the school means that customers (parents) have no way of choosing among schools on the basis of quality. Similarly, ministries of finance have usually not considered whether alternatives such as capitation financing might achieve the same result as vouchers but at less cost.

The type II cell is probably an empty set in the region for most dimensions of the sector. Today's rapid changes in the political, economic, and social contexts for education mean that no education system in any region stays long in the type II or IV categories.[48] Where an ECA country falls into the type II category for a major dimension of the system, the role of the Bank is to monitor that the country is not undoing what were satisfactory solutions.

---

[48] For example, Western education systems now strongly need to change in response to the economic implications of globalization and, in the context of the increasing democratization of institutions, pressures for decentralizing decisionmaking.

The Bank has a responsibility toward type III countries. In some ways type III countries present the greatest challenge to the Bank. The Bank's emphasis on being demand driven, not supply driven, might seem to imply doing nothing with regard to type III countries. Certainly, lending is ill-advised. However, nonlending services organized to help a country compare (benchmark) its education system with those of other countries seem indicated. ECA countries were isolated for decades. This isolation insulated policymakers' concepts and perspectives from the questions inevitably raised by opportunities to compare and benchmark.[49]

Today the mental constructs within which policymakers view their education systems still tend to reflect pretransition values and standards. The lack of market-based prices meant that there was no basis for concepts of efficiency. Educational quality was defined academically as it was in sports: via Olympiads, where a few were nurtured to win, and winning by a few placed the seal of quality on the whole system. Although fairness was a concept during the communist era, it was based on ideological views of the relationships between economic classes. Its connection to human capital, market economies, and intergenerational poverty was neither relevant nor well understood.

A tradition of cradle-to-grave care by the state did not prepare policymakers and citizens for distinctions between public versus private finance or for limits on public finance and on the services that could be publicly supported. Thus, severe limits on public budgets have mistakenly been construed as temporary fiscal crises.

In many countries governance of the sector has changed. However, it is still dominated by government, with inadequate counterweights in the form of competition (choice) and participation (voice). The allocation of functions to different levels of government has not been coherent, and bureaucrats and policymakers in the ministries of education of many countries have little idea what modern public management looks like.

The Bank is a development institution. One of its jobs is to ensure that policymakers bring more realistic premises and information to the decisions that they make about their education systems. In the context of nonlending services, the dialogue between government and the Bank can alter a government's perspectives, causing it to move from a type III to a type I country. The Bank's primary job in type III countries is to multiply chances for policymakers to benchmark and compare their education systems against those of others. Scattershot comparisons will not buy much; there has to be a strategy based on concepts of adult learning.

One part of the strategy consists of creating opportunities for stakeholders to see what "good" looks like.[50] These are similar to apprenticeships, with chances to create a mental model of a good outcome. A long-term strategy for accomplishing this objective is to use mechanisms such as joint Japan–World Bank graduate scholarships to create a cadre of education policymakers for the future. Shorter-term strategies include:

- Study tours to ECA and non-ECA countries that are further advanced in improving a particular function or level of education
- Courses on education for clients, now being piloted by the World Bank Institute
- Small working seminars, in partnership with European bilaterals, the Open Society Institute, and ministers of education with special credibility to ECA ministers of education
- Miniseminars given by mission consultants
- Dissemination of in-country good practices

---

49 The rapid reformation of the Eastern European countries is almost certainly related to their shorter periods of communist domination and to the fact that prior to the communist takeover after World War II, these countries functioned within essentially Western conceptual frameworks.

50 In this context stakeholders include not just the ministry of education but also ministries of finance, labor, and public administration, and teachers' unions.

The second part of the strategy is to gather the necessary information on the sector's performance to allow actors in individual countries to make policy decisions. This means Bank-financed sector work, country economic memoranda, public expenditure reviews, social assessments, and poverty assessments. It means working with countries to create databases of important information needed by management—for example, school mapping databases. It means encouraging countries to participate in international efforts to collect comparative data, such as the following:

- *The OECD's Indicators of Education Systems (INES) project.* This project has developed a tested framework for defining variables, collecting data, and analyzing data on education systems. Indicators include comparisons of public and private costs of education and inputs (e.g., student/teacher ratios, teaching/nonteaching staff ratios, teachers' instructional time, and annual instructional time). These indicators allow policymakers in participating countries to compare the efficiency with which they use inputs with that of other nations. Even if ministries of education are not interested in these data, ministries of finance usually are.

- *Third International Mathematics and Science Study (TIMSS and TIMSS-Replication).* In the first round of TIMSS, nine ECA countries participated in learning assessments for 13 year olds. Twelve ECA countries are participating in the second round, which includes 40 countries from different regions of the world. This ambitious international study has three main components:
  (a) Assessments of students' learning in mathematics and science at ages 9 and 13 and for the final year of secondary school
  (b) Analyses of the characteristics of mathematics and science curricula, such as content, content sequencing, and performance expectations, in 48 countries
  (c) Analyses of videotapes of teaching practice in three countries.

- *International Association for the Evaluation of Educational Achievement (IEA) Civics Education Study.* The CIVICS Study will evaluate the civic and political knowledge of 14 year olds in 28 countries. It will use 38 cognitive items developed by expert panels from the participating countries. The study also includes student, teacher, and school questionnaires that tap concepts, actions, and attitudes having to do with democracy, national identity, social cohesion and diversity, economics, the media, and environmental protection.

- *Progress in Reading Literacy Study (PIRLS).* This IEA program will assess reading literacy at the fourth grade. In contrast to an earlier IEA reading literacy study that employed a somewhat narrow concept of literacy, PIRLS will build on the reading literacy framework of PISA (see below), an assessment targeted at 15 year olds.

- *Program for International Student Assessment (PISA).* This is planned as an on-going OECD program to monitor the learning achievements of students in reading, mathematics, and science. It focuses on all 15 year olds in a country, including those in work-based programs. The test items of PISA reflect key skills that young adults should have mastered to participate fully in their societies and economies. It will be administered on a three-year cycle, starting in 2000. Although each administration will include all three domains, it will focus on one of the three, reading being the focus for the first administration. The Czech Republic, Hungary, and Poland will participate as members of the OECD in the first round. Countries other than OECD countries may participate, but so far Russia is the only non-OECD country in ECA that is doing so.

- *OECD Problem Solving Project.* Network A of the OECD's INES project is planning an assessment of students' problem-solving capacities. After developing and testing items, this instrument will be incorporated into the PISA.

- *International Adult Literacy Study (IALS).* Whereas the TIMSS was constructed around the common denominator of the national curricula of participating countries, the IALS measures the information-processing and interpretive abilities of 16–65 year old adults in real-world work and consumer problems. Four ECA countries have participated in the first and second rounds of the IALS.

- *International Life Skills Survey (ILSS).* The ILSS, an OECD survey, builds on the IALS but is designed to assess a broader range of skills among adults in OECD countries than the IALS does. These skills include prose literacy and document literacy, numeracy, problem solving, teamwork, practical cognition, and computer familiarity. These skill areas will be assessed through direct performance or through behavioral reports. A full pilot survey is scheduled for 2001 and the main survey for 2002.

Having good comparative data is not the same as internalizing, reflecting on, or using the results. Policymakers in type III countries have to "own" any comparative data collection exercise that they enter if they are to change their premises about their country's education system. Where possible, policymakers should be encouraged to help design items. At the least, they should participate in international policy and training sessions surrounding the exercise.

Type IV countries can serve as benchmarks for type III countries. Type IV (and probably type II) countries have gotten much right or are in the process of doing so. As countries within the region, they have a special credibility with their neighbors. With almost a decade of active reform behind them, type I countries, such as Hungary, Romania, and Slovenia, are increasingly assuming the role of type IV countries in the sense of becoming benchmarks for the sector in the ECA region. Where possible, the Bank should work with these countries through nonlending services to expand the perspectives of policymakers in type III countries. In the context of lending services, the Bank should finance type I countries to allow them to use type IV countries for support and guidance. For example, when Albania's Ministry of Education and Sciences prepared its strategy for improving the sector, policymakers within the ministry visited their counterparts in Romania to evaluate a range of reforms undertaken by that country.

What Should the Bank Lend for— and Not Lend for?

Sectoral decisions to lend will be based on several criteria, starting with the five priorities for Bank lending identified in this document:

- Realign education systems with market economies and open societies.
- Combat poverty through educational fairness.
- Finance efforts to improve sustainability, quality, and fairness in education systems.
- Spend resources more efficiently.
- Reorient governance, management, and accountability.

This book specifies the interconnections among these priorities that must be protected. For example, countries should reform the financing of their systems or their upper secondary curricula in ways that protect the access of all children and young adults to education. Fundamental conditions have to be in place for these priorities to be properly pursued through Bank lending. For example, involving the private sector in the provision of educational services and products has to be done in ways that do not simply shift the lack of accountability from the state to markets.

No level of education is out of bounds for lending as long as lending at a given level promotes rationalization of the whole system. All levels, from preschool to higher education, are potentially eligible for lending if lending at that level can leverage rationalization of the system. Relative to comparators, virtually all countries allocate resources inefficiently; a few countries allocate too little to education (Georgia, Armenia, and, recently, Albania), some allocate too much (Belarus and Moldova), and some misallocate by level (e.g., Albania's high unit costs at the tertiary level). Adjustment lending and public expenditure reviews are better mechanisms for dealing with intersectoral misallocations. However, lending by educational level gives leverage over inefficiencies and misallocations at a given level, potentially freeing up resources for levels that are underfunded.

The type of lending will differ by level because the role of government should vary by level. For some levels, such as higher education or vocational/technical education, government should progressively reduce its provision and financing roles in favor of the private sector. For these levels, Bank lending should be focused on helping governments and the private sector create frameworks for private sector or mixed public-private sector provision and financing. These frameworks should address problems of governance, standards for provision, financing, fiscal sustainability and efficiency, management, equity, and accountability of providers to customers.

As long as lending is consistent with the Bank's broad priorities for the sector, lending will start where the client is and build from there. Often, lending cannot start with the Bank's highest priorities for the sector until clients themselves recognize the need. For example, several countries in the region, especially in the FSU, exhibit egregious problems of public sector management and accountability. However, not only may these problems be attacked better in a public sector reform program than in sector lending, but they may be among the last problems that the clients become aware of. They are not visible in the way that decaying infrastructure is. If they are to be perceived, clients need to understand what, for many, are still alien concepts of the role of the state and performance standards for the public sector. Starting with familiar and visible problems, such as reforming curriculum and textbooks, creates an environment for moving to conceptually and politically tougher problems.

The sector should not get involved in lending for humanitarian emergencies. It should, however, be active in postconflict and postdisaster periods. The Bank's mandate precludes providing the immediate help needed in humanitarian emergencies, and the Bank's processes are too slow to provide emergency assistance. The Bank, nevertheless, can help stabilize the economies of countries that border conflict areas and that absorb and provide services for refugees, as was done in Albania.[51] As in Bosnia-Herzegovina, the Bank can cooperate with other international agencies and bilateral donors in rebuilding after wars and natural disasters.

Wars and natural disasters spotlight factors that precipitate conflict or magnify the effects of a natural disaster. For example, a conflict based on the flaring of ethnic hatreds may reflect the fact that the dominant ethnic group used the society's institutions, including its textbooks, to denigrate ethnic minorities. An analysis of the devastating earthquake in Turkey showed that Turkey's lax construction standards (or their lax enforcement) jeopardized the structural integrity of buildings, including schools, in earthquakes. The period that immediately follows a conflict or a disaster provides a rare window of opportunity for new policy precedents. The Bank should be at the table to

---

51 FFor example, at the height of the Kosovar refugee crisis, it was estimated that the presence of refugees housed in host families and collective facilities (not in the camps) meant that the Albanian government faced a 20–25 percent increase in its student population when school opened in September. Had the refugees not returned to Kosovo so rapidly, the budget impact for the Albanian government of financing (let alone providing) these additional services would have been substantial. In the absence of budget support, Albania's ability to provide educational services for its own children would have suffered.

support the development of better rules and better enforcement of them.

Except in situations of natural disasters or wars that destroy large numbers of schools, the sector should not lend just for infrastructure. The Bank's limited project preparation and supervision budgets should be used primarily to achieve policy changes in the education systems of the region. Lending for infrastructure can be part of the package, either to support policy change (e.g., consolidating schools to improve the sector's efficiency or institutionalizing cost-effective school design and construction standards) or as a "carrot" to achieve policy change.

Lending should reflect the comparative advantages of the Bank, relative to those of its partners. The principle of working with partners is sensible and positive. Limited numbers of donors and lenders operates in the ECA region, and the Asian Development Bank is active in Central Asia. A number of partners are anxious to guide the Bank in Southeast Europe and the Balkans, but they bring limited financing. The Soros Foundation/Open Society Institute is active in most countries, but except in a few countries such as Albania, the scale of its programs is small. The European Training Foundation (ETF) is represented in most countries, but on a small financial scale. The European Union's Phare and Tacis programs have refocused their lending on EU accession issues. UNICEF and the United Nations Development Programme (UNDP) have small and infrequent programs. Bilaterals tend to have very limited interests. However, the Bank and bilaterals have cooperated in using their nationals as task team consultants paid by country trust funds.

The five priorities specified in this book were selected in part because they represent the Bank's comparative advantages relative to those of its partners. However, there has been a tendency for the Bank, and not just in the education sector, to slip inadvertently into taking on activities that our partners conduct more effectively than we can.

For example, the Bank has neither the experience nor the staff to deal effectively with handicapped children. Taking on issues better handled by others detracts from the Bank's ability to focus on areas in which its strengths lie. It also sows the seeds of resentment. Our partners have had long experience with certain issues and will see the Bank's (often clumsy) entry into these domains as an attempt to establish the Bank's hegemony. Learning and innovation loans are the types of interventions that might be better financed and implemented by partners, and these need to be carefully scrutinized early in the project preparation cycle. Thus, one task in working with partners is to straighten out each institution's comparative advantages in a given country and to respect these in a disciplined way. The Bank is uniquely suited to introduce issues otherwise best handled by our partners into its policy dialogues with governments, especially with ministers of education and finance. In discussions with national governments, the Bank can help partners who have run successful pilot programs scale these up into national strategies. It can work with partners to help governments develop realistic change strategies and to integrate the actions of partners and the Bank around these strategies. However, the Bank should not finance and implement particular activities that its partners conduct better than it can.

How Will the Sector Handle Lending Risk?

The ECA region and its education sector both have higher than average risks because of a fiscal, legal, and policy environment more unpredictable and volatile than that of most regions. A Bank-financed survey of the private sector found that ECA was the worst or among the worst regions in the world in terms of the policy and regulatory stability conducive to effective investments (Brunetti, Kisunko, and Weder 1997).[52] Respondents noted unpredictable changes in laws and policies, with the unpredictability getting worse over the last decade, and constitutional changes of government that produce large changes in rules and regulations.

The region is afflicted by civil wars among ethnic groups that delay or derail projects. The communist regime papered over unresolved ethnic conflicts that are now re-emerging, the Balkans being the most visible example.

Except in a few countries such as Bosnia-Herzegovina, Hungary, Romania, and Turkey, the Bank's education sector has done little lending in the region, even when secondary and adult training projects are included. (See table 6.2.) Thus, the Bank has few lessons of experience on which to draw. Most current education projects are with first-time borrowers. Both parties (Bank and borrower) have misconceptions and inappropriate expectations of each other. The resulting communication problems, which are typical of new relationships, can be corrected, but often messily.

The Bank's ECA education sector is using several strategies for managing the risks:

- *Base project or program lending on good knowledge about the sector.* By virtue of the criteria that it uses to assess the quality of Bank projects at entry, the Bank's Quality Assurance Group (QAG) recognizes the importance of a base of sector knowledge. Projects based on little sector knowledge suffer rather obviously—for example, from inadequate identification of project risks, or designs whose implementation is problematic. There will always be extraordinary cases where interventions cannot wait for a solid base of sector knowledge. However, in general, decisions by country managers to intervene should be based on reasonable knowledge about the sector.

In ECA education lending has often occurred without sector work, or the sector work has been conducted concurrently with project preparation. Both cases encouraged shallow policy dialogue and priority-setting with governments and have led to "cookie cutter" project designs.

- *Work closely with the country director and country team to put "reinforcing" lending in place.* Sector-specific lending is more apt to succeed if it is coordinated with cross-sectoral interventions that create incentives for a line ministry to implement a sector loan. For example, the objective of a new loan to Albania is to improve the management of the education sector. A second loan and extension of nonlending services reinforce the goals of the education project. A civil service reform loan focuses on conditions for better sectoral management: stabilizing and improving the quality of the civil service and strengthening the core functions of the ministries, such as policy analysis and planning, financial management, and human resource management. In concert with the Bank's nonlending services, the Ministry of Finance has started medium-term expenditure framework exercises that reward realistic planning, costing, and performance monitoring.

- *Design around political risks during project preparation, using political mapping and stakeholder and institutional analyses.* A well prepared project takes into account analyses of whether the players who have to take the actions required to reach the project's objectives have the incentives to do so. Political mapping, stakeholder analyses, and institutional analyses are the types of instruments that can be used to evaluate the incentives that key players bring to the project.

- *Encourage borrowers to manage the political economy of change by building a broad consensus.* In addition to broad consultation and consensus

---

52 Central and Eastern Europe scored better than members of the CIS on these dimensions.

Table 6.2 Education Lending in the ECA Region (FY84–FY02): Closed, Portfolio, and Pipeline

Country	Education/training Closed	$M	In portfolio	$M	Projects Pipeline FY	$M	Education and training components in noneducation projects Closed	$M	In portfolio	$M	Pipeline FY	$M
Albania	1	9.6			1 (FY00)	12.0	1	5.0				
					1 (FY01)	5.0						
Armenia			1	15.0								
Azerbaijan			1	5.0					1	3.5		
Belarus												
Bosnia-Herzegovina	1	5.0	1	11.0	1 (FY00)	10.0			2	5.6		
Bulgaria					1 (FY00)	30.0						
Croatia												
Czech Republic												
Estonia												
Georgia					1 (FY00)	15.0						
Hungary			2	186.4			3	108.8				
Kazakhstan									1	14.5		
Kyrgyz Republic												
Latvia			1	31.1	1 (FY02)	30.0					1 (FY00)	5.0
Lithuania					1 (FY00)	TBD						
FYR Macedonia			1	5.0	1 (FY01)	25.0						
Moldova			1	21.8								
Poland					1 (FY02)	70.0			1	43.0	1 (FY00)	50.0
Romania			3	170.0					1	15.0		
Russian Federation			2	111.0	1 (FY01)	50.0			1	60.0		
Slovak Republic												
Slovenia												
Tajikistan			1	5.0								
Turkey	5	350.0	2	390.2	1 (FY00-01)	100.0			2	35.0		
					3 (FY01)	650.0						
Turkmenistan												
Ukraine												
Uzbekistan												
Total	7	364.6	16	951.5	14	997.0	4	113.8	9	176.6	2	55.0

Notes: FY, fiscal year; TBD, to be determined.
Source: Author's compilation based on SAP (Systems, Application, and Products).

building by the Bank with government, the Bank can help borrowers alter the political risks themselves. There is growing experience with, and knowledge about, how to build a broad consensus for change. Devices include consultation, inclusion of stakeholders in major decisions such as goal setting, social marketing, and publication of credible data on the sector.

- *With new borrowers, pursue modest reform objectives.*

- *Use learning and innovation loans (LILs) in new relationships.* These loans let the Bank begin with a low-key relationship with new borrowers, giving both sides a chance to learn about each other before "going national" or taking on problems that require higher levels of trust and communication. The danger is that the LIL may become a "foot in the door" instrument that does not honor its intended purpose of experimentation, piloting, and innovation. Its intent has to be respected. As long as a LIL is organized around its true purpose, it is a good way to start relationships with new borrowers.

- *Use adaptable program lending (APLs).* This instrument allows flexibility and thus helps the Bank manage political and other risks. APLs let the borrower and Bank adjust the pace to take account of unforeseen changes. The triggers for moving to the next lending phase must incorporate the conditions required for ultimate project success. If these triggers are properly constructed, the Bank can terminate the project in the face of unacceptable changes in the project's political environment. Given the fact that so many borrowers are new borrowers, APLs generally should start small and ramp up over time.

- *Encourage proactive supervision.* Proactive supervision is key to managing risk. Projects can be rerouted to reach the same destination (midcourse corrections). The destination can be changed (restructuring). And the project can be canceled if the conditions for progress have deteriorated. (See the following discussion of exit strategies.)

- *If all else fails, resort to exit strategies.* In the context of the logical framework, project preparation should include a careful analysis of the conditions required to realize the project's development objectives. This analysis should identify the "killer" assumptions—those that, if not met, result in a failed or derailed project. Even if the project is not under APL, the project appraisal document should be clear about the triggers for cancellation. This up-front analysis of those changes in the project that would nullify its objectives can help prevent a slide into what might be, in effect, a different project of dubious value.

The Way Forward

The Bank's development objectives for the region and their implications for country strategies indicate that the Bank's strategy is less about building schools than about changing concepts, expectations, rules of the game, incentives, and capacities. This puts a premium on fielding a staff of high quality and sustained commitment.

The Bank's ECA education sector starts from a singular position. The quality of the portfolio is acceptable, but as table 6.2 showed, education lending in the region has been limited and is mostly recent, and the professional staff has been small. Except for a handful of countries, such as Hungary and Romania, the Bank's sector knowledge based on studies focused only on education is very thin. (See table 6.3.) A larger number of economic and social sector studies, such as poverty assessments, have included education, but they often pay only glancing attention to the education sector.

Table 6.3 Education Sector Work in the ECA Region (FY91–FY00)

Country	Studies Closed	Studies Underway	Studies Planned	Contribution to other economic/sector work and poverty assessments Closed	Underway	Planned
Albania		1 (FY00)		1 (FY97)		
Armenia				1 (FY96)		
Azerbaijan				1 (FY97)		
Belarus						
Bosnia				1 (FY99)		
Bulgaria	1 (FY94)			1 (FY99)		
Croatia		1 (FY00)			1 (FY00)	
Czech Republic				1 (FY91) 1 (FY99)	1 (FY00)	
Estonia						
FYR Macedonia				1 (FY99)	1 (FY00)	
Georgia	1 (FY98)			1 (FY96) 1 (FY99)		
Hungary	1 (FY91)		1 (FY01)	1 (FY91) 1 (FY96)		
Kazakhstan				1 (FY94) 1 (FY96)		
Kyrgyz Republic				1 (FY93) 1 (FY95)		
Latvia						
Lithuania						
Moldova					1 (FY00)	
Poland	1 (FY93) 1 (FY98)	1 (FY00)		1 (FY92)	2 (FY00)	
Romania	1 (FY95)	1 (FY99)		1 (FY92) 2 (FY97)	1 (FY00)	
Russian Federation	1 (FY95) 1 (FY99)	1 (FY00)		1 (FY96)	1 (FY01)	
Slovak Republic				1 (FY99)		
Slovenia						
Tajikistan						
Turkey	1 (FY91)			1 (FY99)		
Turkmenistan						
Ukraine	1 (FY95)			1 (FY93) 1 (FY95) 1 (FY99)		
Uzbekistan				1 (FY99)		
ECA Region		1 (FY99) 1 (FY00)		1 (FY96)	1 (FY00)	
Totals	**10**	**6**	**2**	**28**	**9**	

Source: Authors' compilation based on SAP (Systems, Application, and Products).

Ensuring quality

The five priorities identified in this document imply the need for well trained social scientists (political scientists, economists, sociologists, and cognitive scientists) who are experienced in education. ECA education problems are not narrowly educational in nature; they are heavily entangled with political economy issues, financing problems, institutional and organisational issues, and problems of learning by policymakers and stakeholders.

To ensure a staff of high quality, the sector is adjusting skill mix and the number of staff. For example, it has added sociological capacity to guide the sector's work on social assessments and stakeholder participation. It is constructing a strong core team for each country, consisting of an education specialist, an education economist, an operations specialist, and a team assistant. Since field staff now report to the sector, they are being integrated into core teams. The sector is trying to minimize staff discontinuities within these teams and is starting thematic reviews by external panels.

Recent findings of the Quality Assurance Group (QAG) have shown that the quality of the traditional peer review process is seriously uneven. The sector is rethinking this process with an eye to strengthening it by encouraging each team preparing a project or conducting sector work to convene a mock QAG review (a quality enhancement review) to critique the quality of the work according to QAG criteria.

Regional sector work to fill knowledge gaps

Preparation of this report revealed important holes in our regional knowledge of the sector. Several studies are needed. For example:

- Using the five themes discussed in this book, conduct detailed analyses of the tertiary level of education.
- Using the five themes, conduct detailed analyses of vocational/technical education at secondary and postsecondary levels.
- By sampling countries, assess the provision of preschool. What types of services are being provided, for which subpopulations, and with what apparent effects on children's learning and behaviors in the primary grades?
- In collaboration with UNICEF, expand the TransMONEE database on the sector to include additional policy-relevant variables such as allocation of finances among levels of education.

- Using methodologies developed in the TIMSS, assess the contribution of curricular structure and the organisation of teaching and learning to the poor performance of some ECA countries on the IALS.
- In the context of a broader study of intergovernmental fiscal relations, analyze the consequences of these relations for the provision of educational services.
- By sampling countries and schools, assess resource allocation at the school level.
- To improve the Bank's work on poverty, conduct studies that illuminate (1) the two-way causality between low education and low income; (2) the special educational needs of the poor; and (3) the consequences of the recommendations in this document for serving the poor.
- By synthesizing the results of corruption surveys, build a picture of the types and extent of corruption in the education sector.
- By sampling countries, build a picture of informal payments by parents for education as a percentage of household per capita expenditure (in process).
- By sampling countries, conduct studies of the teaching labor force to assess patterns of human resource policies governing teachers and to measure whether processes of adverse selection have set in.
- By sampling countries, build a picture of school attendance rates, as distinguished from school enrollment rates.

Reflecting intersectoral considerations

The reorganisation of the World Bank established the mechanism of the country team. The country team is a forum for working out intersectoral priority-setting in lending and economic sector work. In the country team context the Bank's ECA education team should exploit relevant intersectoral opportunities.

The sector already prepares education components for rural development, labor market, and social protection projects. The Bank's ECA education sector is also working with public administration members of country teams to improve the public management of the sector in the context of broader public sector or civil service reforms.

The sector needs to be involved in decentralization and tax reform projects, as these affect the financing of education. It needs to be involved in civil service reform projects to help rationalize the staffing and functioning of the sector. It should work more closely with the IMF and with Bank economists in preparing structural adjustment credits and loans and poverty reduction strategy programs to ensure that conditionalities and policy goals fit educational realities. Since education usually absorbs a large share of the public budget, the sector needs to participate in public expenditure reviews (PERs). Poverty rates and levels of human capital are closely related, and the sector needs to collaborate on country economic memoranda (CEMs), poverty assessments, and poverty reduction strategy programs.

The sector should use vehicles such as PERs to strengthen the dialogue between ministries of finance and of education. Ministries of finance need to discard their unhelpful distinctions between the productive (revenue-producing) and nonproductive (non-revenue-producing) sectors. Prior to the transition, education was defined as an unproductive sector, a distinction that persists and that makes ministries of finance reluctant to borrow for the sector. Education ministries must understand the need for fiscally responsible management of the sector. A better dialogue can lay the groundwork for a badly needed rationalization of the sector's financing, for improved efficiency, and for appropriate investments in the sector.

Managing the portfolio

The education sector is entering a new phase. The portfolio is growing, but many of these new projects are with first-time borrowers. In addition to the knowledge and communication problems that new relationships face, many of these borrowers suffer from fiscal and political volatility, rules of the game that distort incentives, and weak managerial capacities. For the foreseeable future, the Bank expects a higher than average percentage of projects at risk, problem projects, and supervision costs. As the portfolio builds, the percentage of staff time used in project preparation will drop and that used in supervision will increase.

Annex Tables

Table A1 Total Population *(thousands, mid-year)*

Country	Note	1989	1990	1991	1992	1993	1994	1995	1996	1997
Central Europe										
Czech Republic	a	10,361	10,333	10,309	10,319	10,330	10,334	10,327	10,315	10,304
Hungary		10,481	10,365	10,346	10,324	10,294	10,261	10,229	10,193	10,155
Poland		37,962	38,111	38,246	38,364	38,461	38,543	38,595	38,624	38,650
Slovak Republic		5,276	5,280	5,284	5,305	5,325	5,346	5,362	5,372	5,383
Southeast Europe										
Albania		3,234	3,273	3,225	3,179	3,185	3,225	3,266	3,304	—
Bulgaria		8,877	8,718	8,632	8,540	8,472	8,444	8,406	8,363	8,312
Romania	a	23,161	23,202	23,002	22,795	22,763	22,730	22,684	22,619	22,554
Former Yugoslavia										
Bosnia-Herzegovina	b	4,457	4,498	2,259	—	—	—	—	2,254	2,346
Croatia	c	4,767	4,778	4,783	4,780	4,778	4,777	4,635	4,533	—
Macedonia, FYR	a d	2,111	2,095	2,115	—	—	1,947	1,966	1,983	1,997
Slovenia	a e	1,996	1,998	1,999	1,996	1,992	1,989	1,990	1,989	1,986
Yugoslavia, FR	a	10,473	10,529	10,496	10,452	10,486	10,519	10,552	10,581	10,604
Baltic states										
Estonia	a	1,569	1,571	1,566	1,544	1,517	1,499	1,484	1,469	1,458
Latvia		2,670	2,671	2,662	2,632	2,586	2,548	2,516	2,491	2,469
Lithuania		3,692	3,722	3,742	3,742	3,730	3,721	3,715	3,710	3,706
Western CIS										
Belarus	f	10,182	10,212	10,223	10,265	10,309	10,308	10,281	10,250	10,220
Moldova	f	4,347	4,362	4,360	4,351	4,348	4,348	4,339	4,325	4,311
Russian Federation	f g	147,342	147,913	148,245	148,310	148,146	147,968	147,774	147,373	146,938
Ukraine	f	51,518	51,637	51,746	51,896	51,925	51,667	51,277	50,859	50,442
Caucasus										
Armenia	i	3,485	3,545	3,612	3,686	3,731	3,747	3,760	3,774	3,786
Azerbaijan	a	7,068	7,117	7,175	7,266	7,333	7,392	7,444	7,488	7,536
Georgia	a	5,407	5,418	5,421	5,412	5,398	5,383	5,374	5,377	5,388
Central Asian republics										
Kazakhstan		16,249	16,348	16,451	16,518	16,479	16,297	16,066	15,921	15,751
Kyrgyz Republic		4,294	4,362	4,421	4,461	4,450	4,440	4,482	4,543	4,605
Tajikistan		5,178	5,303	5,465	5,571	5,638	5,745	5,835	5,927	6,018
Turkmenistan		3,578	3,657	3,750	3,846	3,948	4,218	4,476	4,561	4,643
Uzbekistan		20,114	20,515	20,958	21,455	21,948	22,377	22,785	23,226	23,656
Turkey	h	54,866	56,070	57,049	57,919	58,802	59,699	60,610	61,535	62,866

— Not available.

Notes: Midyear total de facto/present-in-area population (midyear calculation based on January population data).
   a. De jure. b. 1989–90 estimates as of March 31 cover the Yugoslav republic of Bosnia-Herzegovina; 1996 midyear estimate covers the Federation of Bosnia-Herzegovina. c. 1991 de jure census data as of March 31; 1992–95 de jure. d. 1994 census data. e. Until 1992 citizens of the former Yugoslav republic with permanent residence in the territory of Slovenia; since 1992, inhabitants of Slovenia with permanent residence. f. 1989 census data. g. Official midyear estimate. h. 1990 census data (de facto). 1997 census data. Smoothed midyear population interpolated using continuous growth rates. 1985 and 1990 census figures from SIS (1994, table I.7); 1997 census figures from SIS Webpage.

Sources: Based on data from UNICEF-ICDC TransMONEE Database; Council of Europe (various years); CIS StatCommittee (1998a); SIS (1994; Webpage).

Table A2 School Age Population *(percentage of population aged 3–24)*

Country	Note	1989	1990	1991	1992	1993	1994	1995	1996	1997
Central Europe										
Czech Republic		32.6	32.5	32.3	32.3	32.2	32.1	31.9	31.7	31.3
Hungary		30.8	31.0	31.0	30.9	30.8	30.7	30.6	30.4	30.2
Poland		34.5	34.6	34.7	34.8	34.8	34.8	34.8	34.6	34.4
Slovak Republic		36.0	35.9	35.9	35.8	35.7	35.7	35.6	35.4	35.1
Southeast Europe										
Albania		43.8	—	—	—	—	—	—	—	—
Bulgaria		30.6	30.4	30.4	30.3	30.2	29.9	29.7	29.4	29.1
Romania		35.3	35.5	35.9	35.9	35.3	34.6	34.0	33.6	33.2
Former Yugoslavia										
Bosnia-Herzegovina		—	—	—	—	—	—	—	—	—
Croatia		—	—	29.4	—	—	—	—	—	—
Macedonia, FYR		—	—	—	—	—	36.5	36.2	35.9	35.6
Slovenia		32.1	31.9	31.5	31.2	30.8	30.5	30.2	29.9	29.4
Yugoslavia, FR		33.5	33.4	33.2	33.1	33.0	32.9	32.6	32.4	32.2
Baltic states										
Estonia		31.4	31.4	31.6	31.8	31.9	31.9	31.7	31.4	31.0
Latvia		30.6	30.7	30.9	30.9	30.9	31.0	31.0	30.8	30.5
Lithuania		33.0	32.8	32.8	32.9	32.8	32.8	32.7	32.5	32.1
Western CIS										
Belarus		32.2	32.3	32.4	32.5	32.7	32.8	32.8	32.7	32.5
Moldova		36.4	36.7	37.1	37.4	37.6	37.8	38.1	38.3	38.6
Russian Federation		31.7	31.8	32.0	32.2	32.4	32.6	32.6	32.4	32.1
Ukraine		30.7	30.9	31.0	31.2	31.3	31.4	31.4	31.3	31.1
Caucasus										
Armenia		40.0	40.4	40.2	40.0	40.1	40.3	40.5	40.5	40.2
Azerbaijan		44.9	44.7	44.4	44.1	43.9	43.8	43.8	43.8	43.8
Georgia		35.0	34.6	34.4	34.4	34.5	34.6	34.6	34.2	33.8
Central Asian republics										
Kazakhstan		41.6	41.4	41.4	41.6	41.8	42	42.2	42.3	42.4
Kyrgyz Republic		46.7	47.0	47.3	47.6	48.0	48.5	48.8	49.0	48.8
Tajikistan		—	—	—	—	—	—	—	—	—
Turkmenistan		50.2	50.3	50.3	50.3	50.3	50.5	50.9	51.0	51.0
Uzbekistan		—	—	—	—	—	—	—	—	—
Turkeya	a	50.1	49.7	49.3	48.8	48.4	47.9	47.4	47.0	46.5

— Not available.

Notes: Definition of title: number of population in 3–24 age group divided by total population.
 a. Figures for 1989 and 1990 from SIS (1994, table I.10); for 1994–97 from SIS (1995, table A5-1), based on a projection assuming net reproduction rate (NRR) = 1.00 in 2005; figures for 1991–93 interpolated. The NRR is the average number of daughters that would be born to a woman if she passed through her lifetime conforming to the age-specific fertility and mortality rates of a given year. An NRR of 1 means that each generation of mothers is having exactly enough daughters to replace itself in the population.
Sources: Based on UNICEF-ICDC TransMONEE database; SIS (1994, 1995).

Table A3 Total Fertility Rate

Country	Note	1989	1990	1991	1992	1993	1994	1995	1996	1997
Central Europe										
Czech Republic		1.87	1.89	1.86	1.72	1.67	1.44	1.28	1.19	1.17
Hungary		1.78	1.84	1.86	1.77	1.69	1.64	1.57	1.46	1.38
Poland		2.05	2.04	2.05	1.93	1.85	1.80	1.61	1.60	1.50
Slovak Republic		2.08	2.09	2.05	1.98	1.92	1.66	1.52	1.47	1.43
Southeast Europe										
Albania		2.96	3.03	—	2.90	—	2.70	2.64	2.58	—
Bulgaria		1.90	1.81	1.65	1.54	1.45	1.37	1.23	1.24	1.09
Romania		2.20	1.84	1.57	1.52	1.44	1.41	1.34	1.30	1.32
Former Yugoslavia										
Bosnia-Herzegovina		1.70	1.70	—	1.60	—	—	—	—	—
Croatia		1.63	1.63	1.53	1.48	1.52	1.47	1.58	1.67	1.69
Macedonia, FYR		2.09	2.06	2.30	2.18	2.16	2.08	1.97	1.90	—
Slovenia		1.52	1.46	1.42	1.34	1.34	1.32	1.29	1.28	1.25
Yugoslavia, FR		2.06	2.08	2.08	1.91	1.91	1.85	1.88	1.83	1.74
Baltic states										
Estonia		2.21	2.05	1.79	1.69	1.45	1.37	1.32	1.30	1.24
Latvia		2.05	2.02	1.86	1.73	1.51	1.39	1.25	1.16	1.11
Lithuania		1.98	2.00	1.97	1.89	1.69	1.52	1.49	1.42	1.39
Western CIS										
Belarus		2.03	1.91	1.80	1.75	1.61	1.51	1.39	1.31	1.23
Moldova		2.46	2.39	2.26	2.21	2.10	1.95	1.76	1.67	—
Russian Federation		2.01	1.89	1.73	1.55	1.39	1.40	1.34	1.28	1.23
Ukraine		1.92	1.89	1.81	1.72	1.55	1.50	1.40	1.30	1.30
Caucasus										
Armenia		2.61	2.62	2.58	2.35	1.97	1.70	1.63	1.60	1.45
Azerbaijan		2.79	2.77	2.89	2.74	2.70	2.52	2.29	2.06	2.07
Georgia		2.13	2.2	2.15	1.79	1.60	1.50	1.50	—	—
Central Asian republics										
Kazakhstan		2.88	2.72	—	2.50	2.30	—	2.15	2.08	—
Kyrgyz Republic		3.81	3.69	3.67	3.62	3.30	3.14	3.31	2.99	2.79
Tajikistan		5.23	5.05	5.01	4.13	4.30	—	3.90	3.70	—
Turkmenistan		4.40	4.17	4.09	—	4.00	—	3.75	3.25	—
Uzbekistan		4.18	4.07	—	—	3.80	—	3.55	3.43	—
Turkey	a	3.20	3.00	2.91	2.84	2.76	2.69	2.62	2.50	

— Not available.

Notes: The total fertility rate is the sum of age-specific birthrates over all ages of the child-bearing period. It represents the theoretical number of births to a woman during the child-bearing years using the given year's birthrate as a constant.
  a. 1989–93 data from SIS (1995); 1994–97 data from OECD (1998a).
Sources: Based on UNICEF-ICDC TransMONEE Database; Council of Europe (various years); World Bank, World Development Indicators (various years); SIS (1995), OECD (1998a).

Table A4 Demographic Projections by Region *(percentage change from previous year)*

Country	1996	1997	1998	1999	2000	2005	2010	2015	2020	1995–2020
Children aged 3–6										
Sub-Saharan Africa	2.38	2.05	1.39	2.10	2.07	11.34	8.08	6.33	3.03	45.5
Middle East and North Africa	-0.84	-1.30	-1.99	0.07	0.62	7.93	9.83	0.62	-0.61	14.5
South Asia	-0.43	-0.78	-1.45	-0.11	0.17	2.65	-6.80	2.60	2.93	-1.60
Latin America and the Caribbean	-0.31	-0.46	-0.68	0.04	0.25	1.84	-3.90	1.17	0.41	-1.70
East Asia and Pacific	-2.16	-3.49	-5.03	-1.79	-0.80	1.48	-6.42	2.28	2.28	-13.2
High-income countries	-0.21	-0.19	-0.15	-0.25	-0.25	-2.33	-4.58	-2.48	3.71	-6.70
Europe and Central Asia	**-4.07**	**-5.01**	**-6.14**	**-3.14**	**-2.19**	**-3.97**	**4.26**	**-1.89**	**7.24**	**-14.6**
Children aged 7–14										
Sub-Saharan Africa	2.56	2.58	2.50	2.39	2.34	11.17	11.28	9.26	6.65	62.9
Middle East and North Africa	1.74	1.34	0.92	0.50	0.08	-1.45	5.69	8.38	2.68	21.3
South Asia	1.67	1.27	0.89	0.52	0.22	-0.84	1.00	-3.87	0.13	0.9
Latin America and the Caribbean	0.44	0.33	0.21	0.08	-0.04	-0.48	1.02	-2.12	-0.17	-0.8
East Asia and Pacific	2.78	2.56	2.05	1.29	0.30	-7.27	-2.48	-4.71	0.04	-5.8
High-income countries	-0.24	-0.27	-0.29	-0.29	-0.27	-1.60	-2.45	-4.06	-2.71	-11.6
Europe and Central Asia	**-0.25**	**-0.69**	**-1.21**	**-1.80**	**-2.47**	**-15.67**	**-7.12**	**0.57**	**0.58**	**-25.7**

Source: World Bank data provided by Human Development Network.

Table A5 Preschool Enrollment Rates *(percentage of relevant population)*

Country	Note	1989	1990	1991	1992	1993	1994	1995	1996	1997
Central Europe										
Czech Republic	a	89.8	89.8	89.8	83.3	84.9	86.6	88.7	88.5	83.0
Hungary	a	85.7	85.3	86.1	86.9	87.1	86.2	87.0	86.5	86.1
Poland		48.7	47.1	43.9	42.6	42.7	44.3	45.3	46.8	47.9
Slovak Republic	a	91.5	83.7	75.7	78.1	78.0	74.6	70.2	75.2	—
Southeast Europe										
Albania	a b	56.7	57.9	48.9	36.8	36.1	36.8	39.2	38.9	36.0
Bulgaria		63.9	63.9	55.9	57.4	56.2	57.5	61.6	62.6	58.8
Romania		63.3	54.3	51.9	53.3	50.2	55.2	58.4	55.1	52.8
Former Yugoslavia										
Bosnia-Herzegovina		—	—	—	—	—	—	—	—	—
Croatia		29.4	29.4	19.1	20.0	—	26.1	31.0	30.9	—
Macedonia, FYR		—	26.2	24.4	25.3	25.5	26.9	28.0	—	—
Slovenia	c	56.3	56.6	55.8	56.2	60.3	62.8	65.1	66.7	66.2
Yugoslavia, FR		24.1	23.8	21.9	20.5	21.8	24.6	26.3	28.1	29.2
Baltic states										
Estonia		62.2	67.4	60.5	53.7	56.0	58.8	63.2	67.1	70.4
Latvia		52.8	44.8	37.0	28.3	32.6	39.9	47.1	50.8	52.1
Lithuania		63.9	58.6	63.9	39.1	30.1	34.5	36.2	40.0	41.6
Western CIS										
Belarus		63.1	63.3	62.5	58.0	58.3	61.0	62.3	64.0	66.9
Moldova	d e	62.8	61.4	58.7	42.4	36.6	35.1	32.3	32.1	31.5
Russian Federation		69.3	66.4	63.9	56.8	57.4	56.2	55.5	55.0	56.0
Ukraine		65.1	62.3	61.0	57.5	54.7	52.0	48.2	44.9	41.6
Caucasus										
Armenia		65.2	60.5	60.4	51.9	45.3	39.1	31.4	32.4	—
Azerbaijan		20.8	19.7	18.9	18.0	18.1	15.5	14.6	13.5	13.1
Georgia		43.8	42.7	39.1	30.2	26.9	19.0	19.6	21.0	20.4
Central Asian republics										
Kazakhstan		52.2	52.7	52.0	45.9	40.9	30.7	24.6	-	11.7
Kyrgyz Republic	d	31.3	30.3	26.7	23.3	13.4	8.8	7.7	8.2	7.0
Tajikistan	d	16.7	15.4	14.1	11.5	11.5	11.1	8.2	7.7	—
Turkmenistan	d	36.0	35.0	35.0	34.0	34.0	32.0	26.0	22.0	21.0
Uzbekistan	d	38.5	38.8	38.1	34.2	33.0	30.7	27.9	22.7	—
Turkey	f	8.3	8.9	9.9	10.2	10.8	11.2	12.0	13.3	14

— Not available.

Notes: Definition of title: net rates, percentage of 3–6 age group enrolled in kindergarten. Gross enrollment rates for the ECA region must be treated cautiously. The age-specific population numbers are somewhat suspect, since the last credible census was conducted in 1989. (Most countries will conduct a new census within the next two years.) In the intervening decade civil registration of births and deaths has declined sharply, and mobility across borders has increased. Enrollment numbers for countries engaged in conflict are suspect.
a. 3–5 year olds. b. Gross rates; Palomba and Vodopivec (2000). c. Gross rates in public schools. d. 1–6 year olds. e. 1992–97: enrollments exclude Transdniestr. f. 6 year olds; figures refer to the school year starting in the year indicated. World Bank estimates based on enrollment figures through 1996 and for 1997 obtained from SIS (1999, table 1) and Turkey, Ministry of National Education (1998, table 18), respectively, and on population figures for six year olds for 1990, 1994, 1995, 1996, and 1997 from SIS (1995, table A5-1), based on the assumptions that the 6 year old population = .2 x population 5–9 years and that the net reproduction rate (NRR) = 1.0 in 2005. Population for other years interpolated and extrapolated.
Sources: Based on UNICEF-ICDC TransMONEE Database, CIS StatCommittee (1998b, 1998c); Turkey, Ministry of National Education (1998); SIS (1995, 1999); Palomba and Vodopivec (2000).

Table A6 Basic Education Enrollment rates
(gross rates, percentage of 6/7–14/15 age group)

Country	Note	1989	1990	1991	1992	1993	1994	1995	1996	1997
Central Europe										
Czech Republic	a	97.6	98.6	98.7	99.2	99.1	99.5	99.4	99.2	99.1
Hungary	b	99.0	99.2	99.2	99.2	99.1	99.1	99.1	99.2	99.2
Poland	c	97.9	97.5	97.3	97.1	97.2	97.1	97.2	97.4	98.0
Slovak Republic	a	96.8	97.2	98.0	99.8	99.5	97.0	96.5	96.3	—
Southeast Europe										
Albania	b	90.8	90.7	88.5	85.9	86.7	87.6	—	—	—
Bulgaria	a	98.4	98.6	97.3	95.1	94.0	94.3	93.7	93.6	94.0
Romania	c	93.6	89.5	89.4	89.6	90.3	91.4	92.6	93.9	95.0
Former Yugoslavia										
Bosnia-Herzegovina		—	—	—	—	—	—	—	—	—
Croatia	c d	96.0	94.0	81.0	79.0	85.0	89.0	88.0	89.0	—
Macedonia, FYR	c	—	89.4	87.1	86.2	86.2	86.8	86.5	86.9	—
Slovenia	c	96.1	97.1	96.8	97.6	97.8	96.7	97.3	99.8	99.8
Yugoslavia, FR	c e f	95.3	95.0	94.4	72.7	74.3	72.5	71.6	72.7	71.8
Baltic states										
Estonia	g	96.2	94.9	93.6	92.3	91.7	91.3	92.2	92.8	93.7
Latvia	g	95.8	96.4	95.2	90.9	89.5	89.0	89.5	90.3	90.7
Lithuania	c	94.0	93.0	92.6	92.8	91.9	92.2	93.2	93.6	95.8
Western CIS										
Belarus	g	95.8	94.9	94.2	94.2	93.7	93.6	94.1	93.8	94.1
Moldova	g h	95.8	95.6	94.4	92.0	91.6	91.3	91.6	91.5	91.6
Russian Federation	g	93.0	93.6	94.4	93.3	91.9	90.7	91.3	91.4	90.8
Ukraine	g	92.8	92.3	91.5	91.1	90.4	90.6	90.8	91.2	90.7
Caucasus										
Armenia	g	95.5	94.6	91.6	91.1	86.4	82.2	81.4	82.8	82.9
Azerbaijan	g	89.5	90.5	90.5	91.4	92.4	94.2	94.4	95.4	96.6
Georgia	g i	95.2	95.3	92.5	83.3	82.4	80.7	79.8	80.7	—
Central Asian republics										
Kazakhstan	g	93.9	93.1	92.7	91.7	91.5	90.9	90.5	90.0	89.2
Kyrgyz Republic	g	92.5	91.8	90.6	90.3	89.7	89.0	89.1	89.3	89.2
Tajikistan	g	94.1	94.0	94.2	89.6	85.1	86.4	86.6	85.0	85.5
Turkmenistan	g	94.3	94.9	92.5	91.7	92.0	91.8	83.9	83.2	83.1
Uzbekistan	g	92.2	91.1	87.9	87.5	87.9	88.6	—	89.0	89.7
Turkey	c j	86.1	86.8	87.0	86.5	85.4	85.0	84.2	84.1	85.4

— Not available.

Notes: Definition of title: gross rates, percentage of 6/7–14/15 age group enrolled in basic education. Gross enrollment rates for ECA region must be treated cautiously, since the last credible census was conducted in 1989. (Most countries will conduct a new census within the next two years.) In the intervening decade, civil registration of births and deaths has declined sharply, and mobility across borders has increased. Enrollment numbers for countries engaged in conflict are suspect.
a. 6–14 year olds. b. 6–13 year olds. c. 7–14 year olds. d. 1991–96: some areas not reported; estimated rate 95 percent. e. Net rates. f. 1992–97: excludes ethnic Albanians in Kosovo-Metohija. g. 7–15 year olds. h. 1992–97: World Bank estimates based on age-structure data obtained for a pension project in Moldova. i. 1992–96: enrollments exclude Abkhazia and Tskhinvali. j. World Bank estimates based on enrollment figures for 1989–90 and 1997 from SIS (1999, table 1) and Turkey, Ministry of National Education (1998, table 19), respectively, and on population figures for 7–14 age group for 1990, 1994, and subsequent years from SIS (1995, table A5-1), based on the assumption that the net reproduction rate (NRR) = 1.0 in 2005. Data for other years interpolated.
Sources: Based on UNICEF-ICDC TransMONEE Database; CIS StatCommittee (1998c); U.S. Census Bureau (various years); SIS (1995, 1998); Turkey, Ministry of National Education (1998).

Table A7 General Upper Secondary Enrollment Rates
(gross rates, percentage of 15–18 age group)

Country	Note	1989	1990	1991	1992	1993	1994	1995	1996	1997
Central Europe										
Czech Republic		15.9	16.1	15.6	15.9	16.5	17.6	18.8	18.8	—
Hungary		19.7	19.8	19.5	19.5	19.2	20.0	21.2	22.3	23.6
Poland		21.0	21.7	23.3	24.9	26.4	28.1	29.7	30.5	32.2
Slovak Republic		15.6	16.0	16.4	17.1	18.0	19.0	20.0	20.9	21.5
Southeast Europe										
Albania	a	24.4	26.0	28.3	29.6	30.1	29.7	29.1	31.6	33.9
Bulgaria		30.7	29.9	29.4	29.3	29.6	31.3	31.7	31.4	30.7
Romania		3.8	11.6	16.4	17.8	18.4	19.3	19.8	20.4	20.5
Former Yugoslavia										
Bosnia-Herzegovina		—	—	—	—	—	—	—	—	—
Croatia		—	—	—	8.8	13.9	18.0	18.5	18.7	—
Macedonia, FYR		—	—	—	—	—	15.9	17.4	18.1	18.9
Slovenia		—	—	—	—	19.7	20.2	20.6	21.4	—
Yugoslavia, FR		—	4.0	6.1	9.6	12.4	12.8	12.9	13.3	13.7
Baltic states										
Estonia		37.3	36.3	36.7	37.0	39.4	43.5	43.7	45.1	45.8
Latvia		22.1	21.2	20.3	20.3	24.7	26.7	28.7	37.0	39.5
Lithuania		34.7	34.2	32.8	30.6	30.4	32.9	34.8	38.6	39.5
Western CIS										
Belarus		27.5	26.6	26.0	25.2	24.2	24.9	24.9	26.8	28.3
Moldova	b	29.0	26.6	22.6	23.6	24.0	24.6	24.5	26.6	28.7
Russian Federation		24.7	22.5	33.9	22.9	22.6	23.7	24.6	26.0	27.7
Ukraine		25.8	25.2	24.2	23.2	22.7	23.4	24.0	25.5	27.5
Caucasus										
Armenia		35.9	34.3	32.5	31.3	31.2	30.7	29.1	29.6	30.4
Azerbaijan		33.3	33.5	34.5	32.8	28.9	27.0	25.8	28.1	32.2
Georgia	c	38.8	41.3	41.3	35.4	26.6	22.8	21.5	23.4	23.3
Central Asian republics										
Kazakhstan		32.5	33.2	32.6	29.5	28.0	26.1	25.7	29.3	33.3
Kyrgyz Republic		37.8	37.1	36.1	32.6	28.9	27.7	26.7	29.2	33.0
Tajikistan		41.5	40.7	37.7	29.7	26.8	25.3	23.6	22.3	22.5
Turkmenistan		42.4	43.2	40.7	38.3	39.0	35.7	34.1	24.3	24.5
Uzbekistan		37.5	37.7	36.5	31.0	28.0	27.8	—	27.0	28.6
Turkey	d	21.0	21.8	23.9	26.0	27.7	29.1	30.0	28.8	24.7

— Not available.

Notes: Definition of title: gross rates, percentage of 15–18 age group enrolled in general secondary education—typically, two-to-four-year programs. In countries where the typical age range for enrollment is 15–17, coverage and rates may be underestimated. Gross enrollment rates for the ECA region must be treated cautiously. The age-specific population numbers are somewhat suspect, since the last credible census was conducted in 1989. (Most countries will conduct a new census within the next two years.) In the intervening decade civil registration of births and deaths has declined sharply, and mobility across borders has increased. Enrollment numbers for countries engaged in conflict are suspect. a. Palomba and Vodopivec (2000). b. 1992–97: World Bank estimates based on age-structure data obtained for a pension project in Moldova. c. World Bank estimates based on data supplied by UNICEF-ICDC. d. World Bank estimates based on age-structure data obtained from Turkey, Ministry of National Education (1998, table 1), SIS (1995, table A5–1; 1999, table 1), and Turkey, Ministry of National Education (1998, table 23).

Sources: Based on UNICEF-ICDC TransMONEE Database; SIS (1995, 1998); Turkey, Ministry of National Education (1998); World Bank estimates based on data supplied by UNICEF-ICDC; Palomba and Vodopivec (2000).

Table A8 Vocational/Technical Upper Secondary Enrollment Rates
(gross rates, percentage of 15–18 age group)

Country	Note	1989	1990	1991	1992	1993	1994	1995	1996	1997
Central Europe										
Czech Republic		73.6	69.2	62.9	60.6	62.7	78.2	81.0	66.2	65.3
Hungary		62.7	62.7	59.8	56.8	54.3	54.6	57.2	60.0	62.0
Poland		72.2	70.9	69.0	67.8	67.7	68.0	67.6	67.5	67.4
Slovak Republic		70.7	67.6	65.5	64.7	65.0	65.7	66.0	65.9	64.4
Southeast Europe										
Albania	a	54.1	53.1	30.0	17.4	12.3	8.4	7.5	6.9	6.4
Bulgaria		47.0	47.3	46.2	43.1	41.5	42.6	42.5	42.2	42.4
Romania	b	—	79.2	59.8	49.3	45.1	46.4	48.5	47.6	46.8
Former Yugoslavia										
Bosnia-Herzegovina		—	—	—	—	—	—	—	—	—
Croatia		—	—	—	58.5	60.0	58.4	54.7	57.1	—
Macedonia, FYR		—	—	—	—	—	—	—	—	41.8
Slovenia		—	—	—	—	61.5	62.5	63.7	64.9	—
Yugoslavia, FR		13.9	10.7	11.2	12.1	10.0	10.0	11.1	10.6	—
Baltic states										
Estonia		—	37.8	—	36.7	35.8	35.6	36.2	39.2	
Latvia		47.1	46.3	43.9	39.9	36.5	33.7	32.1	32.7	
Lithuania		59.9	54.5	48.2	34.7	35.5	34.6	35.6	34.4	33.4
Western CIS										
Belarus		51.0	48.5	47.5	47.0	46.4	44.3	42.2	41.2	—
Moldova		42.0	38.4	35.6	26.4	24.3	23.1	22.5	22.8	—
Russian Federation		54.1	50.8	49.0	46.4	44.2	41.7	41.8	41.9	41.9
Ukraine		42.1	39.6	39.0	38.8	37.7	35.2	33.7	32.6	30.3
Caucasus										
Armenia		31.6	29.0	25.8	22.7	18.3	14.9	11.3	11.7	10.9
Azerbaijan		27.9	26.0	25.6	21.0	16.4	13.4	11.2	10.7	10.3
Georgia		18.6	17.4	17.2	15.6	15.8	13.2	13.3	12.8	13.4
Central Asian republics										
Kazakhstan		43.2	41.0	39.0	36.7	34.2	31.4	29.8	26.5	—
Kyrgyz Republic		23.5	21.9	21.4	19.7	17.9	17.0	15.1	13.9	13.5
Tajikistan		20.2	19.3	—	16.2	—	—	12.4	—	—
Turkmenistan		25.5	24.3	24.0	22.9	21.1	14.8	10.7	10.7	7.2
Uzbekistan		32.4	29.4	27.8	26.7	26.4	—	—	—	—
Turkey	c	16.1	17.1	18.4	19.8	20.8	22.5	24.0	24.4	22.8

— Not available.

Notes: Definition of title: gross rates, percentage of 15–18 age group enrolled in secondary vocational/technical education (typically, three-to-four-year programs; includes full-time, evening, and correspondence courses). Gross enrollment rates for the ECA region must be treated cautiously. The age-specific population numbers are somewhat suspect, since the last credible census was conducted in 1989. (Most countries will conduct a new census within the next two years.) In the intervening decade civil registration of births and deaths has declined sharply, and mobility across borders has increased. The enrollment numbers for countries engaged in conflict are suspect.

a. Palomba and Vodopivec (2000). b. Based on 15–19 age cohort. c. Based on 15–17 age group. World Bank estimates based on enrollment figures for 1989–96 and 1997 obtained from SIS (1999, table 1) and Turkey, Ministry of National Education (1998, table 23), respectively, and on age-structure data obtained from SIS (1995, table A5-1), assuming that the net reproduction rate (NRR) = 1.0 in 2005. Figures for 1989, 1991, 1992, and 1993 interpolated and projected from figures provided by SIS.

Sources: World Bank estimates based on data supplied by UNICEF- ICDC; U.S. Census Bureau (various years); CIS StatCommittee (1998a); SIS (1999); Turkey, Ministry of National Education (1998).

Table A9 Overall Upper Secondary Enrollment Rates
(academic and vocational/technical secondary education)

Country	1989	1990	1991	1992	1993	1994	1995	1996	1997
Central Europe									
Czech Republic	89.5	85.3	78.5	76.5	79.2	95.8	99.8	85	65.3
Hungary	82.4	82.5	79.2	76.3	73.4	74.6	78.4	82.3	85.7
Poland	93.2	92.5	92.2	92.7	94.2	96.1	97.3	98.1	99.6
Slovak Republic	86.3	83.6	82.0	81.8	83.0	84.6	86.0	86.9	85.9
Southeast Europe									
Albania	78.5	79.1	58.3	47	42.4	38.1	36.6	38.5	40.3
Bulgaria	77.7	77.2	75.5	72.4	71.1	73.8	74.2	73.6	73.1
Romania	—	90.8	76.2	67.0	63.4	65.7	68.3	68.1	67.3
Former Yugoslavia									
Bosnia-Herzegovina	—	—	—	—	—	—	—	—	—
Croatia	—	—	—	67.3	73.9	76.4	73.2	75.8	—
Macedonia, FYR	—	—	—	—	—	—	—	—	60.7
Slovenia	—	—	—	—	81.2	82.7	84.3	86.3	—
Yugoslavia, FR	—	14.7	17.3	21.8	22.4	22.7	24.0	23.9	—
Baltic states									
Estonia	—	74.1	—	73.7	75.1	79.0	79.9	84.2	—
Latvia	69.3	67.5	64.1	60.2	61.1	60.4	60.8	69.7	—
Lithuania	94.6	88.7	80.9	65.2	65.9	67.4	70.4	73.0	72.8
Western CIS									
Belarus	78.5	75.1	73.5	72.2	70.6	69.2	67.1	68.0	—
Moldova	71.1	65.0	58.1	43.4	41.4	40.8	40.6	42.3	—
Russian Federation	78.8	75.8	72.9	69.3	66.9	65.4	66.4	67.9	69.5
Ukraine	67.9	64.8	63.2	62.1	60.4	58.7	57.7	58.1	57.8
Caucasus									
Armenia	67.5	63.4	58.3	54.1	49.5	45.6	40.4	41.3	41.5
Azerbaijan	61.2	59.5	60.1	53.9	45.2	40.4	37.0	38.8	42.9
Georgia	57.4	58.7	58.5	51.0	42.4	36.0	34.8	36.2	36.8
Central Asian republics									
Kazakhstan	75.7	74.2	71.6	66.3	62.2	57.5	55.1	55.8	—
Kyrgyz Republic	61.3	59.0	57.6	52.3	46.8	44.7	41.8	43.1	46.5
Tajikistan	61.7	60.0	—	45.9	—	—	36.0	—	—
Turkmenistan	67.9	67.5	64.7	61.2	60.0	50.6	44.8	35.0	31.7
Uzbekistan	69.9	67.1	64.3	57.7	54.4	—	—	—	—
Turkey	37.1	38.9	42.3	45.8	48.5	51.6	54.0	53.2	47.5

— Not available.

Notes: Definition of title: gross rates: percentage of 15–18 age group enrolled in general secondary education, including academic and vocational/technical tracks. The calculation of enrollment rates assumes ages 15–18 as the typical ages for upper secondary education. In some cases the resulting numbers may underestimate actual enrollments. However, a somewhat arbitrary age range had to be selected because countries differ in their typical ages for general upper secondary education, and across the decade some countries have changed their typical ages for this level; vocational/technical programs vary in length within a country; and data on the distribution of students among these programs of different lengths are not only fugitive but also shift during the decade. Gross enrollment rates for the ECA region must be treated cautiously. The age-specific population numbers are somewhat suspect, since the last credible census was conducted in 1989. (Most countries will conduct a new census within the next two years.) In the intervening decade civil registration of births and deaths has declined sharply, and mobility across borders has increased. Enrollment numbers for countries engaged in conflict are suspect.
Sources: World Bank staff estimates based on data for tables A7 and A8.

Table A10 Share of Students in Upper Secondary Education *(percentage of total)*

Country	Education Level	1989	1990	1991	1992	1993	1994	1995	1996	1997
Central Europe										
Czech Republic	General secondary	17.8	18.9	19.9	20.8	20.8	18.4	18.8	22.1	—
	Vocational/technical	82.2	81.1	80.1	79.2	79.2	81.6	81.2	77.9	—
Hungary	General secondary	23.9	24.0	24.6	25.6	26.1	26.8	27.0	27.1	27.6
	Vocational/technical	76.1	76.0	75.4	74.4	73.9	73.2	73.0	72.9	72.4
Poland	General secondary	22.5	23.4	25.2	26.9	28.1	29.2	30.5	31.1	32.4
	Vocational/technical	77.5	76.6	74.8	73.1	71.9	70.8	69.5	68.9	67.6
Slovak Republic	General secondary	18.1	19.2	20.1	20.9	21.7	22.4	23.2	24.1	25.0
	Vocational/technical	81.9	80.8	79.9	79.1	78.3	77.6	76.8	75.9	75.0
Southeast Europe										
Albania	General secondary	31.1	32.9	48.5	63.0	70.9	78.0	79.4	82.1	84.2
	Vocational/technical	68.9	67.1	51.5	37.0	29.1	22.0	20.6	17.9	15.8
Bulgaria	General secondary	39.5	38.7	38.9	40.5	41.6	42.3	42.7	42.6	41.9
	Vocational/technical	60.5	61.3	61.1	59.5	58.4	57.7	57.3	57.4	58.1
Romania	General secondary	—	12.8	21.6	26.5	29.0	29.4	29.0	30.0	30.4
	Vocational/technical	—	87.2	78.4	73.5	71.0	70.6	71.0	70.0	69.6
Former Yugoslavia										
Bosnia-Herzegovina	General secondary	—	—	—	—	—	—	—	—	—
	Vocational/technical	—	—	—	—	—	—	—	—	—
Croatia	General secondary	—	—	—	13.1	18.8	23.6	25.3	24.7	—
	Vocational/technical	—	—	—	86.9	81.2	76.4	74.7	75.3	—
Macedonia, FYR	General secondary	—	—	—	—	—	—	—	—	31.2
	Vocational/technical	—	—	—	—	—	—	—	—	68.8
Slovenia	General secondary	—	—	—	—	24.3	24.4	24.4	24.8	—
	Vocational/technical	—	—	—	—	75.7	75.6	75.6	75.2	—
Yugoslavia, FR	General secondary	—	27.1	35.1	44.3	55.4	56.2	53.7	55.7	—
	Vocational/technical	—	72.9	64.9	55.7	44.6	43.8	46.3	44.3	—
Baltic states										
Estonia	General secondary	—	49.0	—	50.2	52.4	55.0	54.7	53.5	—
	Vocational/technical	—	51.0	—	49.8	47.6	45.0	45.3	46.5	—
Latvia	General secondary	32.0	31.4	31.6	33.6	40.4	44.2	47.2	53.1	—
	Vocational/technical	68.0	68.6	68.4	66.4	59.6	55.8	52.8	46.9	—
Lithuania	General secondary	36.7	38.6	40.5	46.9	46.1	48.7	49.5	52.9	54.2
	Vocational/technical	63.3	61.4	59.5	53.1	53.9	51.3	50.5	47.1	45.8

(Table continues on following page)

Table A10 (continued)

Country	Education Level	1989	1990	1991	1992	1993	1994	1995	1996	1997
Western CIS										
Belarus	General secondary	35.0	35.4	35.4	34.9	34.3	36.0	37.1	39.4	—
	Vocational/technical	65.0	64.6	64.6	65.1	65.7	64.0	62.9	60.6	—
Moldova	General secondary	40.8	40.9	38.8	47.2	49.7	51.6	52.1	53.8	—
	Vocational/technical	59.2	59.1	61.2	52.8	50.3	48.4	47.9	46.2	—
Russian Federation	General secondary	31.3	33.0	32.8	33.1	33.9	36.2	37.1	38.3	39.8
	Vocational/technical	68.7	67.0	67.2	66.9	66.1	63.8	62.9	61.7	60.2
Ukraine	General secondary	38.0	38.9	38.3	37.5	37.6	39.9	41.6	43.9	47.6
	Vocational/technical	62.0	61.1	61.7	62.5	62.4	60.1	58.4	56.1	52.4
Caucasus										
Armenia	General secondary	53.2	54.2	55.8	57.9	63.1	67.3	72.0	71.7	73.7
	Vocational/technical	46.8	45.8	44.2	42.1	36.9	32.7	28.0	28.3	26.3
Azerbaijan	General secondary	54.2	56.3	57.4	61.0	63.8	66.8	69.7	72.4	76.0
	Vocational/technical	45.8	43.7	42.6	39.0	36.2	33.2	30.3	27.6	24.0
Georgia	General secondary	67.6	70.4	70.6	69.4	62.8	63.3	61.7	64.6	63.5
	Vocational/technical	32.4	29.6	29.4	30.6	37.2	36.7	38.3	35.4	36.5
Central Asia republics										
Kazakhstan	General secondary	42.9	44.8	45.5	44.6	44.9	45.5	45.9	52.5	—
	Vocational/technical	57.1	55.2	54.5	55.4	55.1	54.5	54.1	47.5	—
Kyrgyz Republic	General secondary.	61.7	62.8	62.8	62.3	61.7	62.0	64.0	67.8	71.0
	Vocational/technical	38.3	37.2	37.2	37.7	38.3	38.0	36.0	32.2	29.0
Tajikistan	General secondary.	67.3	76.7	80.4	64.8	76.0	77.0	65.6	—	—
	Vocational/technical	32.7	23.3	—	35.2	—	—	34.4	—	—
Turkmenistan	General secondary.	62.5	63.9	62.9	62.6	64.9	70.7	76.1	69.4	77.1
	Vocational/technical	37.5	36.1	37.1	37.4	35.1	29.3	23.9	30.6	22.9
Uzbekistan	General secondary.	53.7	56.2	56.8	53.7	51.4	—	—	—	—
	Vocational/technical	46.3	43.8	43.2	46.3	48.6	—	—	—	—

— Not available.
Notes: Definition of title: percentage of students enrolled by type of upper secondary education in the total number enrolled in upper secondary education.
Sources: World Bank staff estimates based on data supplied by UNICEF-ICDC.

Table A11 Tertiary Enrollment Rates *(gross rates, percentage of 18–22 age group)*

Country	Note	1989	1990	1991	1992	1993	1994	1995	1996	1997
Central Europe										
Czech Republic		12.7	13.6	13.1	13.3	13.6	14.2	15.0	16.6	17.3
Hungary	a	13.9	14.2	14.8	15.7	16.8	18.5	20.7	22.9	23.8
Poland	b	11.6	12.4	13.0	14.3	15.7	17.0	18.1	19.7	20.6
Slovak Republic		13.2	13.8	13.3	14.2	14.4	15.0	15.6	16.8	17.6
Southeast Europe										
Albania		4.8	5.8	6.0	5.9	5.2	4.6	—	—	—
Bulgaria	c	16.4	18.8	18.7	19.8	20.9	23.0	26.0	27.3	27.1
Romania	d	8.8	10.1	11.0	12.2	13.1	13.4	13.3	18.6	18.7
Former Yugoslavia										
Bosnia-Herzegovina		—	—	—	—	—	—	—	—	—
Croatia		—	—	13.9	14.3	16.0	16.5	16.6	17.2	—
Macedonia, FYR		—	—	14.4	14.4	12.6	11.3	—	—	—
Slovenia	e	18.2	19.3	21.8	21.6	22.9	23.4	24.7	25.7	—
Yugoslavia, FR	f	17.1	16.9	15.8	13.7	14.8	14.5	14.9	16.5	—
Baltic states										
Estonia		—	14.2	14.2	13.9	14.3	15.6	16.9	18.6	21.3
Latvia		15.2	15.5	15.6	15.9	15.8	16.4	18.5	22.8	24.6
Lithuania		17.7	17.2	15.6	13.7	13.3	13.1	13.9	15.4	18.2
Western CIS										
Belarus		16.5	16.7	16.6	17.0	16.1	17.3	17.8	18.7	19.5
Moldova		11.6	11.7	11.4	10.8	10.3	10.8	11.9	12.5	13.5
Russian Federation		16.7	17.0	17.1	16.9	16.4	16.1	16.9	17.6	18.7
Ukraine		15.3	15.3	15.2	15.1	14.6	16.0	16.8	17.9	20.1
Caucasus										
Armenia		16.5	17.0	16.8	15.1	12.3	10.2	13.2	11.5	—
Azerbaijan		8.1	8.6	9.2	8.6	8.5	8.8	11.0	—	12.3
Georgia		14.3	16.4	15.7	13.4	12.7	13.7	12.1	13.6	14.4
Central Asian republics										
Kazakhstan		12.9	13.0	13.4	13.1	12.7	12.6	12.5	12.9	13.4
Kyrgyz Republic		10.9	10.8	10.4	9.7	9.7	10.9	11.8	12.9	15.2
Tajikistan		9.0	9.4	9.4	9.3	8.6	9.2	—	9.4	8.9
Turkmenistan		8.1	8.0	7.9	7.4	7.4	—	7.4	—	—
Uzbekistan		9.1	9.5	9.4	8.8	7.4	6.3	5.4	5.0	5.0
Turkey	g	15.0	16.0	16.7	18.5	22.6	22.5	23.1	—	26.70

— Not available.

Notes: Definition of title: gross rates, percentage of 18–22 age group enrolled full-time in tertiary education. Gross enrollment rates for the ECA region must be treated cautiously. The age-specific population numbers are somewhat suspect, since the last credible census was conducted in 1989. (Most countries will conduct a new census within the next two years.) In the intervening decade civil registration of births and deaths has declined sharply, and mobility across borders has increased. Enrollment numbers for countries engaged in conflict are suspect.
a. Net rate. b. Based on 19–24 age group. c. Includes part-time and full-time students in the 19–25 age group. d. 1996–97: includes students at private universities .e. Excludes advanced degree programs; includes part-time and full-time students. f. 1992–97: number of students excludes ethnic Albanians in Kosovo-Metohija. g. World Bank estimates for 1989–96 and 1997 based on data from SIS (1999, table 1) and Turkey, Ministry of National Education (1998, table 23), respectively, and on age-structure data from SIS (1995, table A5-1), assuming that the net reproduction rate (NRR) = 1.0 in 2005. Figures for 1989, 1991, 1992, and 1993 interpolated and projected from data provided by SIS.

Sources: Based on UNICEF-ICDC TransMONEE Database; U.S. Census Bureau (various years); CIS StatCommittee (1998a, 1998c); Turkey, Ministry of National Education (1998); Laporte and Ringold (1997).

Table A12 Share of University Enrollments by Field of Study, Selected ECA Countries *(percentage of total enrollments)*

Country	Subject	1989	1990	1991	1992	1993	1994	1995	1996	1997
Albania	Humanities	—	11.4	14.1	17.8	21.0	22.8	24.2	23.2	22.2
	Social and behavioral sciences	—	—	—	—	0.3	0.7	1.0	1.5	1.8
	Natural sciences	—	14.4	16.4	16.4	16.1	14.8	12.7	9.8	11.3
	Medical science	—	7.8	8.0	7.0	6.6	7.1	8.9	7.3	6.7
	Engineering	—	17.5	16.2	12.4	10.0	8.6	7.0	5.4	5.3
	Other	—	48.9	45.3	46.4	46.0	46.0	46.3	52.9	52.7
Armenia	Humanities	—	32.2	33.1	34.2	39.6	14.2	21.0	32.1	30.8
	Social and behavioral sciences	—	2.5	2.6	2.8	3.7	2.3	2.0	3.0	3.0
	Natural sciences	—	9.4	9.4	9.8	8.6	5.2	3.7	6.5	6.1
	Medical science	—	8.6	8.9	10.4	9.7	8.3	5.9	8.0	6.7
	Engineering	—	36.1	34.2	31.4	31.8	25.6	13.6	10.2	10.3
	Other	—	11.3	11.8	11.6	7.1	7.6	4.8	6.1	7.2
Azerbaijan	Humanities	34.3	33.0	33.9	35.0	37.2	38.3	39.7	37.3	32.1
	Social and behavioral sciences	2.7	2.5	2.6	2.8	2.7	2.9	2.5	2.5	2.2
	Natural sciences	4.7	7.3	8.5	9.2	10.9	12.3	16.8	20.1	27.8
	Medical science	9.3	9.3	9.4	10.0	10.3	10.9	10.2	9.7	9.7
	Engineering	40.7	39.1	36.7	34.7	31.1	29.0	25.1	25.1	23.5
	Other	8.2	8.7	8.8	8.5	7.8	6.6	5.7	5.3	4.7
Belarus	Humanities	15.2	15.9	16.9	19.7	21.1	21.7	22.6	22.2	23.3
	Social and behavioral sciences	—	—	—	—	—	5.2	9.6	14.1	16.6
	Natural sciences	9.6	9.6	9.6	9.0	8.6	7.6	6.5	5.7	5.0
	Medical science	6.1	6.5	6.8	6.5	6.3	5.5	4.9	4.2	3.6
	Engineering	32.9	32.3	31.3	28.4	26.4	24.0	21.8	20.3	19.2
	Other	36.1	35.7	35.4	36.4	37.7	35.9	34.6	33.4	32.2
Bosnia-Herzegovina	Humanities	2.3	2.3	2.5	2.4	4.0	2.4	1.8	2.5	5.9
	Social and behavioral sciences	37.7	37.3	37.2	37.0	38.6	49.7	57.0	58.5	65.9
	Natural sciences	2.7	2.9	3.3	3.0	2.2	1.1	0.8	1.7	2.3
	Medical science	12.8	12.8	13.4	15.9	19.8	12.7	12.1	8.8	9.1
	Engineering	35.7	36.7	37.3	35.9	33.6	32.5	26.4	26.2	16.8
	Other	8.8	8.0	6.3	5.8	1.9	1.7	1.8	2.4	—
Bulgaria	Humanities	21.2	18.6	18.3	18.8	20.0	15.0	11.2	7.4	7.7
	Social and behavioral sciences	15.2	14.7	16.1	19.1	22.7	28.4	20.6	7.5	8.1
	Natural sciences	7.7	4.7	5.4	5.0	5.1	4.2	3.6	2.8	2.6
	Medical science	8.9	8.4	7.9	6.8	6.0	5.2	4.7	4.1	4.1
	Engineering	37.8	35.8	30.9	29.5	26.1	22.3	19.5	15.4	16.6
	Other	9.2	17.9	21.3	20.8	20.1	24.9	40.5	63.1	60.9
Croatia	Humanities	—	—	—	19.0	19.7	20.9	21.5	21.6	24.7
	Social and behavioral sciences	—	—	—	29.0	29.4	31.1	31.9	33.1	42.2
	Natural sciences	—	—	—	3.3	2.9	3.1	2.9	2.8	2.3
	Medical science	—	—	—	8.8	8.5	7.8	7.9	7.8	9.2
	Engineering	—	—	—	37.0	36.4	34.1	32.4	31.7	47.1
	Other	—	—	—	2.9	3.1	3.0	3.4	3.1	10.3

(Table continues on following page)

Table A12 (continued)

Country	Subject	1989	1990	1991	1992	1993	1994	1995	1996	1997
Czech Republic	Humanities	23.7	24.5	25.5	27.1	28.1	27.8	28.3	28.4	28.1
	Social and behavioral sciences	12.1	12.6	14.8	16.0	18.6	20.8	22.2	22.7	22.7
	Natural sciences	4.1	4.8	4.9	5.3	5.6	5.7	5.9	6.5	7.0
	Medical science	11.6	11.8	11.4	10.7	9.5	8.5	7.6	6.9	6.7
	Engineering	39.5	37.8	35.6	33.7	31.8	30.8	29.4	28.8	29.5
	Other	9.0	8.6	7.9	7.2	6.4	6.4	6.4	6.6	6.0
Hungary	Humanities	3.9	4.3	4.6	4.2	4.3	5.7	5.2	5.3	—
	Social and behavioral sciences	5.7	5.9	5.9	5.6	8.2	8.4	5.3	4.8	—
	Natural sciences	2.0	2.3	2.2	2.4	2.3	2.3	2.0	2.6	—
	Medical science	12.5	12.2	13.8	13.0	11.5	10.1	8.9	8.5	—
	Engineering	12.1	12.4	12.2	11.9	10.6	10.5	10.6	10.4	—
	Other	63.8	62.9	61.3	63.0	63.0	63.2	68.1	68.5	—
Macedonia, FYR	Humanities	6.3	6.4	6.3	7.7	7.7	8.3	8.6	8.9	9.5
	Social and behavioral sciences	17.6	16.9	15.6	15.3	15.2	15.7	16.9	17.0	18.6
	Natural sciences	4.4	4.6	4.7	4.2	4.4	4.1	4.3	4.5	4.2
	Medical science	5.3	4.4	5.9	6.8	7.5	8.9	9.7	9.7	9.9
	Engineering	25.5	28.2	29.2	33.3	23.5	21.0	20.0	21.6	21.3
	Other	31.4	30.4	28.0	23.2	31.8	30.7	28.6	27.8	36.4
Poland	Humanities	11.2	11.5	11.5	10.7	10.6	10.7	9.6	9.3	8.6
	Social and behavioral sciences	3.9	4.4	3.8	4.1	9.7	8.7	9.8	10.3	11.8
	Natural sciences	3.3	3.1	3.2	3.5	3.1	3.1	2.9	2.7	2.4
	Medical science	9.9	10.1	8.9	7.1	6.1	5.0	4.1	3.5	3.1
	Engineering	17.5	16.9	18.2	18.9	19.7	19.5	19.0	18.3	17.6
	Other	54.2	54.1	54.3	55.8	50.9	53.0	54.6	55.8	56.6
Slovak Republic	Humanities	1.3	1.4	1.7	1.7	1.9	2.0	2.0	2.1	2.2
	Social and behavioral sciences	30.7	34.1	36.8	38.9	40.8	41.7	42.2	43.0	44.0
	Natural sciences	3.9	3.9	4.4	4.8	4.9	4.7	5.0	5.0	5.6
	Medical science	8.3	9.0	9.1	8.9	8.5	7.7	7.1	6.3	6.1
	Engineering	47.4	43.6	40.3	38.7	36.8	36.1	35.7	35.2	35.0
	Other	8.5	7.9	7.5	7.1	7.1	7.9	8.0	8.4	7.1
Slovenia	Humanities	—	—	6.9	7.2	4.9	8.8	8.9	5.9	5.5
	Social and behavioral sciences	—	—	4.6	5.3	5.9	6.5	6.5	5.5	5.6
	Natural sciences	—	—	3.9	3.6	3.6	3.5	3.1	2.4	2.2
	Medical science	—	—	6.6	5.9	5.5	6.2	5.5	5.5	6.4
	Engineering	—	—	20.7	21.5	19.6	18.1	14.0	17.2	17.8
	Other	—	—	57.4	56.5	60.4	56.9	62.1	63.5	62.5
Turkey[a]	Humanities	5.2	5.2	5.1	4.9	4.5	4.5	4.9	—	—
	Social and behavioral sciences	59.1	60.2	61.3	63.2	63.9	62.3	61.1	—	—
	Natural sciences	9.2	9.1	8.9	8.6	7.6	8.2	8.7	—	—
	Medical science	8.0	7.6	7.3	6.7	10.1	9.7	9.0	—	—
	Engineering	14.8	14.0	14.1	13.5	11.5	12.4	13.3	—	—
	Other	3.7	3.5	3.3	3.0	2.4	2.5	2.5	—	—

(Table continues on following page)

Table A12 *(continued)*

Country	Subject	1989	1990	1991	1992	1993	1994	1995	1996	1997
Yugoslavia, FR	Humanities	6.1	6.7	6.1	6.2	7.3	7.6	7.8	7.6	7.7
	Social and behavioral sciences	17.4	16.5	16.5	17.6	18.0	18.5	19.5	19.9	20.8
	Natural sciences	9.1	9.6	9.7	9.2	9.5	8.9	8.4	7.8	7.4
	Medical science	9.2	9.7	10.0	10.3	10.4	10.0	10.7	11.0	11.1
	Engineering	28.7	28.0	28.1	26.9	26.0	24.1	21.8	19.8	17.9
	Other	29.5	29.5	29.6	29.7	28.8	31.0	31.7	33.9	35.2

— Not available.

Notes: Definition of title: students enrolled by field of university education as a share of the total number enrolled in university education.
 a. SIS (1997).
Sources: UNICEF-ICDC TransMONEE Database; World Bank estimates based on data supplied by UNICEF-ICDC; SIS (1997).

Table A13 Unemployment by Educational Level, Selected ECA Countries
(percentage of corresponding labor force)

Country	Note	Education level	1992	1993	1994	1995	1996	1997
Bulgaria	a	Total	—	0.0	20.0	15.7	13.5	13.7
	b	Primary or less	—	0.0	29.8	25.1	21.5	20.1
	c	General	—	0.0	20.0	15.6	13.1	14.6
	d	Vocational	—	0.0	15.6	11.6	10.7	12.0
	e	Tertiary	—	0.0	7.7	5.3	4.9	5.2
Czech Republic		Total	—	3.9	3.7	3.6	3.7	4.3
		Primary or less	—	8.8	8.1	10.3	11.2	13.4
		General	—	2.7	2.6	2.0	2.1	2.8
		Vocational	—	3.6	3.7	3.4	3.5	3.9
		Tertiary	—	1.9	1.4	1.1	0.6	1.2
Hungary		Total	9.7	12.0	10.8	10.2	10.5	9.3
		Primary or less	14.3	17.4	16.0	16.0	16.3	16.0
		General	6.7	8.6	7.8	6.8	7.2	6.1
		Vocational	11.3	14.5	12.8	12.2	12.7	10.6
		Tertiary	2.3	2.9	2.9	2.7	3.1	1.9
Latvia		Total	—	—	—	—	22.2	15.9
		Primary or less	—	—	—	—	33.9	19.4
		General	—	—	—	—	26.7	20.6
		Vocational	—	—	—	—	19.6	15.0
		Tertiary	—	—	—	—	11.9	7.7
Poland		Total	12.9	13.8	14.0	12.6	12.4	11.3
		Primary or less	12.0	14.0	15.0	13.8	13.7	14.3
		General	13.8	13.0	13.1	12.0	11.8	10.4
		Vocational	15.5	17.4	17.4	15.7	15.4	13.5
		Tertiary	6.6	6.0	5.2	4.1	3.6	3.7
Romania	f	Total	—	—	8.2	8.0	5.9	5.5
	g	Primary or less	—	—	7.0	5.2	4.4	3.9
	h	General	—	—	11.1	14.8	8.2	7.7
	i	Vocational	—	—	9.1	8.7	6.7	6.3
	j	Tertiary	—	—	3.1	2.2	1.9	2.2
Russian Federation	l	Total	4.9	5.6	7.9	9.2	9.5	—
		Primary or less	5.8	6.7	9.8	11.6	13.0	—
		General	5.8	6.6	9.8	11.5	11.6	—
		Vocational	4.3	5.1	6.8	8.1	8.5	—
		Tertiary	3.2	3.4	4.7	4.8	4.4	—
Slovak Republic		Total	—	12.4	13.4	13.3	10.9	11.2
		Primary or less	—	23.2	28.0	29.2	25.4	26.3
		General	—	11.6	12.9	12.7	12.5	13.5
		Vocational	—	10.7	12.2	11.9	9.7	9.6
		Tertiary	—	3.8	4.0	2.9	2.0	3.1
Slovenia		Total	—	9.1	9.1	7.4	7.3	7.1
		Primary or less	—	10.8	12.2	9.5	10.6	9.2
		General	—	8.4	8.3	6.7	6.3	7.2
		Vocational	—	11.0	10.2	8.3	7.9	6.9
		Tertiary	—	4.3	3.5	2.1	3.0	3.8
Turkey	k	Total	—	—	—	—	—	—
		Primary or less	7.8	—	7.8	5.6	5.4	—
		General	17.4	—	23.5	25.5	20.7	—
		Vocational	23.2	—	33.8	25.9	16.5	—
		Tertiary	7.1	—	6.5	5.6	5.3	—

— Not available.

Notes: Definition of title: number of unemployed, by level of education, divided by the corresponding labor force for that level of education. Data are second quarter labor force survey data

a. 1993 data are for third quarter. b. 1994 data are for third quarter. c. 1995 data are for third quarter. d. 1996 data are for third quarter. e. 1997 data are for third quarter. f. 1994 and 1995 data are for first quarter. g. 1994 and 1995 data are for first quarter. h. 1995 and 1996 data are for first quarter. i. 1995 and 1997 data are for first quarter. j. 1995 and 1998 data are for first quarter. k. April for each year. Household Labor Force Survey Results, State Institute of Statistics. l. 1992–95 data are for fourth quarter; 1996 data are for first quarter.

Source: Based on OECD-CCET Labour Market Database

Table A14 Share of Registered Unemployed by Educational Level, Selected ECA Countries *(percentage of unemployed)*

Country	Education	1989	1990	1991	1992	1993	1994	1995	1996
Azerbaijan	Primary or less	—	—	14.03	7.10	3.10	2.30	1.20	1.04
	Lower secondary	—	—	48.68	41.19	36.40	41.90	60.70	53.15
	Upper secondary	—	—	37.29	51.71	60.50	55.80	38.10	45.82
	Tertiary	—	—	—	—	—	—	—	—
Belarus	Primary or less	—	—	—	—	7.12	9.02	8.77	8.46
	Lower secondary	—	—	—	—	53.79	58.56	61.81	63.62
	Upper secondary	—	—	—	—	21.96	20.57	19.77	19.05
	Tertiary	—	—	—	—	17.13	11.85	9.65	8.87
Croatia	Primary or less	36.18	36.73	37.27	35.97	35.80	36.62	36.26	35.82
	Lower secondary	30.30	30.27	32.17	32.53	32.19	32.57	34.15	34.94
	Upper secondary	23.86	23.50	21.64	22.47	23.30	23.05	22.68	22.50
	Tertiary	9.67	9.50	8.91	9.03	8.71	7.76	6.92	6.74
Georgia	Primary or less	—	—	1.00	1.00	0.80	0.50	0.20	0.10
	Lower secondary	—	—	6.00	5.00	3.20	3.00	1.80	0.90
	Upper secondary	—	—	22.00	24.00	23.00	21.50	19.00	19.00
	Tertiary	—	—	71.00	70.00	73.00	75.00	79.00	80.00
Kyrgyz Republic	Primary or less	—	—	—	0.00	0.00	0.00	0.00	0.00
	Lower secondary	—	—	—	8.02	8.62	7.95	9.00	11.37
	Upper secondary	—	—	—	61.19	65.80	75.45	78.71	78.40
	Tertiary	—	—	—	30.79	25.58	16.60	12.29	10.23
Macedonia, FYR	Primary or less	50.00	49.76	—	47.91	48.05	49.33	51.04	52.11
	Lower secondary	0.00	0.00	0.00	0.00	0.00	0.00	0.00	0.00
	Upper secondary	43.05	43.29	43.59	44.80	44.76	43.90	42.77	41.94
	Tertiary	6.96	6.95	7.05	7.28	7.19	6.77	6.18	5.95
FR Yugoslavia	Primary or less	42.37	42.13	41.73	41.10	40.73	40.23	40.84	41.42
	Lower secondary	16.59	17.41	18.54	19.31	19.85	20.58	21.16	21.58
	Upper secondary	34.85	34.13	33.03	32.35	31.76	31.36	30.96	30.52
	Tertiary	6.19	6.33	6.70	7.25	7.66	7.82	7.04	6.48

— Not available.
Source: Taken from labor surveys.

Table A15 Total Public Expenditures on Education *(percentage of GDP)*

Country	Note	1989	1990	1991	1992	1993	1994	1995	1996	1997
Central Europe										
Czech Republic		4.0	4.1	4.1	4.5	5.2	5.4	5.3	5.3	4.7
Hungary		5.7	5.8	6.3	6.6	6.5	6.4	5.5	4.9	4.3
Poland		—	4.8	5.1	5.4	5.4	5.3	5.2	5.4	5.5
Slovak Republic		—	5.1	5.6	6.0	5.2	4.4	5.1	5.0	—
Southeast Europe										
Albania		4.0	4.2	5.0	4.2	3.3	3.2	3.8	3.2	3.3
Bulgaria		—	5.0	5.1	6.1	5.7	4.8	4.0	3.2	4.0
Romania		2.2	2.8	3.6	3.6	3.3	3.1	3.4	3.6	—
Former Yugoslavia										
Bosnia-Herzegovina		—	—	—	—	—	—	—	—	—
Croatia		—	—	2.9	1.8	1.8	2.9	2.9	2.9	2.9
Macedonia, FYR		—	5.9	6.8	5.4	6.0	5.7	5.7	5.9	5.4
Slovenia		—	—	4.8	5.5	5.8	5.5	5.8	5.8	—
Yugoslavia, FR		—	—	—	—	—	—	—	—	—
Baltic states										
Estonia		—	—	—	6.1	7.1	6.7	7.1	7.3	—
Latvia		5.5	4.8	4.2	4.6	6.1	6.1	6.9	5.8	5.8
Lithuania		—	4.5	—	—	4.6	5.6	5.6	5.4	5.8
Western CIS										
Belarus		—	—	4.6	5.3	6.0	5.8	5.5	6.1	6.6
Moldova		—	—	—	7.8	6.0	7.4	7.7	9.4	8.9
Russian Federation		—	3.7	3.6	3.6	4.0	4.5	3.6	3.8	4.2
Ukraine		—	—	—	—	—	—	—	—	—
Caucasus										
Armenia		—	—	7.5	8.9	5.2	2.5	3.3	2.0	1.7
Azerbaijan	a	6.1	6.6	6.3	5.8	6.8	4.4	2.9	3.3	3.0
Georgia	a b	6.4	6.5	7.0	5.0	0.6	0.5	0.9	1.2	1.4
Central Asian republics										
Kazakhstan		—	—	—	2.1	3.9	3.0	3.2	—	—
Kyrgyz Republic	a	7.9	7.5	6.0	4.9	4.2	5.9	6.6	5.2	4.9
Tajikistan	a c	—	—	—	—	8.5	8.3	2.4	2.2	—
Turkmenistan		—	—	—	—	4.0	2.1	1.7	1.9	—
Uzbekistan	a d	—	10.4	10.2	10.9	10.4	—	7.4	7.4	—

— Not available.

Notes: Definition of title: total public expenditures, current and capital, on education, using the 1995 definition of the United Nations Educational, Scientific, and Cultural Organisation (UNESCO).

a. World Bank data. b. GDP figures adjusted for 1989–94. c. GDP figures adjusted. d. Uzbekistan consolidated government budget. GDP figures adjusted for 1990–93.

Source: Based on UNICEF-ICDC TransMONEE Database

Table A16 Student/Teacher Ratios in Basic Education

Country	1989	1990	1991	1992	1993	1994	1995	1996	1997
Central Europe									
Czech Republic	20.8	19.6	18.7	18.0	17.5	16.7	16.3	14.5	—
Hungary	13.1	12.5	12.1	11.9	11.5	11.2	11.6	12.0	12.2
Poland	18.6	16.7	17.2	16.7	16.5	16.1	15.9	15.6	15.4
Slovak Republic	20.0	19.4	19.2	18.3	18.5	18.2	17.6	17.2	17.1
Southeast Europe									
Albania	19.4	19.3	18.3	17.2	16.7	17.8	17.8	18.1	18.6
Bulgaria	15.6	14.8	14.3	13.8	14.0	13.9	13.6	13.4	13.9
Romania	20.0	16.7	16.6	15.7	15.4	15.0	14.8	14.5	14.8
Former Yugoslavia									
Bosnia-Herzegovina	24.0	23.5	22.5	22.9	25.9	26.4	24.6	23.5	—
Croatia	18.4	18.6	18.7	18.7	18.2	17.9	17.4	16.8	16.5
Macedonia, FYR	20.8	20.5	20.6	20.0	20.0	19.8	19.7	19.6	19.6
Slovenia	15.5	15.4	15.4	15.0	14.5	14.2	13.8	13.5	—
Yugoslavia, FR	19.1	19.0	18.2	18.4	17.8	17.6	17.7	17.3	16.9
Baltic states									
Estonia	10.7	10.5	11.3	10.3	11.1	11.6	11.7	—	—
Latvia	—	—	—	—	10.3	10.5	10.5	10.3	12.0
Lithuania	12.6	12.0	11.3	11.1	11.0	10.7	10.8	10.9	11.3
Western CIS									
Belarus	11.8	11.8	11.6	11.4	11.1	11.0	11.0	10.7	10.5
Moldova	12.5	12.4	12.6	12.4	12.5	12.5	12.7	13.3	—
Russian Federation	14.1	14.0	13.4	12.9	12.5	12.4	12.5	12.1	11.9
Ukraine	—	—	—	—	—	—	—	—	—
Caucasus									
Armenia	11.7	11.7	11.8	11.4	10.7	10.4	10.4	10.4	8.7
Azerbaijan	10.9	10.5	10.5	10.3	9.8	9.8	9.6	9.7	9.9
Georgia	8.4	8.2	8.0	7.8	7.9	8.0	8.0	7.9	9.2
Central Asian republics									
Kazakhstan	13.1	12.8	12.3	11.6	11.2	11.3	11.3	11.8	12.7
Kyrgyz Republic	11.6	10.7	10.8	10.9	12.0	12.2	12.6	13.4	13.5
Tajikistan	—	—	—	—	—	—	—	—	—
Turkmenistan	14.3	14.0	14.2	13.8	13.5	13.5	13.5	13.7	13.4
Uzbekistan	—	—	—	—	—	—	—	—	—
Turkey	33.8	33.9	32.4	31.8	30.6	30.7	29.9	31.2	30.0

— Not available.
Notes: 1996 data are from SIS (1999, table 1). 1997 data are from Turkey, Ministry of National Education (1998, table 19).
Sources: Based on UNICEF-ICDC TransMONEE Database; SIS (1999).

Table A17 Wages in Education in Selected ECA Countries
(percentage of average wage in economy)

Country	1985	1990	1991	1992	1993	1994	1995	1996	1997
Azerbaijan	86.9	88.1	74.1	94.0	97.2	91.4	73.0	71.6	73.1
Armenia	77.0	65.2	78.2	85.8	67.5	41.9	46.6	53.0	43.9
Belarus	85.0	71.2	77.5	82.8	78.7	80.2	78.7	83.8	82.5
Georgia	81.9	73.3	85.0	79.0	47.2	19.1	51.5	50.3	63.1
Kazakhstan	75.0	67.4	72.7	53.9	61.9	52.1	61.6	73.7	75.1
Kyrgyz Republic	90.0	75.2	73.8	62.9	65.4	102.1	84.0	70.9	61.0
Moldova	89.9	66.3	69.7	86.5	83.3	78.6	76.0	84.7	76.9
Russian Federation	77.7	67.0	70.8	61.8	67.7	68.1	64.5	69.8	64.8
Tajikistan	104.3	88.4	79.7	85.2	74.7	81.2	61.3	49.1	—
Turkmenistan	94.1	76.0	62.3	81.4	88.6	56.1	73.2	64.5	—
Uzbekistan	94.7	79.4	77.0	85.1	79.2	64.7	64.1	73.9	—
Ukraine	84.4	70.6	74.4	79.3	71.0	77.5	86.1	77.7	72.3

— Not available.
Notes: Definition of title: education wage/economy wage.
Source: Based on CIS StatCommittee (1998a).

REFERENCES

Allen John S., Keon F. Chi, Kevin M. Devlan, Mark Fall, Herry P. Hatry, and Wyne Masterman. 1989. *The Private Sector in State Service Delivery: Examples of Innovative Practices.* Washington, DC: Urban Institute Press. Cited in Paul (1991).

Balzer, Harley. 1998. "Poverty, Education, and White Collar Trends in Postcommunist Transitions." Prepared for the Workshop on Transition Countries of the Poverty Program, United Nations Development Programme, Georgetown University, Washington, DC.

Berryman, Sue E. 1997. *Preparing for the Global Economy: Focus on Educational Quality.* Washington, DC: World Bank.

Berryman, Sue E., and Thomas Bailey. 1992. *The Double Helix of Education and the Economy.* Institute on Education and the Economy, Teachers College, Columbia University, New York

Brunetti, Aymo, Gregory Kisunko, and Beatrice Weder. 1997. "Institutional Obstacles to Doing Business: Region-by-Region Results from a Worldwide Survey of the Private Sector." Policy Research Working Paper No. 1759. World Bank, Washington, DC.

Consultations with the Poor. 1999a. "Global Synthesis: Summary." Draft. Prepared for Global Synthesis Workshop, September, 22–23, 1999. Poverty Group PREM, World Bank, Washington, DC.

———. 1999b. "National Synthesis Report on Bosnia: Participatory Poverty Assessment in Bosnia for the World Development Report 2000/01." Prepared for Global Synthesis Workshop, September, 22–23, 1999, World Bank, Washington, DC.

———. 1999c. "National Synthesis Report on Kyrgyz Republic: Participatory Poverty Assessment in Kyrgyz Republic for the World Development Report 2000/01." Prepared for Global Synthesis Workshop, September, 22–23, 1999, World Bank, Washington, DC.

———. 1999d. "National Synthesis Report on Uzbekistan: Participatory Poverty Assessment in Uzbekistan for the World Development Report 2000/01." Prepared for Global Synthesis Workshop, September, 22–23, 1999, World Bank, Washington, DC.

CIS StatCommittee (Interstate Statistical Committee of the Commonwealth of Independent States). 1998a. *Official Statistics of the Countries of the Commonwealth of Independent States,* CD-ROM. Moscow. <http://www.unece.org/stats/cisstat>.

———. 1998b. *Sodruzhestvo nezavisimykh gosudarstv v 1997 godu: statisticheskiy yezhigodnik* [The Commonwealth of Independent States in 1997: Statistical Yearbook]. Moscow.

———. 1998c. *Naseleniye i usloviya zhizni v stranakh sodruzhestvo nezavisimykh gosudarstv: statisticheskiy sbornik* [Population and Living Conditions in the CIS Countries: Statistical Handbook]. Moscow.

Council of Europe. Various years. *Recent Demographic Developments in Europe.* Strasbourg, France: Council of Europe Publishing.

De Waal, Clarissa. 1999. "Reports on Rural Education in Mirdita." Draft. Reports prepared for Albania Education Development Program.

Dinca, George. 1998. "Remarks on the Reform of the Financing of Higher Education in Romania." Presented at the Budapest Seminar on Higher Education Finance, June 29–July 1.

Dudwick, Nora, and Helen Shahriari. 2000. "Education in Albania: Changing Attitudes and Expectations." Paper prepared for the Albania Education Sector Study. Europe and Central Asia Region, Human Development Unit, World Bank, Washington, DC.

EBRD (European Bank for Reconstruction and Development). Various years. *Transition Report.* London.

Fay, Robert G. 1996. "Enhancing the Effectiveness of Active Labor Market Policies: Evidence from Program Evaluations in OECD Countries." Labor Market and Social Policy Occasional Papers No. 18. Organisation for Economic Co-operation and Development, Paris.

Fretwell, David, and Sandra Wilson. 1999. "Public Service Employment: A Review of Programs in Selected OECD Countries and Transition Economies." Social Protection Discussion Paper Series, Human Development Network, No. 9913. World Bank, Washington, DC.

Gertler, Paul, and Paul Glewwe. 1989. *The Willingness to Pay for Education in Developing Countries: Evidence from Rural Peru.* Living Standards Measurement Study Working Paper No. 54. Washington, DC: World Bank.

Girishankar, Navin. 1999. "Reforming Institutions for Service Delivery: A Framework for Development Assistance with an Application to the Health, Nutrition, and Population Portfolio." Policy Research Working Paper No. 2039. World Bank, Washington, DC.

Hendrichova, Jana, Jana Svecova, and Lenka Slavikova. 1999. "Inter-Governmental Roles in Education Services in the Czech Republic." Draft. World Bank Institute, Washington, DC.

Ishida, Hiroshi, Walter Muller, and John Ridge. 1995. "Class Origin, Class Destination, and Education: A Cross-National Study of Ten Industrial Nations." *American Journal of Sociology* 101(1):145–93.

Ivan, Gabriel, Mircea Badescu, Paul Blendea Romulus, Brancoveanu Florin Diaconescu, Serban Iosifescu, Dakmara Georgescu, Lucia Marietta Gliga, Ioan Narosi, Roxana Petrescu, Viorica Pop, and Madlen Serban. 1999, "Inter-Governmental Roles in Education Services in Romania." Draft. World Bank Institute, Washington, DC.

Johnstone, D. Bruce, Alka Arora, and William Experton. 1998. "The Financing and Management of Higher Education: A Status Report on World Wide Reforms." Human Development Network, World Bank, Washington, DC.

Joyce, Philip G., and Patricia W. Ingraham. 1997. "Government Management: Defining and Assessing Performance." Unpublished paper. Syracuse University, Maxwell School, Syracuse, NY.

Keefer, Philip. 1998. "Contracting Out: An Opportunity for Public Sector Reform and Private Sector Development in Transition Economies." World Bank, Development Research Group, Washington, DC.

King, Elizabeth M. 1995. "Does the Price of Schooling Matter? Fees, Opportunity Costs, and Enrollment in Indonesia." World Bank, Washington, DC.

Klugman, Jeni. 1997a. "Costs and Gains in Education Financing and Governance in the FSU." Background paper for TransMONEE Project Education Report. UNICEF International Child Development Centre, Florence, Italy.

———. 1997b. "Decentralization: A Survey from a Child Welfare Perspective." Innocenti Occasional Papers, Economic and Social Policy Series 61 (September). UNICEF International Child Development Centre, Florence, Italy.

Knack, Stephen, and Philip Keefer. 1997. "Does Social Capital Have an Economic Payoff? A Cross-Country Investigation." *Quarterly Journal of Economics* 112 (November):1251–88

Laporte, Bruno, and Dena Ringold. 1997. *Trends in Education Access and Financing during the Transition in Central and Eastern Europe.* World Bank Technical Paper No. 361, Social Challenges of Transition Series. Washington, DC: World Bank.

Lockheed, Marlaine. 1997. "Decentralization of Education: Eight Lessons." Presentation at the seminar on Fiscal Decentralization in Developing Countries. World Bank, Washington, DC.

Meager, Nigel, and Ceri Evans. 1998. "The Evaluation of Active Labor Market Measures for the Long-Term Unemployed." Employment and Training Papers No. 16. International Labour Organisation, Geneva.

Milanovic, Branko. 1998. *Income, Inequality, and Poverty during the Transition from Planned to Market Economy.* Washington, DC: World Bank.

Mincer, Jacob. 1993. "Job Training, Wage Growth, and Labor Turnover." In Jacob Mincer, ed., *Studies in Human Capital.* Brookfield, VT: Edward Elgar.

Mingat, Alain, and Jee-Peng Tan. 1998. "The Mechanics of Progress in Education: Evidence from Cross-Country Data." Policy Research Working Paper 2015. World Bank, Washington, DC.

Nunberg, Barbara, and Gary Reid. 1999. "EU Accession and Public Administration in Central and Eastern Europe." Study in progress. Public Sector Management Division, World Bank, Washington, DC.

OECD (Organisation for Economic Co-operation and Development). Various years. *Education at a Glance: OECD Indicators.* Paris: Center for Educational Research and Innovation.

———. 1997. *Literacy Skills for the Knowledge Society.* Paris: OECD; Human Resources Development Canada and Statistics Canada.

———. 1998a. *OECD Health Data 1998: A Software for the Comparative Analysis of 29 Health Systems.* CD ROM. Paris.

———. 1998b. *Human Capital Investment: An International Comparison.* Paris: Centre for Educational Research and Innovation.

———. 2000. *Literacy in the Information Age.* Paris: OECD; Human Resources Development Canada and Statistics Canada.

Palomba, Geremia, and Milan Vodopivec. 2000. "Efficiency, Equity, and Fiscal Impact of Education in Albania." Europe and Central Asia Region, Human Development Unit and Development Research Group, World Bank, Washington, DC.

Paul, Samuel. 1991. "Accountability in Public Services: Exit, Voice, and Capture." Policy Research Working Paper No. 614. World Bank, Washington, DC.

———. 1994 "Does Voice Matter? For Public Accountability, Yes." Policy Research Working Paper No. 1388. World Bank, Washington, DC.

Perkins, Gillian. 1998. "The Georgian Education System: Issues for Reform Management." Background paper for the 1998 Georgia Education Sector Strategy Note. Europe and Central Asia Region, Human Development Unit, World Bank, Washington. DC.

Prud'homme, Remy. 1995. "The Dangers of Decentralization." *The World Bank Research Observer* 10 (2):201–20.

Resnick, Lauren B. 1987. *Education and Learning to Think.* Washington, DC: National Academy Press.

Ringold, Dena. 2000. "Roma and the Transition in Central and Eastern Europe: Trends and Challenges." Europe and Central Asia Region, Human Development Unit, World Bank, Washington, DC.

Rutkowski, Jan. J. 1995. "Labor Markets and Poverty in Bulgaria." Background paper for the Bulgaria Poverty Assessment Study. Europe and Central Asia Region, Human Development Unit, World Bank, Washington, DC.

Shore, Rima. 1997. *Rethinking the Brain: New Insights into Early Development.* New York: Families and Work Institute.

SIS (State Institute of Statistics of Turkey). SIS Website <http://www.die.gov.tr>.

———. 1994. *Istatistik Gostergeler 1923–92* [Statistical Indicators: 1923–92]. Ankara: Prime Minister's Office.

———. 1995. *The Population of Turkey, 1923–1994. Demographic Structure and Development.* Ankara: Prime Minister's Office.

———. 1997. *Statistical Yearbook of Turkey.* Ankara: Prime Minister's Office.

———. 1999. *National Education Statistics, 1996–1997: Formal Education.* Ankara: Prime Minister's Office.

Stewart, Kitty. 1997. "Financing Education at the Level of the Raion: A Case Study of Novgorod." Background paper for MONEE Project Education Report. UNICEF International Child Development Centre, Florence, Italy.

Turkey, Ministry of National Education. 1998. *Cumhurieyetin 75 Yilinda Gelismeler ve Hedefler Milli Egitim* [National Education: Goals and Progress over 75 Years of the Republic]. Ankara.

UNICEF (United Nations Children's Fund). 1998. *Education for All?* MONEE Project Regional Monitoring Report 5. Florence, Italy: UNICEF International Child Development Centre.

UNICEF-ICDC (United Nations Children's Fund International Child Development Centre). TransMONEE Database 3.0 <http://www.unicef-icdc.org/information/databases>. Florence, Italy.

U.S. Census Bureau. Various years. International Database (IDB). International Programs Center, U.S Bureau of the Census, Washington, DC.

U.S. General Accounting Office. 1997. "Air Force Depot Maintenance: Information on the Cost-Effectiveness of B-1 and B-52 Support Options." Briefing report to the Honorable Don Nickles. GAO/NSIAD-97-210BR. United States Senate, Washington, DC.

Vandycke, Nancy, 2000. "Education and the Poor in ECA Countries." Background paper for the ECA Poverty 2000 Report. Europe and Central Asia Region, Human Development Unit, World Bank, Washington. DC.

Varshney, Ashutosh. Forthcoming. *Civic Life and Ethnic Conflict: Hindus and Muslims in India.* New Haven, CN: Yale University Press.

Wetzel, Deborah, and Jonathan Dunn. 1998. "Decentralization in the ECA Region: Progress and Prospects." Draft. Europe and Central Asia Region, Poverty Reduction and Economic Management Sector Unit, World Bank, Washington, DC.

Willms, J. Douglas. 1999. *Literacy Skills in Poland.* New Brunswick, Canada: University of New Brunswick, Atlantic Center for Policy Research.

World Bank. Various years. *World Development Indicators.* Washington, DC.

———. 1996a. "Armenia: Confronting Poverty Issues." Report No. 15693-AM. Washington, DC.

———. 1996b. "Estonia Living Standards during the Transition." Report No. 15647-EE. Washington, DC.

———. 1997a. "Azerbaijan Poverty Assessment." Vol. 1. Report No. 15601-AZ. Washington, DC.

———. 1997b. "Azerbaijan Poverty Assessment." Vol. 2. Report No. 15601-AZ. Washington, DC.

———. 1997c. "Romania Poverty and Social Policy." Report No. 16462-RO. Washington, DC.

———. 1997d. *World Development Report 1997: The State in a Changing World.* New York: Oxford University Press.

———. 1998a. Bulgarian working paper prepared for the Workshop on Inter-Governmental Roles in the Delivery of Education Services in Central and Eastern Europe, Szeged, Hungary, sponsored by the World Bank Institute.

———. 1998b. "Georgia: Education Sector Strategy Note." Europe and Central Asia Region, Human Development Sector Unit, Washington, DC.

———. 1998c. Romanian working paper prepared for the Workshop on Inter-Governmental Roles in the Delivery of Education Services in Central and Eastern Europe, Szeged, Hungary, sponsored by the World Bank Institute.

———. 1999a. "Bulgaria: Poverty during the Transition." Report No. 18411. Europe and Central Asia Region, Human Development Sector Unit, Washington, DC.

———. 1999b. "Civil Service Reform: A Review of World Bank Assistance." Report No. 19211. Operations Evaluation Department, World Bank, Washington, DC.

———. 1999c. "Data Quality Survey for ECA Countries." Unpublished paper. Technical Assistance in Statistics Team, Development Data Group, Office of Vice President, Development Economics and Chief Economist, Washington, DC.

———. 1999d. "Georgia Poverty and Income Distribution." Vol. I. Report No. 19348-GE. Europe and Central Asia Region, Poverty Reduction and Economic Management Sector Unit, Washington, DC.

———. 1999e. "Georgia Poverty and Income Distribution." Vol. 2. Report No. 19348-GE. Europe and Central Asia Region, Poverty Reduction and Economic Management Sector Unit, Washington, DC.

———. 1999f. "Former Yugoslav Republic of Macedonia: Focusing on the Poor." Report No. 19411-MK. Europe and Central Asia Region, Country Department IV, Human Development Sector Unit, Washington, DC.

———. 1999g. "Moldova Poverty Assessment." Vol. II. Draft. Europe and Central Asia Region, Poverty Reduction and Economic Management Sector Unit, Washington, DC.

———. 1999h. "Russia: Regional Education Study." Europe and Central Asia Region, Human Development Sector Unit, Washington, DC.

———. 2000a. "Albania's Education Sector: Problems and Promise." Europe and Central Asia Region, Human Development Sector Unit, Washington. DC.

———. 2000b. "Making Transition Work for Everyone: Poverty and Inequality in Europe and Central Asia." Europe and Central Asia Region, Human Development Sector Unit, Washington. D.C.

GLOSSARY

Accountability. Mechanisms that stakeholders can use to assess the public sector's performance and to pressure the state to honor their interests.

Adult education/training. Includes college, vocational, and occupational programs, continuing education and noncredit courses, correspondence courses, and tutoring for adults. These services are supplied by employers, community groups, and other providers.

Alignment. As used in this paper, the matching of the skills and knowledge created by the education system to the skills and knowledge required by a country's economic and political systems.

Basic education. Primary and lower secondary education combined. ECA countries vary somewhat in the organisation of their education systems and in the ages and grades associated with each level of education. However, in general, primary education can be grades 1–4/5, the normal age range being 6/7 to 10. The lower secondary level can be grades 5/6–8/9, the normal age range varying from 10–14 to 11–15.

Block grants. Grants made to local governments but not reserved exclusively for education.

Capitation financing; demand-driven financing. Funding for education that is determined primarily by the number of students in a subnational unit, such as a school or district. Sometimes called "money follows student", these financing systems are based on capitation ("headcounts"), unit cost, or average cost. The funding formula per student can be adjusted for factors that result in differences in the costs of providing education, as in small villages.

Categorical (or "earmarked") grants. Funding that can only be spent for a specific purpose such as education.

Choice. Giving customers for goods or services, such as educational services, alternatives among which they can select. Although competitive market forces are normally used to provide options, the public sector can structure service delivery in ways that create alternatives for beneficiaries.

Civic mindedness. Playing by the rules of the game that govern communal life—for example, not cheating on taxes.

Cognition. The act or faculty of knowing, or the process of knowing, or knowledge and the capacity for it, or thinking.

Cognitive self-management. See Metacognitive skills.

Contact hours. The number of hours per week scheduled for face-to-face contact between teachers and students.

Continuous education. The availability of educational and training experiences throughout life.

Diagnostic assessment of student learning. Assessment of a student's strengths and weaknesses that teachers can use to tailor instruction that addresses weaknesses.

Distance education. Programs in which students and teachers communicate almost exclusively through correspondence, audio or video links, or computer.

Document literacy. The knowledge and skills required to locate and use information contained in various formats, including job applications, payroll forms, transport schedules, maps, tables, and graphics.

Economies of scale. Realized when an increase in the size of an activity—for example, increased class size—requires less than a proportionate increase in cost.

Educational attainment. The highest level of education completed.

Education mainstreaming. Policies aimed at limiting the grouping of students by ability or achievement in order to avoid exclusion. Mainstreaming implies relaxing rigid divisions between vocational and academic curricula and adopting teaching methods and curricula that allow students in shared spaces, but of different aptitudes, to progress.

Efficiency. For an education system, measured by the relationship between the outcomes achieved and the resources used to produce those outcomes.

Enquiry-based teaching. Method of teaching in which the teacher, instead of giving the learner verbal descriptions of a concept or principle, structures the learning experience so that the student can develop the concept or arrive at the principle himself/herself.

Enrollment rates (gross and net). A gross enrollment rate expresses the total number of children of any age enrolled in a schooling level as a percentage of the total number of children in the relevant age group for that level. Net enrollment rates measure only the number of children of the relevant age group enrolled in a schooling level as a percentage of the total number of children in that age group.

Epistemology. Study or theory of the nature and grounds of knowledge, especially with reference to its limits and validity.

Evaluative skills. Advanced thinking skills that allow the individual to make judgments about the value of materials or methods for a given purpose.

Fairness. In education, equitable opportunities to learn, rather then equality of learning outcomes; for example, all students have the textbooks for a grade.

Foundation skills. The literacy and quantitative skills that provide the base for subsequent learning and enhance the efficiency with which it occurs.

General (academic) upper secondary education. One of three alternatives for students in ECA countries following basic education. The academic, or general, stream leads to matriculation from secondary education and lasts two to four years. (The other alternatives are a technical/vocational stream that also leads to matriculation from secondary education and that lasts three to four years and a vocational program that does not lead to matriculation and that lasts one to two years.)

Gini coefficient. Measures the degree of inequality of the distribution of earnings. It is equal to 0 in the case of total earnings equality and to 1 in the case of total inequality.

Governance. In the education sector, refers to the process of goal setting for the sector as it affects policy and process and monitoring the progress of the sector relative to these goals.

Higher education, or tertiary education, or postsecondary education. Education programs offered to students who have successfully completed prerequisite studies at the upper secondary level. There is usually opportunity for postsecondary technical as well as university training. Program completion is marked by the awarding of a university degree or a recognized equivalent qualification.

Higher order thinking skills. As defined in Resnick (1987), higher order cognitive thinking is evidenced in solving problems that have certain characteristics: the path of action is not fully specified in advance, nor is the path to a solution mentally visible from any single vantage point; the problem yields multiple rather than unique solutions and requires nuanced judgment and the application of multiple criteria that sometimes conflict with one another; and not all of the information needed to solve the problem is available.

Human capital. Investments in knowledge and skills of individuals that increase the individuals' future welfare by increasing the efficiency of their future consumption and productivity. These investments include but are not limited to education and training.

Incidence of poverty. Percentage of the population or of a particular population group living below an established poverty line.

Informal user charges. Payments by service users—such as payments by parents for educational services—that are neither explicit nor public.

In-service teacher training. Professional development programs of varying duration for the existing teaching force, as distinct from preservice training for students before they enter the teaching profession.

Knowing-how-to-learn skills. See Metacognitive skills.

Learning outcomes. The knowledge, skills, attitudes, and values that students acquire as a result of their schooling experiences.

Literacy. As defined in the International Adult Literacy Survey (IALS), information-processing skills, including numeracy, that adults need in order to perform tasks encountered at work, at home, or in the community. These skills include the ability to draw meaning from written symbols—the defining characteristic of higher level reading and writing skills being the ability to draw on an extensive repertoire of knowledge and experiences to expand and interpret the meaning of verbal and quantitative texts.

Lower secondary education. The upper grades of basic education, usually grades 5/6–8/9, with the normal age range varying from 10–14 to 11–15.

Management. How the implementation of goals for a sector is organized.

Metacognitive skills (known also as executive thinking or cognitive self-management). The cognitive ability to observe and reflect on one's thought processes and problem-solving attempts in order to improve their productivity.

Minority language instruction. Teaching subjects in a language of a particular minority group.

Multigrade teaching. Teaching a group of students of different grades combined in a single classroom.

Net reproduction rate. The average number of daughters that would be born to a woman if she passed through her lifetime conforming to the age-specific fertility and mortality rates of a given year. An NRR of 1 means that each generation of mothers is having exactly enough daughters to replace itself in the population.

Paper voucher. A certified document stating the amount of public funding following a student to the school of his or her choice.

Pedagogy. The principles and methodology of teaching and instruction.

Poverty assessment. One of the World Bank's key instruments for analyzing poverty and the public policies, expenditures, and institutions that affect the incidence of poverty.

Preschool. Distinct from nursery care for children ages 0–3; includes children from age 3 to ages 5, 6, or 7. When preschool includes 7 year olds, the curriculum for 7 year old preschoolers tends to approximate that of the first grade in primary schools in other countries.

Preservice teacher training. Training provided to future teachers before they enter the teaching profession.

Primary education. The initial years of basic education, encompassing grades 1–4/5, with the normal age range for these grades being 6/7 to 10.

Prose literacy. As defined by the IALS, the knowledge and skills needed to understand and use information from texts, including editorials, news stories, poems, and fiction.

Quantitative literacy. As defined by the IALS, the knowledge and skills required to apply arithmetical operations, either alone or sequentially, to numbers embedded in printed materials. Such applications include balancing a checkbook, figuring out a tip, and completing an application for a loan or determining the amount of interest on a loan from an advertisement.

Report cards. Periodic formal reports made by a school to a parent or guardian on a student's performance, progress, attitudes, and values, or the report made by a school district or central government to parents on the performance of the schools attended by their children.

Social cohesion. Willingness of groups to cooperate across boundaries that normally divide them (e.g., clan, ethnic, or religious membership). Social cohesion increases economic development by reducing the risk of political instability and civil strife, both of which increase the risk and uncertainty of economic transactions.

Technical upper secondary education. Three- or four-year programs leading to a diploma and the opportunity to continue tertiary studies. Some programs require completion of general upper secondary education as a prerequisite for enrollment in the program; others offer academic courses that let students complete academic upper secondary school equivalency simultaneously with technical training.

Total fertility rate. The sum of age-specific birthrates over all ages of the child-bearing period. It represents the theoretical number of births to a woman during the child-bearing years, using the given year's birthrate as a constant.

Trust. The belief that the other person will honor his or her implied or explicit side of a bargain or a contract. Economic development is based on human cooperation and exchange—on transactions. Trust enhances economic development because it increases the efficiency of these transactions.

Tutor. (1) A teacher; (2) a teacher who works with students individually, perhaps outside school hours, in return for a fee

Tutorial. A meeting between a tutor and a single student (or sometimes small groups of students) in which intensive face-to-face teaching and discussion occur.

Upper secondary education. The level of education that follows basic education and encompasses three tracks: general secondary or academic; vocational secondary; and technical secondary. The normal ages vary from 14/15 to 17/18.

Virtual voucher. A computerized system of allocating public funding among schools based on school choice exercised by students.

Vocational secondary education. One-to-three-year programs providing vocational training in specific occupations or trades through school or work-based programs. Some programs of longer duration also offer academic courses that let students complete general secondary school equivalency along with vocational training, thus giving them access to tertiary education.

Voice or participation. Opportunities for citizens or customers to exert pressure on service providers to perform. Users and beneficiaries can participate in the definition of input and outcome standards. They can also use information on the performance of the public or private sector to press for improved performance and to choose among educational options on the basis of differential performance. The central players for exercising voice include beneficiaries, users, taxpayers, and civic groups.

Voucher principle. Combines the principles of school choice and "money follows student". The voucher principle can be implemented by basing each year's budget on the previous year's enrollment.